GUIDING SPIRITS:

The Haunting Experiences of a New Orleans Tour Guide

Doug Bookout & Friends

Dark Amber Press, LLC

THE REVIEWS ARE IN FOR GUIDING SPIRITS!

Excellent, Entertaining Late-Night Read! 5 Stars!

Do you love ghost stories? Do you love New Orleans? Do you ever wonder about who those people are that work as tour guides in the most fascinating city in the USA? Then why don't you have this book already??? This was a fun read that didn't rehash old stories but put an updated spin on them by connecting to the tour guides and patrons. Some of the stories will give you chills, some of the stories will make you laugh, one of the stories will make you feel terribly sorry for a Toyota Prius, and all of it will make you feel homesick for the city if you've ever visited. I need to put City Park and the Dungeon on my next itinerary. I felt the book was just the right length - my husband wanted to watch a movie I had no interest in last night and I found that Guiding Spirits lasted exactly long enough for me to avoid paying any attention to Bad Boys for Life (sorry Will & Martin). Great job Doug & Friends!!!

Schraderj

Such a fun evening reading this terrific book! 5 Stars!

I have been visiting New Orleans for the past 13 years from my home in Michigan. I've met some really terrific people, and I've seen some things that I couldn't readily explain. New Orleans is indeed a haunted City, and this book will inform and entertain you. It's written in a style that will make you feel like you're sitting around a courtyard talking with your friends. It's not written in the usual lurid spooky ghost story fashion, it's anecdotal and a lot of fun. Definitely worthy of your time and money!

Kindle Customer

If you love NOLA this is a must read! 5 Stars!

I began visiting NOLA in 2014 and have participated in a couple of tours. This book not only brought back those great memories, but it also made me realize there is still so much to explore during future visits! I thought I had seen most of the interesting sites during my nearly ten visits, but I was so wrong. Cannot wait to go on another tour next time we are in town. This book gives visitors many good ideas and provides a great way to learn some history of the fabulous French Quarter. Highly recommend!!

Lisa R. Hensley

i

The spirit of the city comes alive! 5 Stars!

Great read from start to finish. The nitty gritty feel of the City is on each page. The stories are great - the scenes painted in each one of the stories transport the reader to New Orleans. The message of the book? For those of us who love New Orleans there is a call to "Come Home". For Those who have never been --- what are you waiting for?

Mary

Personal Tales from New Orleans Ghost Tour Guides! 5 Stars!

Some unexpected and macabre personal experiences of New Orleans ghost tour guides are recounted in casual, unfettered language, as if we were enjoying drinks at May Baily's bar while the tales were being told. Each storyteller conveys their passion for this most unique city and its dearly departed denizens. Bonus for tourists: Bios of the tour guides, and a list of some of the author's favorite French Quarter haunted bars, haunted hotels, and haunted restaurants. This amazing cultural treasure of a city can't truly be understood unless one visits there. Visit there. And take a ghost tour. This book is not for children

Saavy Consumer

Excellent Read! 5 Stars!

For someone going through NOLA withdrawals, or if one is just curious about ways of life in the Quarter, it was a great time to find this informative and fun to read book. There's no way it's getting put down until I'm done and starting to whine about a follow-up book. You won't go wrong with this!

Ccolor

More than just Ghosts! 5 Stars!

This isn't another book about ghosts in New Orleans, it's about the ones who tell us the ghost stories when we're there. There are plenty of haunting accounts here, but not all of them about those who have passed on, which makes this book even more engaging and interesting. Hearing from several different voices held my attention and made me want to go on all their tours! Thank you to all who share with us your knowledge and time and for bringing us back to New Orleans at a time when we can't get there in person!

M. Deery

Grab your copy now! Before it's too late!

PUBLISHING HISTORY:

Second Edition - Expanded

Copyright © 2025 Douglas E. Bookout

Library of Congress: TX 9-244-700

All Rights Reserved

ISBN: 979-8-9876719-0-0

Published By: Dark Amber Press

All Photographs by Doug Bookout unless specified

Cover Art by MardiClaw

First Edition

Copyright © 2020 Douglas E. Bookout

Library of Congress: 1-8784727161

All Rights Reserved

Published By: BookBaby Publishing

All Photographs by Doug Bookout unless specified.

Cover Art by Drew Cothern

A few words about the revised and expanded edition of Guiding Spirits – The Haunting Experiences of a New Orleans Tour Guide:
When we started this little project a few years back, at the start of the pandemic, it was an avenue for us to channel our pent-up story telling energies during the shutdown and hopefully amuse ourselves and our friends and relatives with our experiences. It also gave me something to do, which I think, during all the pandemic closeness, probably prevented my wife from killing me in my sleep. I had no idea at the time that it would be so well received. But, as you can see from the reviews, it seemed to strike a resonant chord with people who love New Orleans as we do.

So why a revised and expanded version instead of creating another book with the new material? Two answers, Warlocks Press and Iron & Salt Press. I've had the pleasure and honor of working for Christian Day and Brian Cain since October of 2021 when I became the tour guide for their Spirits and Spells Tour. I had known of them for years and their reputation for their professionalism and their attention to detail, which shines through on everything they touch. Then I discovered that they own their own publishing company, Warlocks Press. Their books and products are immaculate, and I can't begin to tell you how excited I was when Christian agreed to help guide me through the process to relaunch this book.

Christian Day & Brian Cain

Then I began talking to my friend and fellow tour guide, Rose Sinister, who started her own company, Iron & Salt Press to launch her new vampire novel, "This Crimson Debt."

Her journey and tenacity to get it done her way inspired me to go out on my own and launch my own company, **Dark Amber Press**. This is advantageous for a couple of reasons. First off, whatever happens to me, I know my baby will be in great hands, as I can pass it down to someone I trust and respect and who loves this city as much as I do, my wife Toni. And second, this also gave us the opportunity to give this labor of love a much-needed facelift and fix some of the glaring issues I was unhappy with in the first edition. Margins were off kilter; pictures were way too dark, and a few pesky grammatical errors that got past us along the way that needed correction.

In addition to that, we've added ELEVEN full chapters of new content along with new anecdotes and even song lyrics with links to original downloadable music available for purchase. All inspired by the city we love. This music acts as a soundtrack to the stories we tell and will even, hopefully, put a few dollars in the pockets of the extremely talented musical artists who created them. These are dedicated people who use the medium of music to share their passion in a way that just leaves me in awe. The poetry of their lyrics, set to music, evokes layers of meaning and emotion befitting a city like no other. Personally, I think you'll be blown away. So, please show us all a little love as we present to you the updated and expanded edition of **Guiding Spirits – The Haunting Experiences of a New Orleans Tour Guide.**

&

"Come here,

Drink a lot,

Do bad things,

Don't get caught."

Mark Pentone, New Orleans Blues Guitarist

ACKNOWLEDGEMENTS:

Christian Day & **Brian Cain** for all of their support, inspiration and generosity. You gave me a boost when I needed it the most!

Rose Sinister for being an all-around amazing, generous and eternally talented human being. Your fangs sink deep.

Sidney Smith & **Haunted History Tours** for the years of inspiration, support, friendship and opportunity. I wouldn't be living this dream if it wasn't for you.

Jonathan Weiss for being not only a fantastic mentor, and a role model, but a great friend. You, good sir, have definitely left a mark.

MardiClaw. Drew Cothern, Tom Harvey & Diana Thornton for the amazing artwork and graphics. You are the true magicians!

To my wife **Toni**. My best friend, the love of my life, my support system, my inspiration, and my rock. I couldn't have done any of this without you. Nor would I have wanted to.

To my favorite bands, **Lacuna Coil** and **Evanescence** for bringing both the darkness and the light! Your songs play on loop as a constant soundtrack in my head!

And to our little fur baby **Chloe**. The sweetest and most precious little guiding spirit I have ever encountered. You took our hearts with you when you crossed the rainbow bridge, but we'll get them back when we see you again.

TABLE OF CONTENTS

ANECDOTES

MUSIC

ഇ൸൸●ഗ൭ങ

PREFACE

What you're holding in your hands is a very different kind of New Orleans ghost and true tales story book. Instead of covering the stories that we relate on our tours, stories of past hauntings and the atrocities in New Orleans history. We're giving you our first-person accounts, as New Orleans ghost and dark history tour guides, of what we've seen and experienced on our tours, in the bars, the streets, the restaurants and in the hotels throughout the city. Oftentimes while in the process of relating those tour stories.

These encounters can range from funny, to spooky, to downright terrifying. Some are paranormal and some are not. But they still haunt us, nonetheless. And we're laying it out here, just for you.

I'm also extremely fortunate enough to work with some of the pre-eminent industry professionals. People I have known and respected for years, if not decades. And not just for their trade craft, but also for who they are, deep down, where it counts. Some of them have graciously agreed to join me in this labor of love and share some of their favorite stories, vignettes and anecdotes as well. So, turn down the lights, pull up the covers, or get cozy in your favorite chair, perhaps along with your favorite New Orleans cocktail, and join us for **Guiding Spirits – The Haunting Experiences of a New Orleans Tour Guide.**

INTRODUCTION

Ahhhhh, that new Tour Guide smell. Freshly minted and bursting with excitement. Bearing a slight tinge of whiskey, a few days stubble and paddle boat loads of information to share. That was me in April of 2016, starting to live the dream of my New Orleans bucket list. I remember how proud I was when I passed the proctored exam and received my official tour guide license from the City of New Orleans. I was now a culture bearer, a liaison, a bonafide representative of the city that I loved, proudly wrapped in Purple, Green and Gold, holding a cocktail aloft and beckoning others to join me on a journey through the naughty bits of New Orleans history.

For me, ladies, and gentlemen, this was an achievement. The culmination of over a decade of daydreams, labor and planning to pursue my retirement bucket list with friends and adopted family in the City that Care Forgot. And I planned on giving it my all, because this is, as appropriately coined by Jason Berry, a "City of a Million Dreams". An old historical city where you can re-create and re-define yourself like no other place on the planet. As long as you're not too concerned about money, that is. And that's because the wages here, well, they're pretty much stuck in the past as well. Waaaaaaaaay in the past. But I digress.

In retrospect, after more than six years, I can honestly tell you, nothing in my background up to that point; no military or civilian law enforcement experience, no 30 plus years in the DoD Military Industrial Complex, no taking grandkids to Target while they were potty training, could prepare me for the monumental task of leading up to twenty-eight somewhat inebriated and wide eyed tourists through the labyrinth of the French Quarter on a Saturday night ghost tour. I mean, seriously. At times I thought I must have lost my mind. I like to joke that sometimes my life was easier when all I had to worry about was national security.

But you know what? I absolutely love it and wouldn't trade this experience for anything in the world! I get to live out my retirement drinking, costuming and sharing amazing stories with some really cool people in the best city on the planet. What a ride! And a privilege.

In general, a tour is an unspoken contract between the guide and their patrons. You come on my tour and I'm going to provide you with two hours of information and entertainment pertinent to the subject at hand. I'll take you to a location, tell you a story, give you details, answer questions, make you laugh (hopefully) and then I'll move you along to the next stop.

We'll lather, rinse and repeat that process several times until we successfully reach the end of the tour, be it in a museum, a historic battlefield or a posh neighborhood of the rich and famous. Oh, and if the planets align properly, you'll tip me at the end.

Now, imagine doing that in the middle of a full-blown raucous party, with brass bands, and street musicians, with amplified sound, performing at various intervals along your tour route. Panhandlers busking for tips or cigarettes, drunk frat bros yelling obscenities, and cars, with monster sub woofers, rolling past your group along with every other bright and shiny object imaginable as your competition. Now you're starting to get a little glimpse of what we deal with on a frequent, almost daily, basis.

Couple that outside sensory overload of activity with disruptive people actually on your tour, who have decided to violate that aforementioned contract of listening, who have been drinking since noon (it's now 8pm) and want to interrupt, tell their stories, have a marital crisis, or show their boobs. Yes, both husband and wife. And now you're starting to get the full picture.

Tour guides in New Orleans are freaking rock stars.

They, day in and day out, deal with situations most city police departments would have a hard time handling, and, all the while, with charm, wit, maturity and professionalism. Well, most of the time. As such, I am honored to be counted as one of their number.

So, my goal, with this book, is to give us all a little spotlight, shine some recognition and provide a platform with which to share some of our own personal stories and experiences, both paranormal and anecdotal.

We're not going to detail the stories we tell on our tours. There are plenty of books out there that already do a fine job of that.

And honestly, we'd rather just have you come visit and take our tours and immerse yourself in the full experience.

In my opinion there's nothing better than hearing a scary story or gruesome tale right on the property on which it occurred. There's a tangible energy in that experience like no other, because this city has a vibe, a hum, an atmosphere, like no other place on the planet. It's a place where it's easy to believe that magic still exists, and dreams can still come true. It's intoxicating.

But beware, there's also a dark undercurrent to the city as well. It can pull you in and drag you down, as we've seen time and time again. Sadly, not all stories have a happy ending, in this gritty city. But that's the allure, isn't it? It's the seductive draw that makes people want to, as Blues guitarist Mark Pentone says, "come here, drink a lot, do bad things, don't get caught." I'm game. How about you?

What mysteries lie beyond the old bookcases at the Toulouse Dive bar? You'll just have to come see for yourself!

CAST
Music by BNSHKR

Lyrics by P. Mangum

Music by R. Stamps

2015

In the mirror, there is a river, dirty deep and wide,
content to be
As it flows to the sea
And in the river, we leave no trace, and in the end, it
will succumb
To the ocean's embrace

We are lost, wanderin' blindly through this world of
madness
We are ghosts, souls separated by a sea of sadness

In the mirror, there is a darkness, heavy thick and
quiet, it covers me
Until I can't breathe
And in the darkness, we are all blind, there is no
hope, there is no true
And what becomes of you

We are lost wanderin' blindly through this world of
madness
We are ghosts, souls separated by a sea of sadness

To listen to this song on YouTube, please scan the QR Code
below

4

Photo courtesy of Paula Mangum

1

THE BOURBON ORLEANS HOTEL
717 Orleans St.

I've always had an affinity for twisted tales and a fascination with the otherworldly. Having grown up in the 60's and 70's on TV shows like Night Gallery, The Twilight Zone and Dark Shadows and books like Red Skelton's Favorite Ghost Stories, The Legend of Sleepy Hollow and the tales of Edgar Allen Poe, the pull of the paranormal and macabre has always beckoned.

My siblings and I also believe that our mom was a naturally gifted sensitive. She could sense things that others couldn't and often see things, through her maternal connection, that happened to us miles away. Later, when we got home, she would question us "did you go back and get your change at the McDonald's counter?", or comment, "I see you found your keys". These occurrences became common place in my early years, but then, as I grew up and moved away, the demands of career and family loomed large and that connection and fascination with the paranormal fell away. That was, until my first trip to New Orleans.

*A single orb drifts to the right of "Touchdown Jesus"
during a full moon over St. Louis Cathedral*

It was January 2004, and I was scheduled to speak at a conference at Eglin AFB. While planning my trip I happened to notice that New Orleans was only about a four-hour drive from the base. Having never been there I requested some time off after the conference and flew my wife Toni out to meet me for an extended weekend. We had no idea that this little trip would forever change our lives.

The Bourbon Orleans Hotel is located right in the heart of the French Quarter at the intersection of Bourbon and Orleans streets. Its grand ballroom was once host to the infamous Quadroon Balls in the early to mid-1800s and the Bourbon Street side was once home to first New Orleans opera house. It's also very haunted.

The second night into our stay was when we had our first strange incident in our room. Getting ready for an evening out in the Quarter, we laid our outfits out on the bed and my wife jumped in the shower while I shaved at the sink. That's when I heard a noise from the bedroom.

It sounded like something fell over. Drying my face, I walked into the suite to find our clothes thrown all around the room and our suitcase turned upside down. I was dumbfounded.

We were on the sixth floor and the only way in or out of the room was through the locked door right next to the bathroom. There was no way anyone could have gotten past me without being seen. When my wife got out of the shower, I showed her what happened and, of course, she thought I was playing a joke on her and trying to scare her. I assured her that was not the case, but I'm not sure I convinced her, until a few days later.

If you're not aware, the Mardi Gras season always begins on 12th night, or Three Kings Day, which always falls on January 6th, twelve days after the birth of Christ. Since we were there in late January, as luck would have it, we were attending our first Mardi Gras season during our first visit, which was really exciting.

Of course, the bead trade was in full effect at that time, so each night we ventured out we would get showered with beads from the balconies above Bourbon Street.

Our first night out we caught quite the haul and I had about 3 pictures left to burn on a roll of film. Once we got back to the room, I had my wife throw on all of beads so I could get a few bead trophy snaps and finish the roll.

The next day we had them developed at the place across the street and when I went in to pick them up, the owner called me over to show me an anomaly in a few of my pictures. Turns out they were the three I had shot the night before in the hotel room. In each shot, there was a serpentine white mist in front of my wife, moving through the picture. It was translucent in some areas and opaque in others.

The developer said "this appears to be a solid object moving through the frame. It's in a different location in each shot and doesn't appear in any of the photos on the roll before this." Another interesting aspect of the "object" was that it was covering my wife's body, regardless of how it moved through the frame. The roll I shot after that, at locations throughout the city, never showed the same anomaly, but we do believe we figured out the reason why.

On our last night in town and intrigued by the weird goings on in our room, we decided to take a Ghost Tour. Our Guide, Julia, was fantastic and during the tour, I began to feel that pull again, towards that long-forgotten fascination with the paranormal.

We stopped for our last story on the tour and lo and behold it was in front of our hotel, The Bourbon Orleans. There Julia told us a tale of the long-ago Quadroon balls, and how a young lady named Henriette Delille, who was destined for that fate of Placage, or becoming the concubine of a rich Creole Gentleman, rejected that life and formed the first African American cloister of nuns known as The Sisters of the Holy Family.

At one point a rich entrepreneur by the name of Thomas Lafon became a patron of their work on behalf of orphaned children and in a gesture of great charity, purchased the ballroom for them to use as their convent. One nun, distraught over being disowned by her family for refusing to participate in the system of Placage, committed suicide by hanging herself in the convent, near the 600 series of rooms in the hotel. Our room. That's when the realization hit us. It was the Nun. She was not happy with our "farewell to the flesh" display of revelry in our room and this was her way of letting us know to mind our Ps and Qs during our stay.

Bead Photo (Insert phallic ghost jokes here)

However, as fate would have it, that was not to be our last encounter with the Nun on the sixth floor.

The next year, in February of 2005, we returned with friends to perform a renewal of vows ceremony at one of our favorite blues clubs. Of course, we had to stay at The Bourbon Orleans and requested a room in the same location as we had during our initial visit.

Our room had a small, stand-alone balcony the jutted out from the building, with the balconies for the adjacent rooms about 6 feet apart. We decided to have a small party in our room with some of our friends and spent several hours drinking and throwing beads off of our balcony to the revelers down below and to other guests in the adjoining balconies. At one point, probably around two AM, we all decided to call it a night, and I pushed two metal patio chairs out to the corners of the balcony so I could pull the double doors shut. I remember joking to my wife that we were probably keeping the Nun up and should head to bed. We had a good chuckle and fell off to sleep.

When I woke up the next morning, I promptly pulled back the curtains from the double doors to find both patio chairs wedged securely against the doors on the balcony, in essence, sealing them shut. Remember, these doors open out, and before heading to bed I had to push them out to the far corners of the balcony so I could get the door to close.

I kind of freaked out. I mean, this was a free-standing balcony, six feet away from the other balconies on either side and on the highest floor of the building. You would have had to have been Spiderman to have gotten up there.

Sadly, in my excitement, I forgot to take a picture before rushing to push open the doors, which was quite a chore. Those chairs were heavy iron cast and were difficult to move.

I can assure you, there were no more jokes about the Nun after that. We continued to stay at The Bourbon Orleans for every visit until the fall of 2011 when we bought our first house in the city and plotted our retirement. We always remained respectful and never had another incident at *that* location again. Unbeknownst to us, we were just getting started.

The Dead are all around us, all the time, in the City that Care Forgot

The spirits await your company at the Ghost Table at Muriel's. (Photo Credit: Carie Ewers - 2025)

ANECDOTE: FAMILY REUNION

My grandfather checking in on our family reunion, which was held at the property on which he passed. Cherryville, NC. 2003.

Family Reunion Photos

2

THE DUNGEON
738 Toulouse Street

The Dungeon is a legendary Goth rock metal bar, established in 1969, and famous for its dark music, creepy S&M themed atmosphere and risqué behavior by its patrons. It is literally my favorite bar in the French Quarter. Word got out fast in the 70's and soon, locals, tourists, movie stars and some of the greatest bands in rock and roll history flocked to the Dungeon during their visits to New Orleans. I mean, we're talking the likes of Queen, Zeppelin, Heart, Lou Reed, Motely Crue, and David Bowie, just to name a few.

There's even a story about the ghost of a young bartender who frequently haunts the bar who committed suicide after Jimmy Paige stole away his smoking hot girlfriend, Patricia. This allegedly happened right under his nose, during one of his shifts at the Venus bar in 1975. Amongst other creepy activities, such as standing where the security cameras can see him, this ghost takes strong exception to people playing Zeppelin on the juke box downstairs. One day I decided to put that story to the test. I'll share the results with you in a moment.

Understandably, in a bar like this, in a city like New Orleans, sometimes that dark mix can result in tragedy, and over the years the bar has been the flash point for a few murders, suicides and other various and sundry bad things throughout its storied history. This all, quite fittingly, just adds to the mystique.

That's one reason why current bands still keep that legacy of rock and roll patronage alive when they're in town. While doing tours, or just afterwards, I've walked in to find members of the Foo Fighters, Alien Ant Farm, Evanescence, Rage Against the Machine, Lindsey Stirling, Machine Gun Kelly, Post Malone, Matt O'Ree Band, Maid of Orleans and Pussy Wolf, reposing in the shadows.

With Rachel Lockett and Terry Corso – Alien Ant Farm

But let's get back to that young bartender who committed suicide and still inhabits the bar. As I mentioned, this ghost often appears upstairs in the security cameras, standing there, with his head down, arms by his side, reclaiming his territory and, in essence, saying "no matter what happened, I'm still here." Downstairs, he harasses patrons who have the audacity to play Zeppelin tunes on the jukebox. When I had just started taking my tours there, probably the summer of 2017, I heard the story

14

and decided to put this claim to the test. I showed up early one evening as Rachel (the bartender) and Drew (the Door Guy) were just opening up.

We were the only three in the bar at the time, so I walked over, put a dollar in the juke box and selected three Zeppelin tunes.

I sat back down, ordered a drink and conversed with Rachel for a few minutes, when suddenly, someone poked me in the back, right between the shoulder blades, hard. So hard, in fact, that it really pissed me off, because, well, it hurt. I wheeled around expecting to find Drew standing there grinning, messing with me, and there was no one. Empty. I was the only living person on the patron side of the bar. And Drew? He was standing outside in the courtyard smoking a cigarette.

Rachel, registering what had just occurred, leaned against the bar with an amused "I told you so" smile and said, "welcome to the Dungeon, Doug." So, that was my introduction to the spirits at the Dungeon. As disconcerting as that was, it would do nothing to prepare me for what was to come next.

About six months after my initial experience, I was conducting a tour on a Sunday evening with a full tour of 28 people. People love this haunted pub crawl. I had just finished telling my group about the notorious 2003 Vampire murder, perpetrated by a couple who called themselves "Never & Worry". They met and seduced their victim at, you got it, The Dungeon. We filed into the bar, as usual, and immediately took over both levels of the establishment. The place isn't that big.

We had been there for about 10 minutes when the upstairs bouncer brought one of my tour patrons over to me at the Venus bar, where I was chatting with a friend. The girl looked to be mid-twenties, blonde, and scared out of her mind. Apparently, something had occurred that really shook her up. I asked her if she was okay and she responded, "I want to leave right now". I asked her what happened and again, she responded "I just want to get out of here. Right now." Fair enough. At that point her husband had joined us with two drinks in his hands and a very perplexed look on his face. The bouncer, her husband, and I, escorted her shakily down the stairs and out to the courtyard where she sat down on the bench that looks like a torture rack. We got her a bottle of water, and that's when the story began to unfold.

15

They were hanging out in the upstairs section known as the Sound Bar, leaning against the wall next to the cage you can dance in, complete with shackles (yes, really) when a spot opened at the bar and the husband decided to go get them drinks. She was causally leaning with her back against the wall, watching the other patrons, when suddenly someone, or something, grabbed her hair from behind and pulled her head back against the wall. Now remember, she's leaning against a solid brick wall on the second floor of a building. At first, she thought her hair got caught or tangled in something.

Reaching back to free herself, she quickly realized that her head was flush against the wall and whatever was holding on to her, was, impossibly, somehow, on the other side.

She struggled to free herself and was unable to do so. She screamed for her husband, who was at bar about five feet away, but his back was to her and the music was loud, so he couldn't hear her. Panicked, she began slapping at the wall with both hands and yelling "let me go"

The bouncer sees her from across the room and thinks she's having a seizure of some kind. He walks over and lays his hand on her shoulder, asking if she's okay. Immediately, upon making that contact, she breaks free… and runs, as fast as she can, across the room towards the stairs. She actually ran so fast the bouncer said that she bounced off of the stairwell wall at the top of the stairs and fell back into the doorway of the bar. That's when he helped her up and brought her to me on the Venus side of the bar.

I have to admit, I was dumbfounded. I had never heard of anything like this happening before. Ashlee, one of the upstairs bartenders who had witnessed the whole incident, came down to check on her. And that's when I learned the story of the Suicide Bride.

With Ashlee & Drew Schmidt (Top) and Rachel Lockett and my wife Toni - Halloween 2018

Apparently, a young couple came to New Orleans with friends in 2005 to celebrate their new engagement.

At some point during their visit to the Dungeon, the girl realized that she couldn't find her fiancé. After checking up and down the bar, she finally approached the door guy with a picture of him on her phone and asked if he had seen him leave.

The door guy responded that he had, in fact, seen him leave with one of her girlfriends about 20 minutes earlier. Knowing that all her girlfriends were with her, she suddenly wanted to know who the skank was that her fiancé walked off with.

Checking the street around the bar and unable to locate him, she returned to the bar and continued to drink. Hard. And she waited, thinking that he would return. After quite a bit of time passed it was obvious that he was not coming back. Her friends convinced her to go back to the hotel and they would deal with "the asshole" in the morning and reluctantly she agreed. Sadly, she was found the next morning having passed away in her sleep from taking too many sleeping pills. Her friends believed it was an accident, too much alcohol had clouded her judgement and she overdosed.

Now she returns, upon occasion, looking for the girl who stole her fiancé. And when she finds someone who fits the profile, she acts out on them by pulling hair, tripping, poking and pushing. Even to the point of placing her hands on the backs of girls seated on the toilet in the ladies room.

Apparently supportive gestures from people nearby, such as the upstairs bouncer, is what breaks the contact (I know, hard to do in a bathroom). From that night on I have generally issued a word of caution to my tour patrons prior to entering. Most of my blonde female patrons make a brunette or ginger sandwich with their friends during their stay. So far it has worked. Well, it did, until something entirely different happened in the summer of 2019. More on that in a later chapter.

Pray you don't have an encounter with the Suicide Bride while visiting The Dungeon.

ANECDOTE: HUMAN RESOURCES CONFERENCE

One Saturday evening I was assigned a Haunted Pub Crawl with a group of 28 Human Resources professionals in town for a conference at the Convention Center. I felt pretty comfortable about this, seeing as I had worked closely with HR in my past life, so no problem, we're all professionals. Let's do this. I watched as newcomers were introduced to conference regulars, members were reunited, and the mood was generally upbeat and positive. It was gonna be a good night.

I kicked off my tour, as usual, took them to our first stop and everyone was drinking and paying close attention to the stories. So far so good. After the second bar stop things started getting a little wonky. People who had just been introduced, maybe 40 minutes earlier, were starting to get pretty chummy with one another, if you get my drift.

By the third bar stop I literally had tour patrons asking where they could find hookers and blow. I'm not kidding. I was awarded the "worst tour guide ever" title by one lady for not assisting with their request. I mean, if you ask me personally, I might know a guy, but when I'm representing a company, sorry, not gonna happen.

Finally, after I finished my last story in front of what can best be described as a somewhat fully clothed orgy, I dragged everyone into the last bar. The tips were meagre, as you would expect from this type of group, but the Coup de Gras was when the lady who had dubbed me the "worst tour guide ever" came over and apologized. She tipped me $20 and said she was sorry she had been so snippy, but since her STD had flared up, it was really impacting her chances of getting laid during this trip. Then she smiled and offered to buy me a drink.

As you can imagine, I was dead! I offered my condolences for her broken lady parts with the just right amount of mourning and got out of there as fast as humanly possible. So, here's to you, my HR peeps, I see you! Respect! With all that buttoned down rule keeping, turns out you guys really know how to party!

3

THE PHARMACY MUSEUM
514 Chartres Street

The Pharmacy Museum. Hands down my favorite museum attraction in the Quarter, just brimming with visual history. This was the first registered pharmacy in the United States opened in 1823 by Dr. Louis Dufilho, a New Orleans native. From the moment you see the large glass urns filled with colored liquid in the apothecary windows, which were used to signal plague outbreaks, you'll be whisked back in time to a certainly simpler, yet more deadly time in New Orleans history. A time where yellow fever, cholera and malaria killed people each year like clockwork in the summer months. Where potions and various concoctions attempted to cure what ailed you, and where the rich would coat their medicines in silver and gold, not realizing they were ironically reducing the efficacy of the drugs meant to save their lives.

Oh, and once you see what passed for a catheter in the early 1800's you won't walk right for a week.

Photo by Tim Brunty

Note: Sadly, as I write this, the Covid-19 virus is hitting the city hard, disproportionately affecting the African American community. For a city who has grown used to tragedy, this situation sadly, feels all too familiar.

On our tours we tell the torrid tale of Dr. Joseph Dupas, an "opportunistic doctor" who, in the mid-1800s, used the plague outbreaks as cover for his nefarious deeds. He would have those who he deemed the lowest in New Orleans society, typically enslaved people, prostitutes and transients, kidnapped and brought to him so he could use them as test subjects for his experiments and procedures. These ghastly operations were usually performed in the entresol storage space above the apothecary on the first floor and always resulted in the death of the test subject, even if the "operation" was a success.

Dupas would generally bribe the death cart drivers to not only find these unfortunate souls for him, but also help him dispose of their remains once he was finished with them. For these services he paid them handsomely with money, drugs, alcohol. Whatever they desired. It also means that the carriage way on the side of the building figured prominently in his operation as the good doctor would raise and lower his victims through the entresol trap door.

Active hauntings on the property include white mists, moaning sounds, orbs, antiseptic smells, moving and displaced objects and the occasional

22

apparition of a man descending the back stairs in a dark brown lab coat. The ghost of Dr. Dupas.

In the four years of doing tours at this location I've had quite a few standout occurrences. Most notably are those of frequent camera malfunctions while patrons are taking pictures down the carriageway. In the instances when patrons bring an actual camera, not a camera phone, to the location, they will experience issues with somewhat bizarre results regardless of whether digital or film. I've had patrons have their camera fail to take a picture down the carriageway, turn and shoot a perfect photo across the street and then turn back to have their camera fail again and again to capture an image down carriageway. I've watched time and again as patrons get white mists, orbs and what I can only describe as a spectral dispersal of energy in their photos. Allow me to share a couple of recent occurrences with you.

In October of 2019, during the Halloween, or Samhain, season, when we believe, as the Celts do, that the veil between the living and the dead is at its thinnest, the following images were captured during my tours.

The first image was taken by a local young man who brought his out-of-town friends on my Haunted Pub Crawl. He confessed to me at an earlier bar stop that he was a skeptic regarding the paranormal but thought it would be fun for his friends. His tone changed significantly when he turned around from the carriage gate to show me the following image.

The trap door

The opaque ectoplasmic mist snaking down from above in this picture is actually coming down from the entresol trap door in the ceiling. The same trap door where Dr. Dupas would hoist and then later, lower his victims. Many viewers of this photo see the images of faces and skulls imbedded in the mist.

Three days later, I was with another tour group taking pictures down the carriageway, when a young lady startled and ran back from gate to the curb across the sidewalk.

I chuckled and asked her if a rat had run across the alley way, because that can happen quite a bit in this old port city. She looked at me wide eyed and said "No. I was taking pictures when this white mist started forming in the alley. With each picture I took it seemed to move closer to me. I felt like it was coming after me, so I ran."

The girl who ran to the curb

Two days after that occurrence the shades on the front doors were open, which is rare, so one lady pressed her camera against the glass so she could take pictures of the darkened interior. The first picture came out very clear, the second one, not so much. Then the third, clear again. I've included photos 1 and 2 below. Judge the results for yourself. Also, she was there alone as the group had already moved on.

No movement of the camera, no change in light, just a spectral discharge of energy that was there one second and gone the next.

White Mist - 2017

Orbs! - 2025

So please, come join us on one of my tours and when we arrive at the Pharmacy Museum, let's see what captures you.

ANECDOTE: CHECKING YOU OUT

We believe that spirits are curious about the living, especially when you're visiting their property, so they come to check you out to see what type of person you are and what you're saying about them. When they do, their energy can affect electronic devices and result in all these camera anomalies we experience. Because I encounter this quite often, my wife has given me the edict, "Do not bring this shit home with you." You'll better understand her concern after you read Chapter 13. This is why I wear a protection ring while on my tours, to keep them from hitching a ride home with me.

Fans (at center) meeting Matt & Eryn O'Ree at BMC

Next photo – Spirits come to visit.

4

A HAUNTED PUB CRAWL HIJACKING OF SORTS
Randy Walker

So this all happened on a pub crawl tour, a haunted pub crawl tour, to be precise. This can be a great tour at times. And at other times, not so much. This is a story of a not-so-great time, where I am in charge of guiding a bachelor party of five to four different bars in two hours. Before the tour even starts, I know this might be a challenge. I have no idea how stupid things would get though.

Our first stop is relatively harmless. We enter this restaurant/bar on the corner of Bourbon and St Peter and go upstairs to the 2nd floor bar to get drinks. So, these guys order drinks, crack jokes and slap each other on the back and all that goofy fun. That's a good sign.

Being the professional tour guide that I am, I join in on the fun, grabbing a beer from the bartender and laughing along with the group acting like I'm just another member of their party. So far nothing bad.

After we get our first round of drinks, I lead my men to a secret room to tell the story. And that goes well too. They laugh at all the right parts, they listen well, gasp at the horror, and even curse at the worst of it. When I finish telling the story of the poor family who were burnt to a crisp in the fire of 1794, they give me a nice round of applause and I lead them downstairs to the exit and I'm thinking to myself:

Oh, this tour will be just fine.

But then, when we are back downstairs, heading outside again to continue to the next stop, I feel a tap on my shoulder and receive the first indicator that this group might be problematic.

"Hey bro," one of the guys says to me, "would it be cool for us to get another round of shots here before we head to the other place."

Now this is the sort of question I can't really say no to without coming across like a jerk, but I really want to say no to this. The next bar is only four blocks away, and I know when groups start going heavy on the drinking early in the tour... it'll only complicate things later. But what I'm I gonna do? I work for tips.

So they take their shots and we exit the restaurant/bar and start walking to the next one.

It's here, on this walk, where these guys start to annoy me. One of them, let's assume Gary, spots a discarded, half full beer can lying on the curb, and proceeds to run up and kick it as hard as he can, sending it crashing down the street. This is followed by a cry of:

"And the kick is goooooooooooood!"

I calmly, but firmly, tell him to please go pick up the can and throw it away, and not to do things like that again, because we're on a tour and I could get in trouble for something like that, plus it's not polite to the neighbors. That's when one of his buddies puts his arm around Gary's neck and answers for him.

"Aw, we're sorry. Gary just gets like that sometimes. He's a wild one. In fact, we are all a little wild, right guys?"

To which a small cacophony of hoots and hollers follow.

Ah yes, so wild, I think, kicking a can down the street, you bunch of James Deans you...

"Oh man, this guy is gonna hate us by the end of the tour!" one of the others says to his friends, like I'm not even there, "He's gonna remember us forever and he's gonna hate us!"

Hearing this makes me cringe.

If there is one statement that I can't stand that I get constantly from my different groups, it is this. I'm convinced the only people who utter this phrase to a tour guide are those that have never worked in the service industry at all. Because those who have know one obvious fact about a job like this, you forget 99.9 percent of the people you serve. As soon as they leave your little world, you forget about them almost immediately. Maybe while you served them, they annoyed you, maybe they were fine, maybe they made your day a little better. Maybe they made it a whole lot worse. It doesn't matter. As soon as they are gone, they disappear from your mind. Only the very great and the very worst get any sort of residency in your brain, the rest vanish immediately. And at this point, I'm positive these jokers aren't qualifying for either position. But I don't bother explaining that. Instead, I just give my standard answer:

"Ah no, you guys are fine. I've had way worse. I actually like you guys." (Did I mention I work for tips?)

Anyway, this renegade crew proceeds to rebel in the following ways:

-Slapping on the top of the occasional trash can as we walk down the sidewalk.

-making loud, lewd comments about the women in their lives back home (note: they were silent about those that passed them by IRL though).

- shoving each other into gallery posts.

-asking one of the bartenders for her number (while the rest snicker loudly).

-making bad jokes while I tell stories.

- telling each other how much I hate them and will always remember them.

So, all in all, this gang of five has devolved into your typical annoying-but-unmemorable pub crawl group, and that's fine. I'm not in a great mood, so it's irritating me more than it should, but it's fine.

On our third stop, we make it to May Bailey's, the one high class bar on the tour that has a delightful brothel story. And would you believe this? While I'm describing the brothel, and the women who work there, my group says things to each other like:

"Matt would go there every day!"

"Eric would never leave!"

"Gary would get a job there!"

"(laughing) Would you guys stop? This tour guide is going to hate us forever!"

So yeah, still just your average pub crawl tour that, if I would have been in a more giving mood, might have even been a little fun. But as I said before, I am just not feeling it tonight, so I do what I always do when I'm working a tour and it's not going well. not feeling the vibe of the group.

I. get. through. It.

Sometimes that's the greatest weapon a tour guide has.

I raise my voice when they make their jokes and little comments and fight my way to the end of the story.

More than halfway through, I tell myself, only thirty minutes to go.

Finally, I finish the third story, and we are on our way down Dauphine Street to our last stop. Now I have a tendency to hold my breath at this section of the tour, because it's the most sketchy area that we travel down. Up until that point, nothing bad has ever happened here during one of my tours, but you have a lot of drug dealers and other criminal elements that frequent the area. I have always felt that I had an unspoken agreement with this sketchy element of the quarter though, which is essentially:

You leave my group alone; I leave you alone.

That might have been wishful thinking, but in all my years doing this nothing bad had happened yet.

And then, as we are about to come up to Toulouse Street, I notice something strange. There's a man on a bike riding alongside me in the street. And he's got a big, stupid grin on his face, like the cat who ate the canary or whatever. And the stupid face with the stupid grin looks awfully familiar. But how would I know this guy? A friend from the neighborhood? A fellow service industry worker?

He rides past me as I'm trying to figure it out. And then, a lot of things happen at once:
- I hear my group behind me start laughing uproariously.
- I see a man who I recognize as being part of the sketchy element that I mentioned earlier running down the street toward us screaming profanely and furiously.
- I recall ten seconds earlier, as we were walking down the sidewalk, that I passed by a bicycle resting against a building wall, while two men discussed something in secret not five feet from the bike.
-Finally, I remember why that man with the stupid grin on his face riding the bike looked so familiar, it's one of the fucking five guys on my tour (let's say Gary).
Oh Jesus Christ, this is bad, I think to myself.

And as I'm processing all this, the running man passes us on the street, screaming again at the idiot who stole his bike, and I hear him clearly shout:

"I'm gonna kill you motherf---er!"

And by God, I believe him. With my whole heart I believe that he means those words. In this area, in the French Quarter, at night, I can safely say that people have been killed for less. And what really gets to me at this moment is the rest of the group behind me is dying of laughter. All four of them slapping their knees and holding on to each other for support as the chuckles vomit out of their drink holes.

"Oh f--king Gary man!"

"Gary's an animal!"

"Look at Gary go!"

In a panic, I turn to them and try to impress upon them how bad this situation is, telling them that they need to go grab their boy before something really bad happens. But their response is to only laugh harder and further praise of Gary's wild heart.

I turn my head back to the nightmare scenario unfolding in front of me and find that it's only grown worse. What I haven't realized til now is that Gary is riding the stolen bike the wrong way down a one-way street, and there's a car not too far away at all heading right for him whose driver seemed to have no idea Gary's pedaling toward him, or just doesn't care.

My mind tries to process this. Violent angry, death-threatening sprinting man on one side, oblivious speeding car on the other, "Wild Gary" in the middle. Simply put, it's the French Quarter sandwich from hell.

Of course, in situations such as these, your life goes into slow motion, and with each turn of the pedal I try to weigh my options here. Do I go after Gary myself and try to save him? Do I save time and just call the ambulance now? Do I just run away from this whole mess and claim the group ditched me after the third stop? None of these options are appealing, so I start thinking of how I'm going to explain this to my boss, when he learns that someone on my tour hijacked a vehicle and immediately got into one of the oddest traffic accidents/murders of all time.

And while I'm thinking on this, the group of jackals behind me are still giggling like children, and Gary is still joy riding, and both the angry man and the car are gaining steam, bearing down on him.

F--- my life, is all I can think.

Now, I don't know how much of this has been exaggerated over time in my head, but as I remember it, Gary's not ten feet away from the front bumper of the incoming car before the bike owner reaches him and throws a right handed haymaker at the left side of his head, causing him to slump over to the left, causing the bike to veer hard to the left so that both the bike and Gary miss the car completely (the car also may have slammed on the brakes at the last minute, but that's honestly not how I remember it. But if it didn't, why didn't the irate bike owner get run over by the car seconds later? These are the questions I have no answer to.)

I breathe a small sigh of relief, as at least Gary wasn't killed by a vehicle. However, my relief is very momentary, because the bike owner is

34

hovering above him as he lays on the ground, with two balled up fists, echoing familiar threats of the recent past. This would have been bad enough, but the fact that Gary's on the ground laughing hysterically while looking up at the bike owner...well, I feel like this is an added insult to injury that does not help the situation. And of course, behind me, I hear the familiar calls of:

"F--king Gary man!"

"He's a legend!"

Even now, his friends make no effort to help their friend, or take the situation serious. This infuriates me so much; I almost want something bad to happen. Just so they will finally understand that you don't pull this dumb shit in the quarter, and if you do, you don't laugh it off like it's nothing, because it's not.

The next thing I know, I see the bike owner back on his bike, pedaling past us. Behind him, Gary is still on the ground, still laughing like a maniac. As the biker passes us, I see him turn to me with angry fucking eyes and say:

"And f--k you too."

Oh dear, I think, whatever deal we had before is over now...

Gary's friends finally run over to their fallen friend and help him up. All of them are laughing. Especially Gary.

"Gary, you're out of your mind, buddy!"

 I quickly get them back on the sidewalk and march them a few blocks away before laying into them. I explain to them how dangerous that was. I explain how stupid that was. I explain that if they pull anything like that again, this fucking tour is over (some tour guides here will admonish me, saying if it was them, that would have been the end of the tour right then and there. I can't argue this, all I can say is I am a whore for tips, and in the back of my mind I'm hoping that this guilt trip will help with some major cash love at the end [spoiler alert- it didn't]).

I tell them all this, in my angry AND disappointed tour guide voice. When I'm done, one of the guys turns to his friends and says as if I'm not standing there:

"Oh man, this tour guide is gonna hate us forever by the end of the tour! He'll never forget how awful we were!"

Amidst their cackling, I can't help but finally agree with this sentiment. I will never forget how awful they are.

ANECDOTE: **KARMA TAKES A TOUR** – *Stella Salmen*

I have had all kinds of people on my tours. Some are believers, some are skeptics, but I hope all of them are at least a bit open minded and curious. I do my best to present things in a manner that, while not "converting" anyone, might make them at least question their idea of normal. On one tour, however, I believe I converted and entire group into believing in psychic energy.

While giving a tour presentation about the basic history of Voodoo, I had a group of people that decided they would disrupt my tour. OK, that happens frequently enough, but these people decided that they would NOT stop. They had balloons, loud music playing, clown make-up. (If you don't know New Orleans well, you might think this strange. Trust me, it is not.)

After several polite requests to kindly move on, they got rather nasty with me… then they did, indeed, proceed to walk further up the street, yelling foul insults at me. Again, these things happen. But this time it was more annoying than usual. I looked at my group, who were in awe that this had happened, and just smiled.

One man made a comment about how I really "kept my cool". I responded, not loudly, but in a low speaking voice that my entire group did hear, "I hope she breaks her ankle", followed with a rather sardonic smile.

At that precise moment, we hear a loud "Yelp" halfway down the block, as the woman at the back of the obnoxious group turns her ankle and falls in the street.

The look of shock on every face was simply precious.

I resumed the tour with, "Now, to continue with Voodoo…"

Best. Coincidence. Ever.

5

DEAD KIDS

Dead Kids. They absolutely terrify me. From the screaming boy in the Grudge, to the Grady Twins from The Shining and the tongue clucking little girl of Hereditary, if you're at a scary movie with me, that's when I'm coming out of my seat. REDRUM? Yeah. Fuck that.

Yet the city of New Orleans, where I live, is filled to the brim with ghost lore and the tales of dead children. It seems that they occupy practically every building in the French Quarter. Yay. So, the next few chapters are dedicated to these young denizens of the afterlife and their interactions with we earth bound souls. Some are innocent, some are tragic and some, like the tale I'm about to share with you, are wickedly mischievous.

One of my favorite ghost tales, ever, is a story we were told on our very first ghost tour in the city as we stood across Royal Street from the Andrew Jackson Hotel. Apparently, at one point in this property's fascinating history, it was a boarding school where five young boys tragically died in a fire and who still occupy the grounds, playing amongst the guests of the hotel. Watching them sleep. Touching their stuff.

The story we were told was of a young couple visiting from Texas in 2002. They checked into the hotel, excited about their visit to New Orleans, and promptly got to unpacking. The wife takes her toiletries to the bathroom and is startled to see a little boy standing in the bathroom. He's dressed in a shirt and overalls and appears to be about eight years old.

Astonished, she kneels before the little boy and asks,

"Sweetheart, are you lost?"

"Where's your family?"

The boy doesn't respond, just stands there stoically, staring right at her.

After a few additional attempts to talk to him, she tells him "Wait here, we'll find them."

With visions of Home Alone, she runs into the room, past her stupefied husband and grabs the phone. She shushes him as he's asking, "what is going on and who were you talking to?" and begins talking to the desk clerk;

"There's a lost little boy in our room and I need you to help me find his family right away."

The Desk Clerk responds, nonchalantly; "Ma'am, just leave him alone and he'll go away."

She says "What? What do you mean he'll go away? His parents must be frantic!"

Again, the clerk calmly restates "Trust me. Just leave him alone and he'll go away. This happens quite often."

Suddenly it dawns on her. She's heard the stories, the ghosts of dead kids on the property. She abruptly hangs up the phone and grabs her camera from the dresser, runs into the bathroom and levels it at the little boy with the intention of taking his picture. He screws up his face in a little grimace, clearly unhappy, and disappears, instantly, before she can snap the shot.

She's stunned.

To the surprise of her husband, she decides she wants to stay, in that room. Her heart has been touched by that little boy and she desperately wants to make contact with him again. Her husband reluctantly agrees. It becomes kind of an obsession for her during their trip, her husband having to pry her away from the room to attend outside activities. But the face of that little boy keeps haunting her.

Sadly they have to leave and return home and she, try as she may, has not been able to reach the little boy. She's extremely disappointed by this. They arrive home and unpack and later the husband drops off their film for processing.

A few days later they're sitting on the couch, going through their pictures and reliving some of the fun moments, when they both stop dead in their tracks. She is holding a picture in her hands of her and her husband asleep in the hotel bed in the middle of the night, taken from the vantage point of the dresser where she would always leave her camera.

So, who took the picture?

They believe it was the little boy's way of asking "how do you like it when someone tries to take a picture of you when you don't want them to?"

Um, yeah, again… no thank you!

ANECDOTE: THE CHILD ON THE TOUR - *Sidney Smith*

Many years ago, I was leading a Haunted History ghost tour throughout the French Quarter. Our tours are primarily geared toward an adult audience. Not that there's anything inappropriate for kids, it's just that the material is more easily digested by a more mature audience. This particular group included a single mother and her son who looked to be about 6 or 7 years old. He was the ONLY child on the tour.

About 30 minutes into the tour, the child started walking alongside of me, as kids are often drawn to the tour guide with questions. I could easily see the mother toward the back of the group the entire time. About 30 minutes into that, the mom comes running up to me frantically screaming, "Have you seen my child???" I pointed downward at the kid who was standing right next to me the whole time. After a sigh of relief, she then stated, "WOW! He was with me just a second ago." And I'm thinking to myself, NO... He's been with me for the last 30 minutes.

She then looked down at the child and in a frustrated tone asked him, "Why did you leave me???" He innocently looked up at her and said..."Because you were holding that other boy's hand, mommy."

Ghost kids in Williamsburg VA –
Photo by Dionysios Evangelopoulos

EULOGY AT JOSHUA TREE (BALLAD OF GRAM PARSONS) by Jaime Lynn Vessels

If they find me in Joshua Tree
Don't let them take my body
They'll be riding that dragon away
Through the fire and the flame

In a room far from home
Drinking whiskey all alone
Planning cross-country
To claim my bones
And steal me home

What daddy didn't know
Before the wheels hit the road
The gasoline and heroine were
Set to explode
At Cap Rock stone

If they find me in Joshua Tree
Don't let them take my body
They'll be riding that dragon away
Through the fire and the flame

Speeding down the runway
Trying to catch my plane
Two friends in a hearse took my coffin
They knew what I'd say
If they stole me away

All they ever found
Was a box above the ground
Thirty-five pounds and
A legacy of sound
To bury in the ground

If they find me in Joshua Tree
Don't let them take my body
They'll be riding that dragon away
Through the fire and the flame

Oooh, oooh
Oooh, oooh

A silent grave in Metairie
Is all that remains of me
In Louisiana swamp land,
In New Orleans
Take me back
Take me back
Take me back to Joshua Tree

If they find me in Joshua Tree
Don't let them take my body
They'll be riding that dragon away
Through the fire and the flame

To purchase this song on iTunes, please scan the QR code below

THE KIDS IN THE PARK

Charmaine Swan Rich

This chapter is about my job and all the people I come in contact with, the ones that are alive…and dead. I am a tour guide in New Orleans. In doing this job, I found my "gift" or "curse". People call it different things – depending on their perspective.

I always knew I was able to hear, see, and feel the spirits, but never really talked about it. I guess those few naysayers invaded my confidence. This job has taught me that, and so have the spirits. I started working as a tour guide 2 years ago and one of the main tours I give is our bus tour. We escort groups all around the city to haunted locations and regale them about the history of the city. It truly is a wonderful, fun job. I have a great time with the tourists, being a people person, but I have also reestablished my connection with the spirit world.

I always knew it was there, ever since I was a little girl. Our stiff concrete society dictates I don't talk about that. But the spirits kept coming, little by little… and this job and one of my wonderful bosses, who has become my mentor, helped me understand my connection with

44

the spirits. Let me clarify my boss calls me an empath, a spirit magnet. They have been coming to visit me all my life. Some time ago, I finally fully accepted it. I am not a psychic or medium and will never claim to be. The spirits just visit me. At times I can see them, hear them, feel them – but the level and amount of contact is up to them. At first, yes, I was scared, and felt like I was crazy, but now, you get used to things happening, sometimes they just startle me. This leads me to my City Park story.

On our bus tour, one stop is in City Park. It was founded as a park in 1854 by John McDonough who bought the land from a man named Louis Allard. The park was formally known as the Allard Plantation. So, as you can guess – there are lots of spirits who inhabit the park. The tour bus always stops by an exceptionally large live oak tree (about 300-400 years old) next a lagoon. It is the perfect place for spirits to roam and, it is my favorite location on the tour. A live oak growing next to water is the best ingredients for a portal for the spirits. Especially in New Orleans. We honor our dead and talk to them, call them for advice, for support and thank them for our many blessings. We also love to raise the vibration in New Orleans. We do this through music and food, as well as by celebrating and being together, being a family. We are all connected through our energy with one another, and this energy connects us to our ancestors. But the main reason why this is my favorite location is that my "kids" are there, always waiting for me.

The tour originally went to this location to tell our guests a story about Lisa. Since she is a highly active spirit, this location is very popular with the tourists, and they can take lots of pictures of her. Her story dates back to when City Park was the Allard Plantation. Legend tells us that since Lisa drowned herself in the lagoon, and sometimes she still makes her appearance there. We encountered other spirits there – lots of them – and it happened by accident.

Child Spirits visit with Charmaine Swan Rich during her story at City Park – Photo by Charmaine Swan Rich

One night my boss was giving this particular tour and her friend who was tagging along, just happened to be a psychic medium. Upon arriving at the lagoon, the medium begins to walk away from the group. Naturally, my boss realized he discovered someone. And she was right. That was the first time the kids made an appearance. That night, the medium found 9 children there – who had been brought to this location, killed there and either buried or thrown into the lagoon. We suspect that we are the first to find them.

Then, later tour groups began taking pictures of a little boy at this location. He showed up a lot. We had to find out who he was, who the kids were, and what had happened here. My boss then scheduled a ghost hunt at this location. She brought in another medium (who had no idea what the first medium found out) who brought out equipment. I went on this hunt and was the one filming the psychic. Which, by the way, is easier said than done. I will never forget that night – we did find out who the little boy was…and more.

Child Ghost in a Dress, City Park, 2019
— Photo by Charmaine Swan Rich

That night our psychic connected with the little boy in the pictures, and we found out his story. This little boy's name is George. George is there with 3 other little girls. The four kids stick together. George told us they are all about 9-12 years old and died in the 1920s. George told us a serial killer killed them. Since he always carried around a bag of toys, he would give them a toy and whistle a fun tune to get them away from their parents, either at home or from the amusement park just down the street. He would walk them to the large oak tree by the lagoon.

This is where he would kill them and bury them. That night George told our psychic he is here playing with his yo-yo and waiting for his older brother. We asked George if this was the toy the killer gave him. He said it was. We then asked him how he died? How did the kids die? George told us the killer crushed their skulls.

George also talked about how the killer used to whistle and so he thought this man was a hobo. He traveled from city to city – by jumping on trains. We did some research and found that the large street at this location, called City Park Ave, was a railroad line.

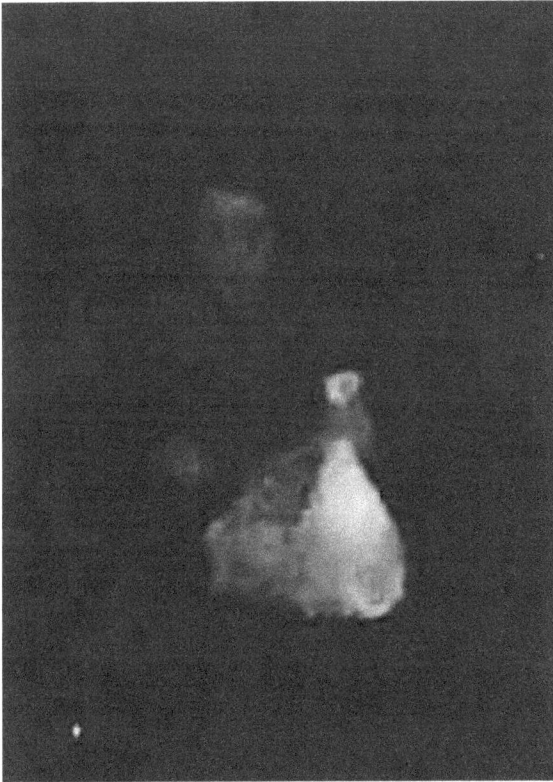

. ***Ghost with a Bag, City Park, 2019***
– Photo by Charmaine Swan Rich

That night George also told the psychic that the kids now love to watch people in the park, their favorite thing to do. There is a beautiful pavilion across the lagoon where City Park hosts large events, like fundraisers or weddings. When there is an event there – the kids will sit at the water's edge and watch the people dance and listen to the music. They love to do this.

I wondered why the kids are still here. I read and researched to find out that some earth-bound spirits stay with us because they have unfinished business. The more I go to this location, the more I realize the kids want us to know that they are there. They want people to know their story. Since we did this hunt, George and the girls have constantly made themselves known. Just about every tour I conduct, the group leaves with pictures of the spirits. Spirits show themselves in many different ways. Also, as we bring more and more groups there – the spirits get more and more energy to manifest.

The more I did this tour, the more George connected with me. A common question which tourists ask me now is, "don't you get scared?" The answer, "Yes-at first." But when you are around the same location and, probably, the same spirits, night after night, you know which ones are scary and which ones really need company. Do not get me wrong, there is also an evil spirit at this location, sometimes, but I will talk about him later.

Every time I got off the bus, I could feel and hear George saying – "she's here again!" They respond to the excitement that I came to visit and brought some company for them. There were some nights when George and the girls were so excited, they would, for lack of a better way to say, clog up my brain. I would hear their thoughts, their excitement, and it was so overwhelming I couldn't speak, I couldn't give the tour. I didn't know these people on the tour, but they expected me to tell a story. There were times, when I had to excuse myself for a minute and let the kids know I would give them attention AFTER I told their story. You know how kids are – very impatient. As I did this and would turn back to my group, I saw looks of fear, amazement, and skepticism on their faces. Some people, actually most people, were amazed and wanted to know what the kids were telling me and how I could feel them and hear them. But there were the few who thought I was nuts and "acting" – those doubters always gave bad reviews. I have now learned to ignore them and feel a bit sorry for them.

I not only hear George in my head, but I sometimes see him and the girls. Early on, George told me he would really like it if the people sang to him and the girls. They loved music. I would tell my groups this, and those that sang – did get wonderful pictures of orbs, mist etc. George really didn't care what they sang or how they sounded. He would always connect with people that either sang to him or talked to him –

sincere people. George and the girls would usually pull me to one area or another. I would tell the people on my tour to "take a picture over there." Most of the time they would go home with a wonderful picture of a spirit.

George Visiting the Tour, City Park, 2019
– Photo by Charmaine Swan Rich

I have had lots of experiences with the kids. One night, the kids just couldn't wait until I got off the bus. As we pulled up to the location, the driver looked at the bus door and told me not to move. I stood still as he took a picture of the door. He was a bit shaken. I asked him what he saw. He said, "I'll tell you later." Now, for all of our tours, the driver stays on the bus, and does not know the story about the kids. The tour continued and the next stop was the bathroom break. At this point I asked the driver what he saw. He said, "I saw kids standing by the glass door, gazing into the bus."

I told him those are the spirits that are always here, as it was 10:30pm and there were no kids anywhere that night. The bus driver became confused and said, "Well, the picture didn't come out because of the flash, but these kids looked evil!" I reassured him the kids were not evil and asked him why he thought this. He answered, "There was something wrong with their heads, they were misshaped, crushed." I then told him how the kids died. He got very pale. Now this driver never gets off the bus on our tours!

As I mentioned before, there are many spirits at this location. There is at least one evil, scary spirit that we know about. It is the serial killer, at least we think it is. There have been times I have gotten off the bus and felt something was horribly wrong, a dreading feeling, like I should not be there. These are the times you need to leave – trust your instincts when it comes to the spirit world. But, in this case, the show must go on. I would take my groups out and tell them the story.

During these times, I have learned not to stay long at this location. One night, during a feeling of dread, a couple of teens asked me specific information about the serial killer. I do make it a point to not talk about him as much as possible. He is part of the story, but that's it. Well, this one night, I didn't listen to my instincts, I wanted the tips, and admittedly, I got cocky.

Right by the oak tree I went into details about the serial killer as much as we knew. The tourists were hanging on my every word, and the dread was spreading. We got back on the dark bus and I felt something crawling on my neck, right by my vocal cords. Mind you, this is 11pm at night. I instinctively crushed the thing and to this day, I have no idea what it was. I threw it on the floor of the bus and felt my neck. There was a stinger about ½ inch long in my neck. Panic hit me in front of my tour group. This is not good. I pulled the stinger out and tried to continue with the tour. No one really knew what was going on, as the bus was very dark. And thank God the next stop was our bathroom break. Everyone always runs off the bus to the bathrooms.

I then looked in the mirror on the bus, lights on, to see a hole in my neck, and it was swelling up the size of a lemon! It was right in my vocal cords, and I could not speak! The bus started to spin, and I had to sit down with help from the bus driver. As he ran to get me water, I took Benadryl from my purse. A good tour guide always carries a knife, ibuprofen,

Benadryl, and bug spray, which may have helped in this situation. I took the Benadryl – actually two – with my water.

As I sat and tried to calm myself down, I realized what I had done. Never, never talk about him. He is evil. I paid the price, the serial killer had sent me a message right where it hurt me as a guide, in my vocal cords. I got the message. I have never talked about him while standing in the location. Luckily, I was able to continue and thanks to the Benadryl, I was quite happy and mellow the rest of the tour.

The last time I saw George was early March 2020…one of the last times I did the bus tour thanks to the COVID-19 virus. I was telling my group the story of the kids and I looked to my right by an azalea bush. George was standing there, smiling at me. I gasped and froze for about 5 seconds – which seemed an eternity when you have 28 people starring at you. Of course, no one else saw him and I didn't reveal what I saw. I then just continued with the story. I know George wanted me to come to the azalea bush. When I finished, a couple of girls did ask me why I gasped. I told them. They were amazed and happy that George was there. I did walk over to the azalea bush – which had just started blooming pretty white flowers. I could hear George telling me that he wanted to show me the pretty flowers.

It has been about 8 weeks since I did this tour and I miss the kids terribly. Later I did go back to the tree during the day for a walk. I brought my kitty, Minnie. She is an exceedingly rare black kitty who loves to walk on a leash. I walked her to the tree that day to meet George. I explained to him that day why we were not doing tours and that one day, when the virus goes away, we will do the tours again. I hoped he understood, as much as a kid can. So, I guess this virus has even affected the spirits – they really are not seeing many people in the park. Thus, not getting the energy they need to materialize.

I always have tourists ask me, "Does anything ever follow you home?" I always find this question odd – anything? It should be anyone. And that answer is yes. I think the kids come home with me sometimes. But, not for long, and I do not know why. My good friend, who is also an empath has told me she believes the kids know that I am a mom and feels that motherly bond with me. And that's OK with me. I love being a mom. It really is who I am in my soul.

Twice when I was home alone, I heard a male, child voice saying "Mom!" At other times things have been moved around in the kitchen and sounds coming from the kitchen when no one is there. There have been two occasions when my husband has come to me yelling, "Someone is here!!!! There is something going on in the kitchen!!" All I do is smile and laugh when he leaves the room. I do believe it is the kids making him a little nuts – as kids do.

Finally, I will leave you with a thought – the spirits are all around us, every day, every night. Trying to communicate. We just must know how to listen, what to look for. The very last bus tour I did before the COVID 19 virus outbreak was a private tour. Lots of drunk people, so lots of energy. And a good percentage of naysayers. Sometimes my favorite tour. We went to the live oak tree at City Park and right away I could tell the kids really did not want to come out for drunk adults. So, I thought, well, they may only see spirits because of the spirits they are drinking. Ha! Once again, the spirits world proved me wrong. That was the tour they were trying to send a message – a dark one, one no one wants. I realized this after our sobering lockdown for the COVID 19 virus.

This last picture, of the dark, menacing soul, is the very last picture taken on my bus tour before COVID 19 came to New Orleans. I did not realize this was a sign until I was sitting in my house, day after day, becoming a bit dark myself.
  So, if one day, you find yourself wanting to take a vacation, after all this COVID 19 virus leaves us, come on down to New Orleans. George and the kids are waiting for you, and maybe, someone else.... I would love to introduce you to them.....

A Lady in Black at City Park – Selfie Takers to the right are unaware of her presence. This figure appeared on Charmaine's last tour before the Covid 19 shutdown. (Both photos courtesy of Charmaine Swan Rich)

ANECDOTE: **THE PUB CRAWL OF THE TRAVELING PANTS**

My early Sunday evening Pub Crawl started normal enough, semi drunk bachelor party, about a dozen nice young guys having fun, nothing out of the ordinary. I'm standing just off the curb, as we guides always do, telling them about our first in ground cemetery at Burgundy and St. Peter, when a car comes up really close behind me and stops. The window rolls down and a gentleman about my age is driving. He turns and grabs something off of the passenger seat and moves to stick it out the window, just as a member of my tour group steps off the sidewalk behind me and approaches the vehicle. The guy in the car hands him what appears to be a pair of tuxedo pants on a hanger, and that was, in fact, exactly what it was. This kid on my tour had left his tux pants at home and was supposed to be in the wedding the next day with the guys on my tour. His dad drove out from Biloxi to drop them off and tracked him down right to the corner on which we stood. Well done good sir, you didn't even have to exit the car. The kid finished the rest of the Pub Crawl carrying those pants around on a hanger. He never dropped his pants, and he never spilled a drop. Not all heroes wear capes!

7

THE WATCHER ON THE ROOF TOP
727 Toulouse Street

Vampires play a significant part of New Orleans folklore, dating back to the late 1720's, where it is said that they made the trek from the old world (Europe) to the new world hidden securely in the dowry boxes of the Casket Girls. Jacques St. Germaine, a prominent figure in New Orleans society in the early 1900's also plays heavily into this vampire lore and was reportedly a character influence in Anne Rice's Interview with a Vampire.

So one evening I'm standing with my tour group across the street from Molly's Bar discussing Comte St. Germaine when I glance back toward the bar and I see, what I can only describe as a dark figure hunched on the rooftop by the chimney, watching us. Then suddenly, it stands up, unfurls, and disappears in an instant. It happened so fast that I, as they old saying goes "didn't believe my own eyes."

I remember pausing for a moment as my brain registered the event and turned to my group to ask if anyone else had witnessed what I had just seen. That's when I saw a lady in my group standing with her mouth agape, eyes wide and completely motionless. I asked her if she just saw something on the roof. She said yes. I asked her to describe it to me, and she did. Exactly as I had seen it occur. A few others in my group also attested to seeing a "blur of motion" on the rooftop, but not in the detail in which the lady on my tour and I had witnessed.

The Dark Rooftop on Toulouse

My wife and I were living on Frenchmen Street at the time, and I remember walking home after the tour, a little unnerved and paying special attention to the rooftops. I posted on Facebook that evening about my encounter and Kalila Smith, a New Orleans paranormal expert, friend, and mentor, weighed in.

She stated that this is a frequent occurrence, though rarely observed, and believes that they are watching to see if we treat their stories with respect. Recent documented encounters have occurred at Maison De Ville (where we were standing), Jackson Square and The French Market Inn.

The Jackson Square incident was documented, as it was reported to police in 2013. Three young ladies, walking through Jackson Square around midnight one evening, noticed a man standing on the roof of St. Louis Cathedral watching them as they passed on the walkway below. He leaned out further and they immediately "felt threatened". One of the girls screamed and the figure was suddenly "gone in a flash".

Many locals believe this to have been an encounter with Jacques St. Germaine, or as he is known now, Vampire Jack. His impending arrival is usually heralded by an intermediary who will approach the intended victim on the street or sidewalk and utter the phrase "It's a nice night for Jack to be out." Most people brush off these odd encounters with a "good for him" type response and then go on about their business. That is, until they meet a strange dark figure further along their path and come to the realization that they are missing time, and also have strange cut, or wound, on their bodies which they can't recall how they received.

Since my little tour encounter, I always endeavor to keep my stories respectful and walk with one eye on the rooftops. You never know. In a city like New Orleans, perhaps this is not just folklore after all.

Vampires on my Tour!

Amanda the Vampire Hunter

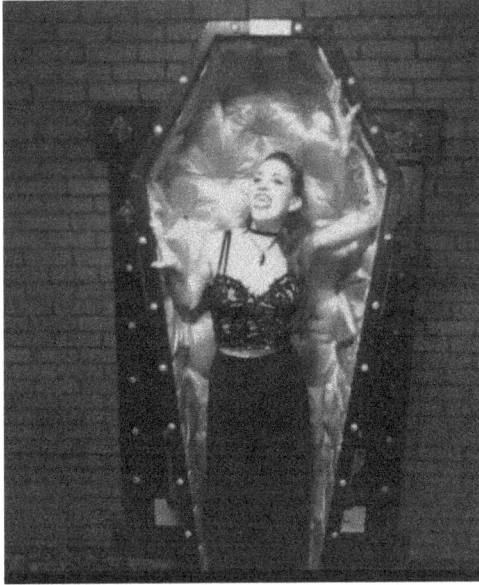

Alex coming to life for her shift at The Dungeon

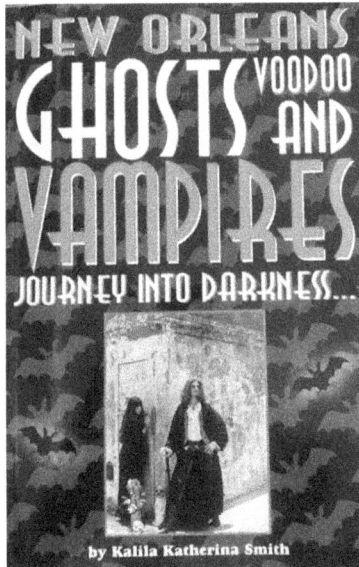

Author's Note: If you're interested, Kalila Smith relates similar stories in her book New Orleans Ghosts, Voodoo and Vampires, Journey into Darkness, which is a must have book regarding the paranormal in New Orleans, in my opinion.

ANECDOTE: QUEEN FOR A DAY

In 1981 Queen came to New Orleans to rehearse prior to launching their South American tour. They posed for an iconic picture on the corner of Royal and Toulouse (Goggle: Queen New Orleans) which we stop and recreate on my Haunted History Pub Crawl Tour.

Note the very important role, that one guy has taken (bottom left), that I have dubbed "Nose picking guy". Check out the back left of original Queen photo online and you'll see what I mean.

8

GHOST RENTALS

Whenever I give a Haunted Pub Crawl tour, I feel the responsibility to act as a good host for my tour patrons. During the decade my wife and I were visiting as tourists we were always fortunate to get friendly and engaging tour guides that treated us well. It made for a more fulfilling experience.

Now that I'm in that position I make an effort to get to know the people on my tour, converse with them about their stay and offer my assistance whenever possible, because I sincerely care that they also have a good experience. It's just part of being an ambassador for the city. This means that while people are watching me give a tour, I'm also watching them and looking for non-verbal cues and body language to gauge their reactions, good and bad.

One Sunday evening in May of 2018 one such experience really stood out and left an impression on me. I had the usual full twenty-eight-person tour group on a Sunday evening, and I noticed during my first story that these two young couples, who were standing together, were extremely quiet and disengaged. Almost to the point of deep sadness, like they had just received some really bad news.

At our first bar stop I made a point of introducing myself, asking where they were from (Southern California) and if there was any special occasion they were celebrating on their visit to New Orleans. They were polite enough during the conversation, but still seemed down, so I asked them if there was anything wrong. They all dropped their heads in unison and told me that they'd had a pretty horrifying experience on their way home from partying Saturday night and it had nothing to do with the paranormal.

They told me they had a really fun night partying in the French Quarter, where they stayed until about 2am. Because it was a beautiful spring evening, they decided to walk back to their Airbnb instead of getting a cab or an Uber. It was only about a mile outside of the Quarter. They were talking and laughing, and the girls decided to race each other for fun, and soon left the guys walking back about half a block behind. As they girls got close to a neighborhood bank they slowed and resumed walking, still a good distance from the guys, lagging behind.

That's when a man exited the passenger side of a parked car, leveled an AK-47 at them and demanded their purses. The two girls screamed and started to run. Their two husbands, hearing the screams started running and yelling in their direction. Apparently, it startled the perpetrator enough that he decided to jump back in the car and they made a fast get away before the husbands caught up with them. They were all understandably terrified and traumatized.

They got to the Airbnb and spent time, into the wee hours of the morning, going over the incident with the police. At one point they started packing their things and were just going to cut their losses, end their trip, and get as far away from the city as possible. But as they started to relax a bit, and the adrenalin wore off, fatigue set in and they to get some sleep. They ended up sleeping most of the day and decided to go ahead and keep their reservation on their ghost tour. My tour.

Honestly, I was speechless. And heartbroken for them. I remember telling them, over and over, how sorry I was. They accepted it graciously and we continued on the tour. I kept tabs on them at each stop and noticed, with each gruesome and haunting tale, that they began to relax and enjoy themselves and that their spirits were lifting. At the end of the tour, they came up and hugged me and thanked me for "saving" their trip. They said the experience was just what they needed to give the city another chance. We took pictures together (which I won't post since I don't have their contact info to obtain permission) and had a few drinks together. I gave them my number, but failed to get theirs, which I regret, because the AK-47 robber was eventually arrested a few weeks later and jailed. I would have liked to have let them know.

That encounter, to this day, is still one of my proudest moments as a guide in this city that I love and call home. It also deeply saddened and angered me. Angered me because in that particular neighborhood where the incident occurred, well, it hasn't actually been fair to call it a neighborhood for quite some time. Since Katrina it has turned into blocks and blocks of empty corporate Airbnb investment properties. This lack of community infrastructure also makes these areas a haven for criminals as ill-informed tourists, unaware of the circumstances, are ripe to become victims.

Fortunately, in the summer of 2019, the City woke up and realized that whole historic communities were being decimated by this practice, and families, some who had spent generations in some of these houses, were forced out because they could no longer afford the artificially increased property taxes.

So, the city did the right thing for these neighborhoods and ended the whole house rental practice. At the time of this writing property values are starting to return to somewhat affordable levels again, and hopefully we'll soon see families back populating these ghost communities, many which surround the periphery of the Quarter, once again.

I also make it a point to end my tours by reminding my guests that this city has a dark side and can be very dangerous, so to be careful, act with caution, don't get so drunk that you become unaware of your surroundings and get transport home if it's outside the Quarter. Especially late at night. We all want you to be safe, fall in love with the city the same way we did, and come back and visit us over and over again. It's what truly makes this all worthwhile.

ANECDOTE: SNAKES IN THE GRASS

A few months after launching the Haunted Pub Crawl in early 2017, things were blowing up and the Crawl was becoming quite popular. Sidney threw some of his best guides, Drew Cothern, Randy Walker and Chrissie McArdle on the tour, and working together we were putting together a really solid tour experience with great bar stops.

Soon after, that's when I learned that espionage wasn't just limited to my Defense Department experience. One Monday evening I had a fair-sized group, maybe about ten people, on my early tour. We launched right at 5:30, got drinks and I started in on my first story. A tale of the most devastating fire in New Orleans history, and a few of the victims who still occupied the building in which we stood.

About halfway through the story, two young ladies walked into the room where we were gathered and demanded to know why we didn't wait for them. Taken aback for a moment, I welcomed them, told them they hadn't really missed anything and that I would catch them up on what they had missed between stops. That didn't satisfy them, and I could see the rest of the group was getting impatient with the interruption, so I asked them to have a seat and we would talk at the conclusion of the story.

They sat with their arms folded, like petulant little kids, and glared at me until I finished. That's when I laid it out for them. They were 15 minutes late. Out of respect for our clients, we start on time. If someone is late, they have two options; realize that they're now on the tour, albeit late, relax and continue with the group, or go ask for a refund. That's it.

Unfortunately, they decided to continue on, which I later discovered, was by design. They refused to buy drinks at the stops, not spending any money, which is a tell-tale sign, and asked bizarre and pointedly skeptical questions at the end of each story. Something didn't feel right, so I pressed them a few times for details about themselves in the form of casual chit chat. They always responded with vague and sometimes contradictory answers. They were definitely up to something. I snuck a picture of them at one point and after my tour, reported the incident to my management. Something was off.

A few days later I got my answer. They were guides from a rival tour company sent to undermine my tour and find out what stories we were telling and why we were becoming so popular. They even posted a bogus negative review mentioning that their company did a much better job of this tour and review readers should come and take it from them instead. Pretty cutthroat and low class. Fortunately, our management was on top of that and had the bogus review removed.

This is why I always recommend that people read several reviews prior to going to a restaurant, taking a tour, checking out a band, etc. Sometimes people have nefarious motives in their reviews, they have a vendetta, they got their feelings hurt somehow, or, in this instance, they're trying to steal customers. Reviewer beware. It's a jungle out there.

Things are getting pretty cutthroat on St. Peter Street
with Claire Christine Sargenti - 2018

9

THE LALAURIE MANSION
1140 Royal Street

I'm sure many of you are already familiar with the story of the LaLaurie Mansion, from either taking one of our tours or perhaps from watching American Horror Story, Season Three, Coven. I can't think of anyone better than incomparable Kathie Bates to portray Delphine Marie McCarty LaLaurie, a 1800s New Orleans socialite who is considered to be amongst America's first female serial killers. Most notably for torturing and murdering her enslaved people, sometimes even during her lavish dinner parties.

In July 2016 I had only been a tour guide for a few months when I got the assignment for my first private tour. I was to meet my point of contact outside Muriel's restaurant at 8pm, on the edge of Jackson Square. I showed up a little early, texted my contact that I was waiting outside and then, promptly at 8pm, eighteen bachelorettes, with Bride Tribe tank tops and glowing penises on their heads, marched out of the restaurant and lined up in from of me. I... was terrified. Not because of who they were, but rather, because of who I was. I mean, here's an old, retired dude pushing sixty taking out a group of young girls on a private tour.

I was afraid that they would have wanted a younger guide, somebody they could party with and relate to. I learned a valuable lesson that night. Never judge how you think the tour is going to go based on how the crowd looks when you walk up, because, you know what? These girls were awesome. They were fun, accepting and totally embraced the tour and me as their guide. Oh yeah, they were also terrified. Of everything. Which makes my job a whole lot easier and a lot more fun. I pulled out all the stops that I could muster with my whole three months of tour guide experience and, towards the end, when they asked if could go to the LaLaurie Mansion so that they could take pictures. How could I say no?

I led them there, told them the story, in gruesome detail, and then motioned for them to follow me across the street so they could look at the property and maybe even get a peek in the windows. I got halfway across the street and realized I was by myself. I turned to look, and they were all still standing firm where I left them. Not one of them had budged. I yelled back "come on guys!" and they yelled back "NO WAY!" And I said, "Seriously, no one is home" and they responded, "Not the living people we're worried about." I shrugged it off, fair enough, and rejoined the group while they finished taking pictures from the safety of across the street. We said our goodbyes and I went home feeling pretty good about myself at that point and hoped they would leave me a good review.

Two AM. My phone started blowing up. "OMG, OMG, do you see what is in this picture!!!???" So, I sat up in bed, looked, and was pretty much blown away. Check it out for yourself.

The LaLaurie Mansion – Original Photo - Circled

Bachelorette Party Photo - Zoom

There is a superstition amongst some of the guides and investigators that walking in a cavalier fashion under the gallery at the LaLaurie Mansion will result in a curse. Now, as a rule I don't particularly subscribe to those types of things, but this one certainly gave me pause. Remember, this is New Orleans and the rules, well, they don't apply much down here. And this lady in black, grey face and dark hooded cloak, staring back at the girl taking the picture, to me, that's a big fat nope.

Now, before you think maybe I'm not as skeptical as I should be on some of these things, I did take the following steps to verify the authenticity of this photo. First, I spoke with the girl who took it the next morning. She claimed that they were sitting in Laffite's Blacksmith Shop after my tour having drinks and going through their pictures. As soon as she saw the picture in question, and zoomed in to look at the apparition, her phone died in her hand, in spite having more than half a battery life left on her phone. It freaked her TF out.

Once she could get back to their hotel and recharge her phone, she did. It took over an hour. Super drained. And once it came back, that's when she started blowing up my phone at two AM. When I spoke with her, she said she hadn't slept much that night.

Next thing I did was drive to the location the next morning to see if I had somehow missed something in the window. Did somebody leave a raincoat hanging in the window? Nope. Nothing there. Now I had already checked the alarm system, which is visible, through the side window of the entry door when we were there the night before. That's why I was confident during our visit that no one was home. I checked it again and still set. No one home.

Next step was to send the picture to a forensic IT specialist friend of mine that works in DOD. The verdict; authentic. No evidence of manipulation whatsoever. Final step, send it to a paranormal investigator for validation and comments. What I got back was a little lesson in Paranormal Investigation 101.

So, why do investigators on shows like Ghost Hunters and Kindred Spirits (one of my personal favorites) go dark during their investigations? Is it for mood? To make it look scarier? No. It's because we believe spirits need to draw on energy in order to manifest and interact with the physical plane of existence. That's why investigators put out those boxes that light up, or go beep, pumping out a lot of energy so spirits can draw from that energy and communicate.

From my experience there is probably no greater power source on the planet than a bachelorette party visiting New Orleans and this spirit came out to warn them, not in my house girls.

Terrified Guests outside the LaLaurie Mansion

Okay bachelorettes, who's next?

"THE SPACES IN BETWEEN – WE PLAY MUSIC"

With Ro Lopez, Halloween 2017

Halloween 2016

With Wild Card – Alice Cooper in Wonderland – 2018
With Claire Voorhies-Chighizola, Chris Primm & Jim Mitchell

Halloween 2018 with Wild Card

The Away Team: Ro Lopez, Chris Primm & Jim Mitchell – 2017

Dark Amber at Santos – August 2019 with Joey Laborde on Bass

Olas Ortwein, Kyle Cripps & Amber Mouton – Quarter Life 2019

AND WE LOVE TO COSTUME... FOR EVERYTHING!

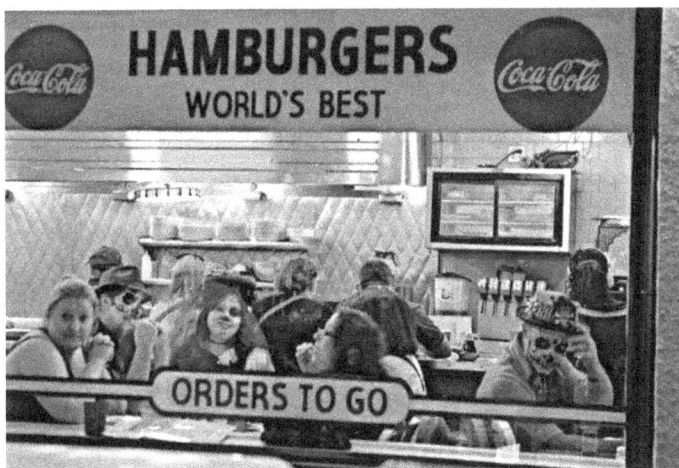

GHOST TOWN LYRICS

Written by Kelly Walls, Troy Walls & Lexi Lew

Everybody tried to warn me
That strange things happen here
They say that every February
Fools are gathered on the Square
They don't know that in the shadows
There's blood stains on these walls
From the last poor souls who came for Mardi Gras

When you're walking down the street
You ought to know that here in Nola
It's hardly ever what you think, so be careful what
you drink
And who you invite inside
If you wanna keep your soul
Listen close to what I told ya
Keep your guard up and your head down
When the spirits come around
I'll be your guide
I'll help you survive
In this Ghost Town

That's the last words that she told me
When she led me to this room
Lit the candles and poured the potion
That I'm pouring out for you
I know you're thinking you won't drink it
Honey you already did
You don't remember but the bitter taste
It lingers on your lips
You'll be just fine

When you're walking down the street
You ought to know that here in Nola
It's hardly ever what you think, so be careful what
you drink

And who you invite inside
If you wanna keep your soul
Listen close to what I told ya
Keep your guard up and your head down
When the spirits come around
I'll be your guide
I'll help you survive
In this Ghost Town

Now that you know what to do
You better do it well
Find Papa Legba, lots of souls
Or find yourself in hell

When you're walking down the street
You ought to know that here in Nola
It's hardly ever what you think, so be careful what
you drink
And who you invite inside
If you wanna keep your soul
Listen close to what I told ya
Keep your guard up and your head down
When the spirits come around
I'll be your guide
I'll help you survive
In this Ghost Town

Follow the QR Code below to get to Lexi's link tree for purchasing options.

LexiLew.com

10

NIGHTS SPENT IN THE GUTTER WITH THE RATS AND THE PUNKS
Drew Cothern

The French Quarter is famously a place of personalities. Ruthie the Duck Girl, who wore brightly colored furs and roller skated the old Creole streets accompanied by a small flock the birds in the latter days of the Twentieth Century; the Traffic Tranny, who up until recently would help motorists safely pass through the throngs of revelers on Bourbon Street at St. Ann; Twerkin' Granny, who can still be found delivering her message of God's love as she pedals through the neighborhood on her improvised bike/billboard/party-wagon, stopping every now and then to dance with her fans in groovy, geriatric gyrations. These eccentrics add the color, vivacity, and unpredictability that makes the Quarter famous around the world, and they are beloved while they're here and mourned when they're not.

Then there are the gutterpunks.

Oogles. Crust-punks. Traveling Kids. Neo-Hobos. There are plenty of terms for them, but in New Orleans, we call them gutterpunks. You've no doubt seen them in your city, in whatever passes for an economic or cultural center, crowded in vacant doorways and alcoves and cluttering up corners, uniformed in earth tones and face tattoos and body odor and contempt, all alike in their desperate attempts to be different, often with dogs in tow.

Some of them had hard home lives that they had escaped, perhaps too young to be out on the streets and hopping trains alone. Some of them had dependencies on drug or drink that dragged them down and put them out. Some seem to be doing it for a lark, retaining a credit card or a trust-fund for their endeavors. Some have a philosophy built on anarchism, Beat generation romance for a life *On the Road*, and the DIY sensibilities of punks that had come before. They can be crude, obnoxious, and mean, but on a personal level, I find that I can often get along with them well enough when I'm not working. I've always sympathized with the outsider. When I'm trying to guide a tour, it's another story.

Gutterpunks are the enemy of French Quarter tour guides.

I understand the impulse. When you're on the fringe of society, why not shake things up, provide some much-needed distraction from your hunger, your withdrawals, or even just your boredom? You come upon some jerky-looking asshole dressed in a bowler hat and red-checkered vest, carrying a cane, telling tired old bullshit ghost stories to a bunch of square tourists, and friend, you've got your distraction.

Looking back over the years at the way I used to dress in an attempt to add a touch of theatricality to my presentation, I'd have bullied me too. But I quickly learned that the only thing it really adds is a signal to the gutterpunks that you're still green, still unsure, and totally ready to be fucked with. At five years in, I don't dress like that anymore, and the gutterpunks tend to recognize me as one who has been taken in and accepted by the Quarter, no longer shakable, and ultimately not worth the trouble. But that was not always the case.

Photo by Drew Cothern

I recorded the first interaction I had with a gutterpunk while on tour. He was drunk, I was working. I was dressed in the outfit I wore my first season, a bowler hat, red checkered vest, and black pants. I also carried my grandfather's cane. This is the exchange that followed, documented shortly after it occurred:

"Thass all bullshit."

"Excuse me? Which part?"

"Alla it."

"Oh, my mistake. Ladies and gentlemen, I didn't realize we had a true historian in our midst. Would you like to lead the tour?"

"Put down your stick, dude."

"No, I need it. Gummy leg. Besides, I'm sure you'll do fine without it. Go ahead. Tell these fine people what you know about New Orleans history."

"Do y'all know about the House of the Risin' Sun?"

"I do, actually, yes. But go on."

"Well...iss been the ruin of many poor boys..."

"Uh-huh. Go on."

"Put your stick down."

"Why?"

"Because I'm gonna fight you."

"Oh. In that case, no way. Why do you wanna fight me?"

"Because you tol' me to lead yer tour."

"Oh, I'm sorry! I got the impression you knew what you were talking about. But you DON'T know what you're talking about, do you?"

"It was my birfday yesterday. Somebody stabbed me in the foot and I'm PISSED OFF about it!"

"Well, I'm sure it was just karma paying a debt."

"PUT YOUR STICK DOWN!"

"LOOK! This is gonna go one of two ways - you're either going to mosey on your way, or I'mma get NOPD down here. Which's it gonna be?"

"Aww, man, I just wanted to fight, dude. You ain't gotta call the cops, man, you ain't gotta call the cops."

"Phone's ringing."

"You're skinny and quick and I'm slow. You ain't gotta call the cops, dude, you prolly coulda taken me. Pussy."

He hung his head as he hobbled away, careful not to put any weight on his stabbed foot. My group applauded. For a brief moment, I pitied him. A *very* brief moment. So, this is the way these interactions typically go. Words, threats, insults, but nothing more. On a couple of memorable occasions, though, that was not the case.

I'll never forget this one, because the fellow was wearing a white t-shirt displaying the Ten of Swords from the tarot as seen in the Rider-Waite deck, with a figure evoking an assassinated Julius Caesar lying on the ground in a pool of blood, run through with ten swords. It represents betrayal, loss, defeat, failure, and death; in other words, not necessarily something one would normally wish to have hanging over them. It was a card he seemed to be living.

I had an unusually courteous group that night. Normally, I have to keep reminding them to leave a walking path behind them so as not to block traffic on the sidewalk, but not this time. In spite of this, Ten of Swords came sauntering by and seemed to have a problem that there were people gathered on the sidewalk. He said something snide to one of my guests, who responded in kind. I was going to ignore it, but it kept going and the gutterpunk was getting more aggressive. So I stopped my story and said, "Is there a problem?"

The gutterpunk said, "Yeah, all these fuggin white people are blocking up the sidewalk! It's giving me anxiety- white people give me anxiety!" Now, it's worth noting that this fellow was white, whiter than my group, even, which was maybe a quarter Hispanic.

Confused by his statement, I said, "White people give you anxiety? Man, looking in the mirror must be tough for you." Then, after noting his scruffy state, "Although I guess you haven't done that in a while."

He turned on me, "FUCK YOU! Eat your Chick-Fil-A!"

"What?"

"Eat flesh, breathe chemicals, GET FUCKED!"

I cocked my head and looked at him. "You're cute. You're really very cute. With your half-baked philosophies, your sense of entitlement, and your hate. Just adorable!"

"I'll show you fucking CUTE!" he roared, throwing down his skateboard and box of take-out to rush me.

As I have learned to do in these situations, I did not flinch. I did not back down. And all of a sudden, he lost the courage of his convictions. He glared at me for a moment before casting his eyes down to his spilled take-out.

"That was my fucking DINNER!" he moaned.

"Then why'd you throw it on the ground?"

He knelt down and grabbed a fistful of runny noodles off the dirty St. Phillips Street sidewalk and took a bite out of it. It was only then that true disgust washed over me. He glared at me, then hurled his fistful of noodles at me. His aim was bad. Very bad. The noodles flew over my head without even having to duck, landing in the street behind me with a wet splat. I laughed. My group laughed. And with a final fuck-you, he stalked off into the night, leaving the rest of his dinner behind. Other tour guides would see him following our altercation getting into a fight with a parked car on Bourbon. I would see Ten of Swords only once more, a few weeks later, being thrown out of the St. Louis Cathedral. His shirt, which had been white when he assaulted me with Alfredo, was torn and brown. I wouldn't see him again.

Photo by Drew Cothern

Perhaps the most memorable interaction I've had, though, came while I was telling a story in Dutch Alley by the River. I was near the end of my tour with a group that, frankly, didn't care for me. They were disengaged, dead-eyed, like goldfish in a bowl, gawping at me as I talked, but not really hearing. I hate groups like that. May as well be telling ghost stories to a brick wall.

Enter: a gutterpunk. He comes oiling by, passing in between me and my group. It seems that he's just passing through, but then he stops. He stops right in front of a girl that looks like she just graduated high school in Cornfuck, Nebraska. He eyes her before holding up his grubby hand, bringing it right up to her face. She reacts the way you might expect any valedictorian of Cornfuck High might - she gasps and cringes away.

I sighed. I approached him and said, "Hey, man. You gotta go. I'm working here, and you're bothering these people."

"I ain't goin' nowhere until I get my high-five," he snarled, turning back to the girl.

"Yes, you are," I said, feeling uncharacteristically heroic, "One way or another."

He wheeled around on me, got right in my face, smashing his nose into mine. "You gonna head-butt me?" he said.

I gripped my cane, ready to smash him in the temple as soon as he made a move. My adrenaline began pumping hard. I was wearing steel-toe boots and ready to stomp him right into the ground if necessary. I had plenty of witnesses who would say I was justified. Just as soon as he made the first move. I waited. He waited. We were breathing each other's air. I'd put him in a bad position, I realized. If I hit him first, then he was justified in giving me a beating. But if he just walked away, then I would win. So he settled on the third option, to attempt to humiliate me. So he kissed me, full on. Open-mouth.

But here's the thing. I'm not about to be humiliated by some goddamn gutterpunk.

I kissed him back with tongue.

A power-move! He pulled back, his eyes wide with surprise. I wiped my mouth and fixed him with my most intimidating gaze and growled, "*Yeah!*"

In that growl, I had asserted, *Yeah, that's right. Fuck with me. I can be crazy. I can live in the ditch with you. Yeah. Fuck with me. I dare you.* But he didn't. We'd met as shameless equals. There was nothing more to be said. Then, he was gone, down the road to the river. As he went, I realized I could taste his rancid sweat on my mustache. I grimaced and spit before turning to my group.

"Y'ALL BETTER TIP ME FOR THAT!" I bellowed.

For the first time all night, these dead-eyed fish-people that I couldn't get to even chuckle began rolling with laughter.

And tip they did. They tipped very well.

Photo by Drew Cothern

None of these interactions have ever escalated to violence, but I can honestly say that the years of working in the Quarter has had an effect on me. I don't take shit, and though I will work to avoid it, I'm ready for violence should violence come. The Quarter can be a violent place, after all, and being able to stand your ground is necessary to survive.

Though no violence has come to me, I have witnessed it coming to others. Sometimes, unfortunately, in front of my tour group.

I was standing outside MRB on St. Phillip Street with a group one November evening and I had to pause my story as a cop, an ambulance, and a firetruck went screaming down lower Decatur. I wondered what the matter was, but I didn't worry for long. A moment later, as we rounded the corner onto Decatur, I saw the source of the commotion.

It was a gutterpunk, sitting halfway up the block on the curb, and he was being attended to by a medic. Blood gushed down the side of the gutterpunk's face, but I couldn't see its source due to his thick, blonde dreadlocks and the medic attending him blocking my view. As we approached, I heard the medic say, "Okay, man, we have to take you in to get you stitched up."

The gutterpunk nodded grimly before replying, "Well...should I get my ear?"

He turned and pointed, and I saw it. Not a piece, not a part, no. *His entire right ear had been severed and was lying behind him on the sidewalk.*

Which put me in an awkward position. Do I stop the tour and turn around? Do I do as I typically do and try to ignore it and keep on my route? *How does one simply ignore a severed human ear?* Luckily, I didn't have to make that choice. Another paramedic saw us coming, and like an angel of god, swooped in and rescued the ear, getting it out of sight. The only ones to see it were me and four frat boys walking behind me.

One of them didn't handle it well. I'd never seen anyone literally turn green before, but he did, having to lean on one of his bros to keep steady as we continued down the block. After he stopped gagging and caught his breath, he said to me, his voice shaking, "Did...did you see that guy's *ear?*"

Trying my best to maintain composure, I smiled at him and said, "Oh. First ear, huh?"

Photo by Drew Cothern

89

One question I am often asked is, "What's the weirdest thing you've seen in the French Quarter?" You'd think a whole human ear lying - like *Blue Velvet* - on the sidewalk would be it, but no. Friends, I have seen things that would make you laugh, make you cry, and scenes that would turn your hair white. But the weirdest thing came, happily, not while I was on tour, but after I'd had a late night that had turned into an early morning in the Quarter.

It was nearing seven o'clock and the sun was coming up and I was sobering up and it was time to go home. I'd parked my car on St. Peter Street, and as I walked towards it, I saw something unexpected down the block. Now, those of us that are in the Quarter every day expect the unexpected, but this was beyond that.

Down the block, I saw a man. Wearing a blue dress. Squatting like a bird on top of an orange Prius. As I got closer, details of this scene started to become clear. His thin, yellow hair was standing out at odd angles, and he was gnawing on the crust of old pizza the way a dog does a bone. I noticed there was a puddle of vomit on the hood of the car. About half a block away from him, we locked eyes and I realized with horror what he was doing.

HE WAS FUCKING HIMSELF WITH THE ANTENNA OF THE PRIUS!!!!!

We both screamed. He hurled the crust at me before reaching into the greasy pizza box beside him for more ammunition. I hastily apologized. What else could I do? I apologized for interrupting him and said I would go to the next block.

Blurred for your protection – Photo by Drew Cothern

You probably don't believe me. I wouldn't if I were you. I couldn't believe what I'd seen myself and tour guides, after all, are known to indulge in hyperbole. But it did happen, and I knew that no matter how insistent I was about what I had seen, no one would believe me. As I shakily opened my car door and closed it behind me, I had a realization. In order to leave the Quarter, I would have to drive down St. Peter Street. I would have to drive right past him. My phone was at less than 5% battery. Just enough. The video I took that morning is proof, friends, that you should *always* believe your tour guide because, in the French Quarter at least, the truth truly is stranger than any fiction we could ever dream up on our own.

ANECDOTE: HOPE IN THE FRENCH QUARTER -
Charmaine Swan Rich

Today I went for a walk. Because of the Covid-19 Quarantine, I had not been to the French Quarter in a month - which was weird since I am a tour guide and work in the quarter.

Today, the French Quarter was quiet, still and empty. It really freaked me out at first. Then, after a few quiet moments...I felt Her. The City. She is still here, just sometimes She has to recharge Her strength, Her energy.

I felt Her calmness. Her silence. And She was breathing. As I walked around thru the silence I felt Her love - "I am still here, just resting" is what I felt in my heart. But, I still wished I could hear something other than silence with my ears... if only..... Something....the kids hitting the buckets, the clop, clop of the mules, the horns playing....oh the horns...the music... that would help.

As I walked down St. Ann Street and Pere Antoine Alley I guess She heard me. Through the deafening silence I heard him... the guy I had heard him thousands of times, in the same place, by Cafe Du Monde. I walked by him, actually ran by him when I was late for a tour, but now, my heart exploded, and tears came to my eyes.... "This little light of mine, I'm gonna let it shine..."

He was here, singing and clapping, as he always did. It's the "guy that only knows three songs and only about four lines in each song!" And he is here, with his tip bucket - singing!!!!

After I took this picture of Cafe Du Monde, I went over to him and gave him, well, let's just say, it was more than a dollar. He looked at me, right in my eyes and had tears in his eyes - "oh, oh, wow! Thank you ma'am! You spent me out! I can go have lunch now!" Not expecting this, I stumbled with my words, saying "oh, good, stay safe, have a good day!" He got on his bike and took off.

I can't explain the loving, happy, feeling deep in my heart that made me feel warm and fuzzy all over. With what is going on now, She gave me all that I needed... and then I gave that to someone else... and all I am gonna say is "This little light of mine, I'm gonna let it shine...."

11

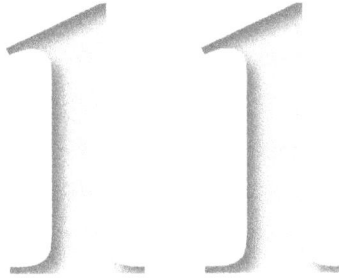

HURRICANE WARNING
Ariadne Blayde

In my experience, there are two types of tour guides. You've got the ones who prefer small groups so they can lean in close, make chit chat, get to know everybody; these guides basically treat the tour as an informal stroll, a conversation between friends. And then you have prima donnas like me, who call it "My Tour" with capital letters like it's the newest hottest off-Broadway event of the season and demand as large an audience as possible. In my case, My Tour is a one-woman theatrical performance complete with perfectly-crafted turns of phrase, accents, and occasional sections of mime. Horribly cheesy or breathtakingly compelling? I don't give a shit, really, but my tour guests usually tip well enough that I feel good about how I've chosen to use my theatre degree.

 On the night in question (a balmy evening in early March, if I recall correctly) only about a dozen people showed up for the 6:00 Ghost Tour. Some tour guides would be happy to have a small group, but I was not. What star likes a tiny audience? Having a small group makes my scenery-chewing appear awkward and over-the-top, and requires me to tone the tour down to a conversation by going off my usual script. I can't turn on tour-autopilot when I have a small group; I have to actually *work* at my job, and who wants to do that? I almost turned down the tour, but this was immediately post-Mardi Gras and I had some poor spending decisions to make up for.

I stood next to the ticket seller for half an hour before the tour as the customers trickled in. They included: five French-speaking Canadians, a nice stocky couple from Texas or Florida (I can never distinguish nor remember; tourists from these states are equally unpleasant), another nondescript family or two from I don't know where, two exuberant young women of color, and a 25-year-old white girl all by herself. The minutes ticked by and I prayed that more would show up. But it was a slow night, and a Tuesday, and I knew I'd just have to work with what I'd been given. At 5:55 I put on my lipstick and at 6:00 I led them away down the sidewalk, already cranky.

At 6:03, it started to rain.

I am usually prepared for rain. I keep a small umbrella in my bag, and as long as it starts raining before the tour begins, we're good to go: the tourists understand that the tour will continue rain or shine, and have taken the time to buy ponchos or umbrellas. But when it starts raining *after* our start time? Bad, bad news. They're not prepared for it. Doesn't matter that they all keep devices in their pockets that can predict the weather; if it's not precipitating when the tour starts and then starts to rain halfway in, they are all 1) terrified, 2) unprepared, and 3) mad at me, since I am, as they always seem to think, single-handedly responsible for the quality of their New Orleans experience.

I stopped in a different spot than usual so that they could huddle under a small overhang and rushed through my intro, prepared for an already difficult small-group tour to be made more difficult by the rain. But, surprisingly, my introduction went better than I expected. There's a very interesting phenomenon in tour groups, wherein one or two people with a bad vibe can bring down the whole group, and one or two people with a good vibe can elevate the experience for everyone. This tour seemed to be trending toward the latter; the two young women of color were clearly prepared to have a wonderful time, and their enthusiasm was infectious. I apologized for the rain and told the group I hoped they were up for an adventure. "We ain't sugar, we ain't gonna melt!" one of the young women called in response, raising her drink. Some of the other group members laughed and nodded.

How 'bout that, I mused to myself. *Might not be such a bad tour after all.* I breezed through the rules -- one benefit of a small group is that you don't have to be such a stickler about crowd control -- and gave my usual teasing guidelines about drinking, which of course is allowed on the tour as long as it doesn't get out of hand. "Don't get wasted, that's not fun for anyone but you," is my usual line. "I'm looking at y'all with the two-for-one hurricanes," I said, nodding toward the pair of women and single girl, who were all holding pleasantly pink drinks in go-cups. The bar next door offers buy-one-get-one hurricanes for our customers, so the pair of young women had split the deal, and each had one. But the solo white girl had apparently decided to drink both herself; one of them was free, after all, so she was double-fisting, one hurricane in each hand. They laughed at my joke and promised to behave.

I launched into my first story and the pair of young women continued to be interested, engaged and talkative. In a big group this can be a problem -- "This is not a conversation," I often have to remind drunken dads who want to interject comments every three sentences -- but in small groups a little back-and-forth with the group can work. I found myself enjoying the conversational tour style that I normally hate so much, and the rain didn't seem to be bothering the group at all. If anything, it seemed to have created a sense of camaraderie. Two teenage boys from separate families seemed to have a snarky teenage-boy thing going, and the solo white girl had jumped onto the duo's vibe train. As we walked to our next stop I heard her laughing and joking with them in the way young women often do in bar bathroom lines, tipsy and quick to make friends with strangers. She had finished her first hurricane and was onto her second, which honestly should have been a red flag, but I was just pleased that they all seemed to be having a good time.

The rain picked up. I did an excellent job keeping the group tucked away under balconies, but I myself got soaked as I stood in the street to deliver the stories. By our third stop, the downpour showed no sign of ceasing and the temperature had dropped ten degrees. I was freezing, and I could tell the group was becoming uncomfortable. I wrapped up the story at the LaLaurie Mansion a little more quickly than usual and hustled them toward the bar where we always take a break, eager to warm up.

On the walk I chatted with the three young women, who had become a unit. I asked the white girl what brought her to town; by now she was quite tipsy and all she could tell me was that she was here with her "woo-woo girls." She referred to her fiancée several times, and I was able to piece together that she was in town for a bachelorette party: her own. "Where are your friends?" I asked, and she said they would all be arriving tomorrow. She stumbled on the sidewalk and one of the duo caught her arm and pulled her close. I looked down at her hand and saw she had sucked down most of her second hurricane in the last 15 minutes. This was an alarming development.

"Make sure she gets some water at the bar," I whispered to the other ladies, and they nodded.

Across the street from the bar I told the group where they could buy ponchos and dismissed them for a ten minute break, then hurried around the corner to my car to get my rain jacket. I was deeply chilled and felt much better after putting it on.

When we returned from our break, the rain had slowed but the white girl was visibly very drunk. She interjected slurred comments as I spoke, but it wasn't cute anymore. "You have to be quiet, honey," I told her in the same voice a kindergarten teacher might use. The other women were now firmly entrenched on either side of her, steadying her as she swayed and murmuring to her in hushed voices to keep her under control.

You may have heard of the famous drink called a "hurricane," invented in New Orleans at the popular Irish tavern Pat O'Brien's in the 1940's. It consists of 2 ounces light rum, 2 ounces dark rum, various fruit juices, and a floater of 151 (which is 75% alcohol by volume). A hurricane is easily two to three times as strong as any other cocktail, and the kicker is, it's sweet and tropical and goes down easy, easy, easy. This girl -- who, might I add, was about 5'2" -- had now had *two* of these concoctions in one hour, and I was pretty sure she hadn't had dinner. Bad news bears.

At our next stop she started vomiting.

Now here's the thing. As a tour guide, I am absolutely allowed to kick disruptively intoxicated people out of the group. I've done it before; the quickest it ever happened was when a basic bro and his girlfriend were so drunk and annoyed at each other they started kicking each other in the shins during my introduction, then made up, which emboldened the dude to start yelling "PENIS" at my next stop. Kicking drunk folks off is not a problem; the boss has our back, and the other patrons are always so relieved to be rid of the assholes that they usually tip better and leave better reviews.

This girl was beyond the point of disruptively drunk. The other group members edged away and tried not to look at her as she huddled behind a car, throwing up pink liquid the same color and consistency as the hurricanes she'd just gulped down. In any other circumstance I'd have kicked her out of the group, but I realized with horror there was absolutely no way I could do that. She was all alone, not only in the group but *in the whole city*. Her other bachelorettes hadn't arrived yet. This girl was tiny, wasted, and sending her out into the streets of the Quarter by herself was out of the question.

I announced an emergency break and ran across the street to the coffee shop to get her a bottle of water, while the two young ladies held her hair and patted her back. The French Canadians announced politely that they would be leaving, and I felt a surge of frustration; they were nearly half the group, and clearly did not intend to tip me before they departed.

When I got back from the coffee shop the girl was apologizing through a haze of tears, horribly embarrassed. "It's okay, it's okay," her new friends said reassuringly as they patted her back. "Happens to everybody. You're gonna be okay."

I very frankly told the rest of the group that I had no choice but to keep the girl with us, for her own safety. They were understanding enough. We were almost finished, anyway -- just a couple more stops. During the next story the girl made a valiant effort to seem like she was interested and paying attention, nodding vigorously at every sentence and occasionally taking breaks to step away and vomit. She seemed to get most of it out and was marginally more sober by the time we got to our last stop. I rushed through my sleep-paralysis story and sagged with relief when I finally got to my outro, possibly more desperate than I'd ever been for a tour to end. Tips? Abominable. Ones and fives, probably fifteen bucks total; normally I hit at least $60, even with small groups.

The other group members wandered away, leaving me, the young ladies and our drunken charge alone on the wet sidewalk. She was now openly crying, horrified at her own behavior, and the young ladies -- who, I was now convinced, were literal angels sent from heaven -- soothed her and tried to cheer her up. "Hey, there's no crying in baseball!" one said. "Yeah, chin up, girl, you're gonna be okay in no time."

"She's gotta get back to her hotel," one of them said to me, and I nodded. "Girl, where you staying?"

We got the information out of her after a few tries: a hotel in the Central Business District, on the other side of the French Quarter.

"I guess we ought to put her in an Uber or something?"

I shook my head. "Nah, she'll barf. And that's a giant fee."

By now it was clear what I had to do. "I've got this from here. Y'all go enjoy the rest of your night," I said, thanking them profusely. "I literally could not have gotten through this tour without you."

"Oh, it was no big deal! Just hope she's okay tomorrow," they laughed.

Can I actually give you a hug?" I asked and embraced them each. Never in my five years as a tour guide had I been so grateful for someone in my group.

"Oh! I'm so sorry, we don't have any cash to tip you," one said.

"My god, are you kidding?" I laughed. "I'm the one who should be tipping you."

I said goodnight to them, and they went off laughing and cheerful, totally unphased by the last two hours' nightmarish events.

"Come on, babe, you're coming with me," I said, hauling the white girl to her feet.

"Where are we going?"

"The only place you *can* go, honey. Back to your hotel to sleep this off."

I took her to my car -- my most prized possession, by the way, a convertible red Mini Cooper -- and got her buckled in. "I'm gonna drive you back, okay? Barf out the window if you need to."

"I'm so sorry," she burbled through hiccups and more tears. "This is so-
- so embarrass-- ing. I'm not like this, I promise. I'm not this-- this kind
of ind-- individual."

"Happens to everybody," I said. "I'm just glad I'm here to make sure
you're safe."

Her cheeks filled with vomit as we hit a pothole. "Out the window, out
the window!" I hollered, lowering it for her. But short as she was, she
wasn't able to get her head out the window far enough for a clear shot,
so she opened the passenger door a crack.

"Woah woah woah! Don't open the door!" I said, rolling up to a
stoplight. She spat vomit out the gap and wiped her lips. "Don't do that
again, okay? And put your seatbelt back on!"

She did it again five minutes later, luckily when the car was stopped,
and then again one or two more times. Between the constant door-
opening and endless apologizing, my patience quickly wore thin. Add to
that the fact that it was still raining, and visibility wasn't great, and the
ten-minute drive felt like it took thirty. After navigating through a
frustrating series of one-way streets I finally pulled up to her hotel.

"Okay. We're here. This is it, right? This is where you're staying?"

"Yes," she said vaguely. "I think so."

"Get some room service once you get up there. You have to eat."

She started to cry again. "This is the worst night ever. I'm such an idiot."

"Hey," I said, putting a hand on her shoulder. "No, it's not. Your friends
aren't here yet, nobody has to know. Tomorrow's a new day, okay? And
now you've learned your lesson, so you'll have a much better time for
the rest of the week. And you really will have the best time. It's hard not
to, in this city," I smiled.

She sniffled and nodded, then started wailing again. "You're such a
saint. And I'm the worst tour customer ever."

I laughed, considering this. "Well, maybe. But at least you have the self-
awareness to acknowledge it. Most of them don't," I said, remembering
Penis-shouting guy and his awful girlfriend.

I jotted down my number on a slip of paper. "This is my name and number, okay? Text me if you need anything. And for God's sake, do not leave this hotel until morning."

"I won't," she promised.

She clumsily gathered her things and got out of the car. I made sure she hadn't left anything behind, watched as she stumbled into the hotel past the totally-unphased doorman, and drove away through the rain, hoping it would wash away the trail of vomit down the side of my car door.

The next day I got a text at 1 pm. "Hello from the most embarrassed person in the world!" it said. We shot a few texts back and forth, she apologized again, I made some jokes to help her feel better. "What's your Venmo?" she asked. "I at least owe you a car wash."

"Oh, don't worry about it," I texted back, hoping she would see through the lie. Sure enough, a few seconds later my phone made that delightful cash-register sound. Fifty bucks. My eyes popped with money signs, like a cartoon character's. I thanked her and told her it wasn't necessary.

"By the way, I loved your tour," she said. "What I remember of it, anyway. You're really good at what you do."

Hell yes I'm good at what I do, I thought, immediately and gratefully transferring the fifty bucks to my empty bank account. "Take care of yourself," I texted back. "And enjoy the hell out of New Orleans."

My first Halloween in this city, I "pregamed" with a hurricane and ended up so drunk that I had to miss the big party and go home, sobbing, at eight o'clock. On New Years' eve two weeks after I turned 26 I got so drunk that I wandered down the train tracks by the river and then let myself into the tour company's storage closet and fell asleep, my boyfriend frantically searching for me all the while. I've thrown up in people's yards, cried in bar bathrooms, become overly friendly with strangers. What woman hasn't, in her twenties? I don't hold a thing against that girl, and I'm glad I could get her home safe. Countless women have done the same for me. She seemed like a sweet, responsible person whose overdrinking was an accident, and we've all been there. Hell, many of us have indulged in overdrinking on purpose, on the regular. I hope she learns her lesson and doesn't make that mistake again

Of course, some people never grow out of the binge-drinking and bad-decision-making phase. We get a lot of visitors like that in New Orleans, some of them well into their 40's and 50's and 60's and still struggling with finding and managing their own limits. I grew out of my unhappy relationship with alcohol; I had to. It would be impossible to walk the streets of the French Quarter every night if I didn't have a handle on myself, my drinking, my coping skills. I know how incredibly lucky I am to live the life I do and have the job I do. And the reality is, sometimes the cost of that is dealing with people who aren't so lucky. People whose lives are hard and boring and painful, people who need an escape. For some, New Orleans is the only place they really get to let go. And whenever I have an inconvenient, annoying, or downright exhausting experience with someone who has let go a little too much, I try to remind myself how fortunate I am to be in New Orleans telling ghost stories for a living.

No amount of bachelorette barf can take that away from me.

ANECDOTE: **DAVE GROHL** - *Rachel Lockett*

So, it's a busy weekend before Halloween, Saturday night at the Dungeon. They usually are. But this one, even more so because it's also Voodoo Fest weekend and the city is packed.

I'm working the downstairs bar, which is my domain, when I notice our doorman, Alan, is waving, trying to get my attention and yelling "1942! 1942!" At first, I thought he was having a stroke, or something, so I yelled back "1942 what? I follow his gaze to find Dave Grohl and his entourage taking a seat at the bar. Okay. Got it.

Now, to Alan, 1942 actually means something. You see Alan was working at Yo Mama's Burgers on St. Ann one day a few years back, when Dave Grohl walked in and sat down at the bar. The Foo Fighters were in town filming Sonic Highways across the street at Preservation Hall and he came in for drinks. They did this a lot all over the Quarter.

Ironically, the bartender didn't know who Dave Grohl was, so when he ordered shots of Don Julio Tequila 1942, she says "Hey, this is $20 a shot. You sure you can afford this?" And he smiled and replied "Yeah, I got it covered." So, Alan remembered this and getting a little stunned and flustered that Dave had just walked into The Dungeon, that's apparently all he could get to come out of his mouth.

Now I have to say, working at a place like the Dungeon, you get to meet a lot of celebrities, and, over the years, let's just say I have a really long list. But Dave Grohl, he's in a class unto himself. He is literally the coolest person I have ever met. He's so humble and grounded. He's very generous. He looks you in the eye when he talks to you. For me it was magical.

In the midst of everything that's going on, there's a group of people in the cage. One had a ball cap on. Now I don't get star struck often, and I never do this, but I went over to the people in the cage and said, "Dave Grohl is here!" And they laughed and it was fine. I guess I let my excitement get the best of me.

But as the night progressed, with everything that was going on, the people in the cage began to irritate me. So, about an hour had transpired, when I finally got pissed off at something that they did, went back to them and said "Alright, you guys are gonna have to pay up, or leave, or do something, because you just can't sit around and stare at Dave Grohl all night." To my surprise they were actually really nice about it. Some are not. They ended up leaving and I kind of felt like I'd maybe been a little bit of a jerk, but, oh well.

Then I find out that the guy in the ball cap was Tom Fucking Morello of Rage Against the Machine. Whoa! And I remember his face when I told him that he couldn't be staring at Dave Grohl. What was that look? Shock? Amusement? I can't quite recall. But, in my defense, he kind of was just sitting there staring at Dave Grohl. In retrospect, I'm sure they knew each other and I'm sure that's why he was staring, but he was kind of incognito in a ball cap, looking like an average Joe, and Dave Grohl was getting all the attention.

So, that's my tale of how I rescued Dave Grohl from Tom Morello at the Dungeon. Just remember, not all heroes wear capes. Some of us wear horns.

Photo by Rachel Lockett

12

THE DISAPPEARING FACE

Stella Salmen

Muriel's Restaurant: Jackson Square

Muriel's Restaurant is one of the most popular haunted locations for ghost tours in the city. Having been heavily damaged by the Good Friday Fire of 1788, it was sold to a wealthy man... with a gambling problem. As one would expect in a ghost story, the tragic events were, play poker, bet mansion, lose mansion, commit suicide.

Although his family had to depart the mansion to satisfy the gambling debt, his spirit remained. He also took issue with the location being turned into a restaurant, as he mistook well-dressed people partaking of fine food and spirits as being parties... he loved parties, and evidently felt insulted that he was not invited. The more successful the restaurant, the more active the hauntings... until a psychic medium communicated his reasons to the owners. To make him feel more welcome, there is a special "Ghost Table" in the old carriageway. Private dining for our restless spirit. Groups visiting can look down the long hall and view the table from the street. They also get the opportunity to take pictures.

I always caution my guests that the plexiglass on the gate is quite warped and scratched, so many times "anomalies" that appear in photos can be attributed to that, but not always.

I ask my guests to wait until we take our mid-tour bar break to show me odd photos, because if I looked at them after each stop we would never get through the tour. Yet on this occasion I made an exception.

Stepping down from the carriageway to allow my guests to get photos, I wait for my group to gather. One woman who had been front and center, and got her pictures right away, walked up scrolling through her shots, and suddenly froze in place with her eyes as wide as saucers! I had suggested using the "burst" setting on phone cameras… it takes 10-12 pictures in a fraction of a second and can capture images that pass too quickly for the human eye to see. She had taken my advice, and on seeing her shock, I asked to see what she captured. Why not… others were still at the doorway taking photos. Fully expecting to see just an odd reflection, I instead got quite a shock!

She scrolled through the pictures:

Table, Table, Table, FACE, Table, Table…

I physically jumped!

Ok, people were gathering, and I told her that I really wanted to see that again when we got to the bar break.

3 stories later we break, and I ask the woman to show me that photo burst again. She was a bit nervous, but also glad to have confirmation.

Opened the photo series, and:

Table, Table, Table, Table, Table, Table, Table… it was gone.

My favorite picture with Stella, stealing her soul at The Funky Pirate Blues Bar, October 2016

STRANGER IN MY HOUSE
Eryn

One day I woke up
And I saw him standing there
He looked so familiar
I knew him from somewhere
Maybe the grocery store
Or walking down the street
He did not frighten me
But where did we meet?

Who is the stranger in my house?
I recognize something in his eyes
I'm not sure why or how
Who is the stranger in my house?

He was there on my wedding day
And when my children were born
I found a piece of my heart
By his feet on the floor
The cat seems to know him
And the dog doesn't cry
He's in my memories
With me trapped inside

Who is the stranger in my house?
I recognize something in his eyes
I'm not sure why or how
Who is the stranger in my house?

Everything is spinning
He somehow knows my name
Am I really dreaming
Or did I really wake with this pain

Who is the stranger in my house?

I recognize something in his eyes
I'm not sure why or how
Who is the stranger in my house?

One day I woke up
And I saw him standing there
He looked so familiar

Go to **erynoffical.com** to listen to this song and many others in her amazing catalogue.

13

BRINGING THEM BACK WITH YOU

When dealing with the paranormal, especially as much as we do, there is always a very real possibility of spirit attachment. My wife and I learned this in a very real way after our visit in 2005. We were living in Maryland at the time and had friends from California and Maryland join us in New Orleans for a benchmark vow renewal ceremony and to celebrate Mardi Gras. This was the same visit I discuss towards the end of Chapter One where we experienced the balcony chair spirit activity at the Bourbon Orleans Hotel.

Our group took a fascinating cemetery tour to St. Louis Cemetery No. 1 and I was immediately hooked on the cemetery culture here. The cities of the dead. Our guide was great. Polite, informative and very proud of the city. It made quite an impression on me. He also mentioned that he was a Voodoo practitioner and I watched as our group squirmed a little.

You see, the only thing we knew about Voodoo was what we had seen in the movies, with zombies, frightening potion induced rituals and frantic orgies. At the Marie Laveau tomb he dispelled a lot of those myths and explained the religious aspects and practices in a way that relaxed some of the tension in the group. Towards the end he invited those of us who were interested to attend a blessing ceremony at the Voodoo Spiritual Temple and Cultural Center on Rampart Street, to be conducted by Priestess Miriam. I'll admit, I was a little nervous, but also very intrigued, so our group decided to do it. I believe a little more than half the tour participated.

Once we got inside Priestess Miriam greeted us and I remember thinking "what a beautiful soul". She radiated inner peace and immediately put us at ease. We all sat in a semi-circle while she swept the negative energies away from us and replaced them with good. If remember correctly, we were given these little sachet type bags, containing herbs to keep us safe and protected.

Back in the room I promptly tossed them in my suitcase and forgot about them, until we returned home a few days later. That evening, back in our own bed, I settled in to begin reading a new book I'd purchased during our visit entitled "Searching for Spirits by Kalila Smith". If you'd told me then that 12 years later, I would be working with her at Haunted History Tours, I would have said you were crazy. Seems the fates knew what they were doing even then.

Around 11:30pm I turned out the light and we settled in to sleep. Having drifted off, we were both awakened with a start by someone pounding on our front door. I glanced at the clock, and it was straight up 12 midnight. Grabbing my robe, I figured it must be an emergency of some sort for one of our neighbors to be acting that way. As soon as my foot hit the landing at the bottom of the stairs, the pounding stopped. I turned on the porch light, quickly opened the door and found... that there was no one there. Not a soul and not a sound.

I walked out to the sidewalk, listening for noises. Nothing. I checked around the house. Again, nothing. Scratching my head, I went back inside and up to bed where my wife was waiting, sitting on her side of the bed. "What was it?" she asked. "No idea. Maybe kids, who knows." I turned my bedside table lamp off and we both snuggled back into bed.

That's when the oddest thing happened. The overhead chandelier lights in our bedroom came on. By themselves. No. I'm not kidding. We both immediately sat up in bed and I have to admit, my heart was pumping, and my mind was racing a mile a minute. A knock at midnight, our lights coming on by themselves. What the hell was happening? Then my wife, who is not into this paranormal stuff even a little bit, spoke out loud and said "whoever you are, I don't want you here. We don't want any trouble. Please leave peacefully." Two minutes later the lights turned off and in the next seven years of our living there, it never happened again,

We may never know what it was, but I felt somehow that we had dodged a bullet. A few days later, cleaning out the rest of the stuff from my suitcase, I found those two gris gris bags that we were given at the Voodoo Shop. Do I think they were responsible for what happened that night? On the contrary, I think they may have protected us and I had a new respect for a religion that was very foreign to the way I was raised. But, as I would find out later, this little incident was a walk in the park compared to what some experience.

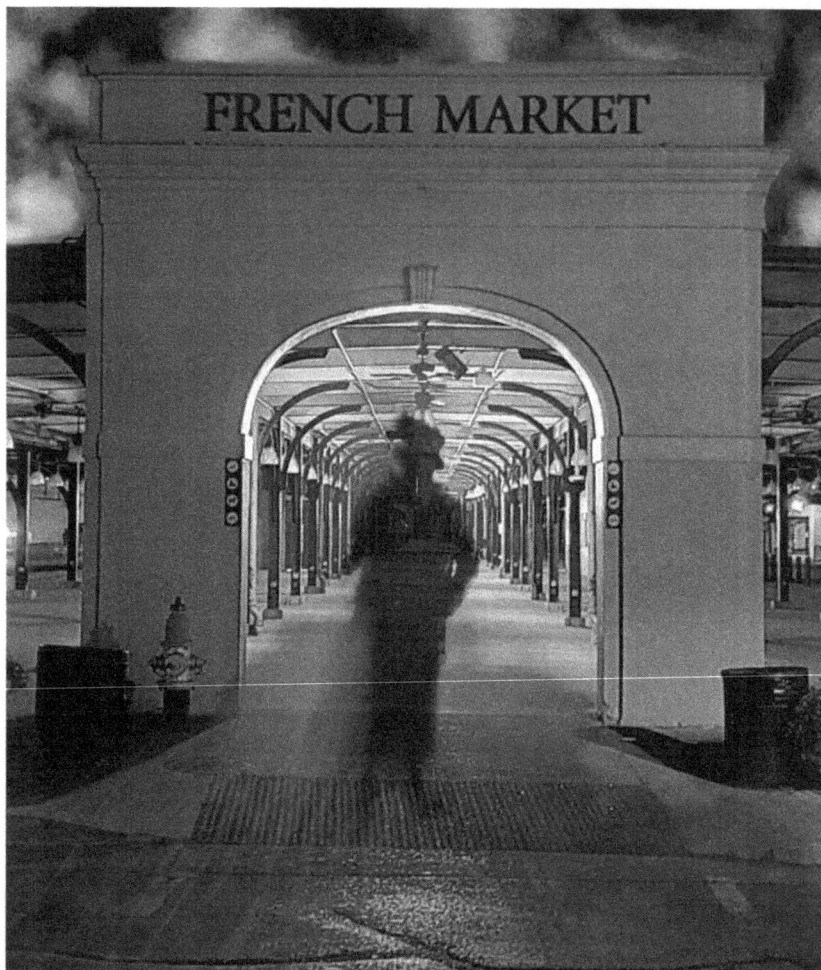

Shadow Figure Art Concept by Drew Cothern

Remember earlier in the book when I promised you another creepy Dungeon occurrence? I saved the best, or scariest, for last. Here goes.

At one of my tour stops, The Chartres House, on a Monday evening in May 2019, I ran into two couples from SoCal who were on my Sunday late tour the night before. They were eating dinner and as soon as they saw me, they started frantically waving me over.

Smiling and happy to see them, I walked over and asked them how they'd been and if they'd had fun last night. The husband of one of the couples admitted that they had a "really rough night". "Too many

Dragon's Blood shots?" I asked, thinking they were suffering from hangovers. "No", he replied, "We believe dark spirits attached themselves to us at The Dungeon and followed us back to our hotel." Um, what?

Apparently, after I left them at The Dungeon at the end of the tour the husband of the couple said he kept seeing a shadow figure hovering by them when they were at one of the upstairs bars. This went on for quite some time. Wherever they would go, it seemed to follow them. Hanging back, but just on the edge of his peripheral vision. At one point he said he saw it lunge towards them from behind and it scared him so badly that they decided to leave and go back to their hotel.

Once there, they brushed their teeth, got ready for bed and kind of nervously laughed about the tour and the weirdness they experienced at The Dungeon.

They crawled in bed, kissed and turned off the light, and that's when his wife saw what appeared to be the shadow figure of a man standing by the end of the bed watching them. She screamed and her husband immediately turned on the light and the figure disappeared. I'd like to note that at this point of recounting the story, both the husband and wife started getting teary eyed and shaking a little. I told them to be calm, that they would be okay, and I would help them. He continued.

Turning off the light again, they discovered that there were now two shadow figures in the room, one male and the other female. The wife told me that at one point she felt what she described as "an invisible woman" crawling on top of her, starting with her feet. She could feel her hands and the shape and weight of a woman's body on top of her and felt as if her own body was "frozen." Again, she screamed, her husband turned on the light and the sensation of being pinned lifted. Surprisingly, that's not the really terrifying part.

The husband said that they turned on all the lights and eventually drifted off to sleep. When he woke up it was daylight, and he was relieved that they had somehow survived the night. And, as he turned to look over at his sleeping wife, he felt a presence beside him who leaned in and whispered in his ear "slit her throat."

114

It upset him so badly that he started crying and he jumped out of the bed, his legs collapsing underneath him. His wife, hearing the commotion, woke up wondering what was wrong.

He said it took him a while to even find himself able to utter the words to her to describe not only what had happened, but the grim task he was instructed to accomplish. It took about five minutes, and once he was able to tell her, then she became afraid of him. I mean, these two kids literally had a night from hell.

They were still visibly shaken and teary-eyed telling me the story. I referred them to a friend who could help them smudge and protect themselves and showed them the protection ring I wear on my tours. This is, hands down, truly one of the most bizarre and terrifying experiences I've encountered while doing tours here.

Amanda showing the shadow figures who's boss at the Dungeon

ANECDOTE: **THE HOUND FROM HELL**

Remember, my bartender friend Rachel, the one who saved Dave Grohl? Well, she started having odd things happen with her cell phone thru the month of October 2018. She usually keeps it under the counter at the bar next to the register where it had mysteriously started taking pictures on its own, of the shelves under the bar. These were not photo bursts, but photos taken at different intervals throughout her shift. In one instance there were 13 pictures taken over the span of an hour, even though her phone was locked, and no apps were open.

The last time it happened was on October 31st, 2018, and she heard it click. She grabbed her phone and went out to the courtyard and there was one picture that had not only taken itself, but it was linking to Instagram. It was trying to upload the photo to the page of some chick from Romania, who she didn't know. She killed that from happening and that's when she noticed something in the pic. Something that had not been in any of the others. She zoomed in and this is what she found. Hound from hell, anyone?

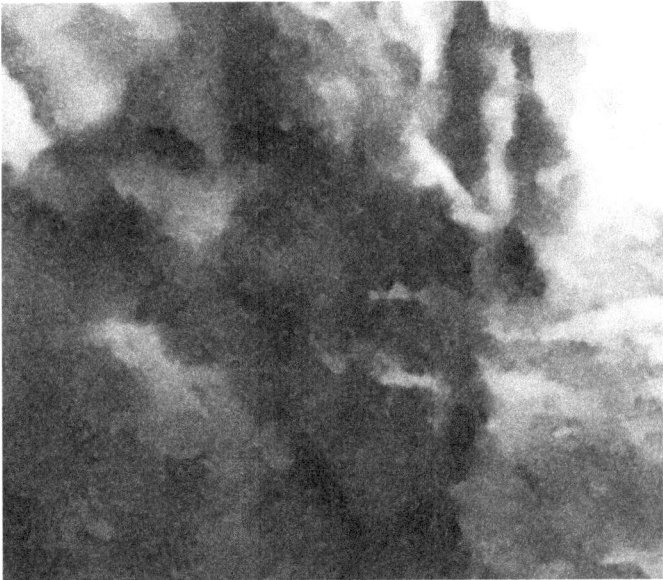

Demon Dog – Photo by Rachel Lockett

116

14

NIGHT STALKERS

Jonathan Weiss

I've always loved the city of New Orleans, and of all the things I've loved, more than any is how different she is at night than from the day. While it has that feel now, in the days before Katrina it was truly remarkable, and something that was easily experienced.

Over and over, the new to the city, the inexperienced, the tourist would find themselves in an area that they couldn't recognize, the brows would furrow, they would look again and again over their shoulders in trepidation and worry, sure that they would remember something, and more shaken when for all their efforts, it only seemed more alien.

While we residents of the old city knew our locations, the feeling of something terrible, something... watching was always there, lurking just out of view. It's so simple, yet so strange how, like a Stephen King novel, the benign just starts to twist until what was something charming begins to fill you with dread, and the realization comes: you're in someplace *different*. And something simple and bizarre happened to me soon after my most recent return to the city.

In 2003, I was working as a bartender on Bourbon Street as my main gig - and no, that's definitely not the weird part - guides used to apprentice for their positions (and generally you're not considered local till you've done your time on Bourbon!).

I would go to work at 9pm, and often not leave till 9am in the days when the city didn't stop. While this being the case during the weekends, on slow nights I was done in the dead hours, just after 3am, when the city oftentimes finally slows into an uneasy slumber.

I lived on the downriver lakeside of the Quarter, on Burgundy and Governor Nicholls, the area of the city that things traditionally happen to tour guides. The things that make *us* uncomfortable, the things that even *we* don't want to talk about and usually then amongst ourselves alone and usually while drinking.

I'd left work early that night and was walking the shadowy blocks home feeling quite satisfied with myself, money in my pocket, breathing in the rich thick air and relishing in the relatively cool, jasmine-scented night. And as I neared my home, I saw something moving in concert with me to my left along St. Philip street - turning my head I realized that it was a cat, one of the many ferals that have always hung around our ancient port, and it was walking along the line of cars, keeping pace with me, head low-slung, eyes locked on me.

Photo by Chastity Yvonne

I thought that was kind of cool, really. Like I was being escorted home by a fellow gentleman of the Quarter, like-knowing-like, as it were, and I smiled and greeted him. He didn't respond.

As I neared Burgundy, I realized that he'd been joined by another, and they were leaping from car to car, gateway top to walk, pacing, and... watching. When I turned onto Burgundy, and was within a block of my home, the traffic pattern changed and the cars were now on the right, so these two abandoned the cars, trotted across the road and began to slink along the shadowy doorways, never turning their gaze.

Photo by Elliot Gorton

I admit, at that point I was getting a bit unnerved, but continued along towards home just ahead, when a motion caught my eye to the right - a third had joined the first two, it was now keeping pace on the right, eyes glowing in the pale streetlights.

Then I spied another, this one crouched and moving furtively along underneath the cars, glaring and glaring. I stopped. They stopped. I moved, they followed, unblinking and bearing what now began to dawn on me was a fascination, a cold malice in their narrowed eyes.

Suddenly I realized that the breeze had died, and how very still it had all become, seeming as if everything was holding its breath, frozen in place and desperately trying not to be noticed. A stillness of *age.*

I looked ahead, and as the hairs on the back of my neck began to stir, a large, scarred male slowly strolled into the middle of Burgundy Street, for all the world as if he owned it, sat, curled his tail around his legs and *glared.* I didn't want to, I guess because I *knew* already what I'd see, but slowly turned around to look behind me. And crouching there were two others who'd moved into the street behind me, tails twitching. And in a feeling, I can't easily describe I understood something that must have been a familiar fear of our oldest ancestors: I was being stalked.

I immediately broke into a run towards the iron gate of my old home, shouting and waving my arms like a lunatic, but not looking back at whatever might have been behind me - slammed through it, and crashed it closed, raced upstairs to my tiny garret apartment, and looked into the lamp lit street below. Then double checked the lock on the door and drew the curtains tight.

Photo by Jonathan Weiss

Because there they all sat. Staring upwards. Right into my eyes.

Truth.

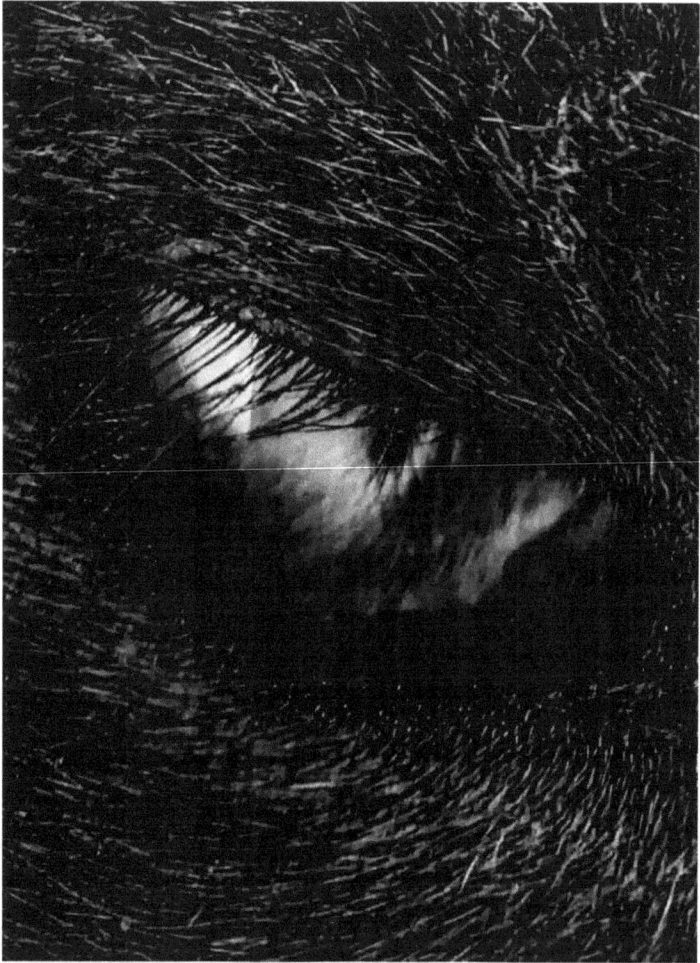

Photo by Kelly McMillian

15

BLIND AMBITION
Rose Sinister

I qualified for my City of New Orleans Tour Guide License in September 0f 2013, but I didn't get a chance to perform my first ghost tour until mid-October, in the lead-up to Halloween. That's the way it is in my profession; the new guides start at the bottom of the seniority totem pole and either take the tours that the more experienced guides don't want or get assigned the last dredges of tourists who show up at the last minute on particularly busy nights in the high season.

The months that follow Halloween in New Orleans are *not* the high season for tourists. The weather cools, the revelers leave, and work is scarce until the lead up to Mardi Gras starts.

All of this to say that I was still pretty green, as far as experience goes, by the time Carnival was about to hit us full force in the face in early March 2014. The weather was cold, the streets were crowded and polluted and *filthy:* I mean, really, truly, filthy, saturated with every variety of human and animal bodily fluid you can imagine- yes, even that- washed down with stale beer and sickly sweet, melted daiquiris.

I'd probably performed fewer than two dozen tours by then, enough to have my stories pretty memorized, but not fluidly. I knew my route well enough, but not intimately. I was getting decent tips, but not great ones.

By this point I'd dealt with a few hecklers and a few belligerent bums, and I'd seen enough poop on the cracked and uneven sidewalks to instantly be able to tell the difference between human and canine. Besides, I'd been a resident of New Orleans for the better part of a decade already, I'd worked in the French Quarter nearly the entirety of that time. I'd seen the Jesus freaks with their bullhorns next to the body-painted naked people covered in beads next to the passed-out Oklahoma tourists on the sidewalk often enough that they hardly registered anymore.

I thought, in my hubris, that I'd seen it all.

Enter Lundi Gras night. That's "Fat Monday" in French but it's only an "official" part of Mardi Gras in New Orleans, and only recently at that. It's basically the night before the last hurrah. The last night to take a ghost tour before Carnival is over for yet another year.

So, despite the chill in the air, the tourists came out in droves, crowding the ticket window on the sidewalk and I watched, bottom of the tour guide totem pole as one, after another, after another full-to-capacity tour group departed along the sidewalk as the clock moved closer to 8 pm. That's when the last ghost tour leaves for the night, and it was looking like another no-work night for me. The crowd along the sidewalk had started to thin, and those of us left over started to pack up the signs and the credit card machines and lock them away for the night.

I don't know if I'm the one who saw them first, or if it was someone else who said, "Oh, no..." but we all looked up at once and noticed both groups hurrying down the sidewalk toward what was left of the Haunted History tour setup with the deliberate intention in their step clearly indicating that, while they were late, they expected to be accommodated for a tour.

Two clusters of tourists, arriving at the same time but not together- one cluster of six was a group of fraternity brothers from some university up north, already so drunk that they were slurring their words and complaining that it had taken too long to find our sign-in location.

The other group of tourists, also around a half dozen in number, were also students- of the Ruston Louisiana School for the Blind.

At the last minute, I had my work cut out for me after all. As I straightened my license and prepared to step out with my last-minute cluster of a dozen or so students, roughly half sighted, half blind, I could already hear the groans from some of the frat boys that this was going to *suuuuuck.*

I can't say that I expected much better myself. I'm ashamed to admit that my first thought was selfish, indignant, and downright ableist: what the hell kind of blind person comes out and takes a ghost tour of the French Quarter on one of the busiest nights of the year? And what the hell was I supposed to do, stand in front of buildings they couldn't see and tell them stories of ghost sightings they wouldn't perceive, tell them to take photographs so that maybe, when they went home, they'd find orbs or ectoplasm or some other visual proof of ghosts in the images captured by their cameras?

I arrived at Pirate's Alley, where I normally began my tours, with my mismatched group in tow, and looked down, at the flagstone pavers beneath my feet. I'd often wondered, '*if these stones could talk...*'

And I realized, suddenly, how distinctively different the flagstones of the alleyway were from the other parts of the sidewalk we'd just walked down, and I looked at the canes that my blind tourists were using to navigate the crowds and the filth and the obstacles, and suddenly I thought, "what *better* night than Lundi Gras in the French Quarter, to really put those navigational skills to the test?'

And what better night than this, when I was unlikely to snag any prime real estate for storytelling in front of the most famous buildings anyway, to focus on all the non-visual elements of hauntings and paranormal activity that I'd formally glossed over in my scripted recitations of terrible things happening to terrible people and the terrifying legacies of those long-ago traumas?

New Orleans is for everyone. *Stories* are for everyone. And my job, as a storyteller, isn't a route, static performance about me- my job is to reach people where they are and communicate to them on the level they best understand, why this history matters, why these stories are important, and why these tragedies are *haunting*.

I'd only really known that in a bland, rather intellectual way before that night.

But what does a haunted house mean, if the visuals are irrelevant? I can describe the texture of stone and peeling paint, the hollow echo of angry voices in the night, the icy cold of ghostly hands wrapped tight around your neck as you are sleeping...

There's the ichorous, palpable, sticky quality of hot blood from a disemboweled Romeos dripping slowly off a cast iron spike above you, the deafening jeers of a mob at an execution, the stench of rotting bodies piled chest high down the street, waiting to be gathered and thrown into the river, or the frigid cold of icy wind and sleet pummeling the naked flesh of a doomed young woman in love, freezing to death on a rooftop on a cold December night.

Storytelling is about creating an image in the mind's eye. You don't need to see in order to experience that, in order to feel that.

There are defining moments in all our lives that indelibly crystalize our values and our ambitions in one fell swoop. I'd never stopped to consider, before that night, how I could- and *should*- strive to make my tours more inclusive and accessible for everyone. But it's a story I bring up every single time a new tour guide asks me for advice about the job.

"Your job is to tell a story. Your performance is not about you. A decade from now, people will probably forget the minutiae of historical details in your stories, so don't get too bogged down in those. Remember, you're in a position to create a memory that someone might carry with them for the rest of their lives, and what they will remember most is how you made them *feel*."

The blind students loved the tour. The Yankee fraternity brothers loved the tour so much they decided to forgo drinking at the bar break so they didn't get any drunker and miss out on the tour- and that's high praise coming from frat bros in town for Mardi Gras.

I got my tour guide license in September of 2013. But Monday night, March 3rd, 2014, was the night I became a Storyteller.

Rose Sinister in Pirates Alley – Photo by Ryan Miller Lane

ANECDOTE: **THE SPIRTS TOLD ME**

In addition to sharing stories with people about the city I love, one of my favorite aspects of being a tour guide is watching the reactions of the tour patrons while I'm espousing some of these truly gruesome tales. For instance, I had one lady burst into tears in an upstairs event room one evening. She somehow thought that because we were sitting at tables that we were going to have a séance and she was terrified. Even after I assured her several times that that was not going to happen, she continued to be afraid as long as we were in that room.

On another occasion this young lady was absolutely so not digging my recounting of the dark history of torture and execution in Jackson Square. Her friends were so amused by her reactions that they snapped pictures and sent them to me later (see below).

And that was at the very beginning of the tour.

5 Star Review Coming My Way!

My all-time favorite reaction, however, was from a lady from Clemson here with her husband for the division title game against LSU in January of 2020. They were very sweet and her husband, as we were walking between stops, told me that he was a firefighter, and his wife was a pharmacist.

A few stops later we're at the Pharmacy Museum and I'm telling the gruesome tale of Dr. Dupas when I look over to see this lady staring at me, wide eyed, and nodding.

Acknowledging her I said, "That's right, you're a pharmacist, aren't you?"

She screamed! Loud. Dropped her drink and stepped back, both hands covering her mouth. Astonishment awash all over her face. She replied, "How did you know?"

Obviously, she had not heard us talking earlier.

I looked at her husband and he winked. I replied, "The spirits told me." And she literally freaked da fuq out. "OMG! That's...that's not possible!"

After a few moments her husband started laughing and said, "I told him earlier." After punching him several times in the shoulder and calling him a few choice names we were finally able to settle down and get back on track. The whole tour cracked up.

At the end he thanked me and tipped me $100.

Terrorizing your loved ones, it's a service we provide.

16

BAR MON CHER
817 St. Louis St.

Bar Mon Cher was a beautiful little oasis of a bar on busy St. Louis Street between Bourbon and Dauphine. Good drinks, great music and old creole atmosphere. It literally transported you back to a simpler time. It's the place where a wonderful burlesque performer by the name of Lefty Lucy captivated us and taught us the joys of Burlesque Bingo. For almost two years, until it changed ownership, Bar Mon Cher was a wonderful stop on my Haunted Pub Crawl. It was also, of course, extremely haunted.

The owner, Jeanette, was kind enough to share a story, and a picture, with me from the day she moved in. She pulled up to the front of the locked and alarmed building and stepped back across the street, to take it all in for a moment, before she turned the key and all the transformational hard work of restoring the interior began. That's when she noticed a lady in a white dress watching her from an upstairs balcony window. But wait, wasn't the building supposed to be empty? Weren't the doors locked and the alarm system set, as promised? Making her way into the building she discovered that all was as it was supposed to be. She unlocked the door, turned off the alarm and headed upstairs to investigate. No one was there. But she had a picture. She had proof.

The Lady in White – Original Picture (left) and Close Up

Unable to let go of the mystery Jeanette did some investigating in the City archives. That's where she found records of a 1800s cabinet maker named Barthelemy who fell into a forbidden love affair with the young slave woman who was purchased by his sister, Madame Bacas, to care for her daughter. The young woman's name was Adalaide.

Barthelemy and Adalaide took up residence at 817 St. Louis in 1822 and lived, with their ten children, on the property for 36 years. Yes, you read that right, ten children. His woodworking shop was downstairs, and their residence occupied the upper two floors.

After what we believe to have been a long and happy life, Adalaide, the Matriarch of the house, died in 1855 at the age of 72. But that doesn't mean she left the property. She apparently continues to watch over her old abode and Jeanette believes that it was her, in the window on that first day, checking out the new owner to see if she met with her approval.

Jeanette continued to draw Adalaide's attention and would catch glimpses of Adalaide watching her as she prepared the upstairs room for a party or accomplished some other task in the bar. She also frequently felt her presence on the staircase and the second-floor landing.

Oddly enough, Adalaide would also mimic Jeanette's voice so that employees would think she was talking to them, when Jeanette was actually locked away in the apartment upstairs. The employees would hear her call their name, or ask; "what are you doing?" They would turn around to see, out of the corner of their eye, a fleeting glimpse of who they believed to be Jeanette quickly passing by their station, dressed all in white.

Jeanette witnessed this occurrence for herself one evening during Burlesque Bingo. Honey Tangerine, the performer that evening, was on the stage in between bingo games. She was staring at Jeanette, who was across the bar, maybe 20 feet away, and mouthing "What, Jeanette?" Jeanette just stared at her, dumbfounded, and then watched as the sudden realization crossed Honey's face that Jeanette wasn't saying anything. Honey was hearing Jeanette's voice in her ear, talking to her, while Jeanette was across the bar, too far away for a casual conversation. She was literally hearing Jeanette call her name while watching Jeanette standing silently across room.

We also believe that the lady in white is not the only spirit occupying the building. The door man, Jonathan, would frequently tell me stories of seeing children running up the stairs and of chasing phantom children around the first floor.

The first time it happened he thought somehow someone had managed to sneak past him. He caught a glimpse of them turning the corner of the foyer entering the bar and gave chase, only to find that no one was there. This apparently happened quite often.

We know that four of Adalaide's family members died on the property: Barthelemy, Adalaide and two of their children. One child, Louis, died in infancy and the other, Felix, died at the age of 15 when he tragically drowned in the Mississippi River during a 4th of July celebration.

The Casket in the Courtyard at Bar Mon Cher

Jeanette, and her staff received a surprising answer to the mystery of the children during a séance that was conducted in September of 2017 where the departed spirits of a woman and two children were contacted who resided on the property.

The séance, conducted by Eevie Ford, Cedric Whittaker and Michael Bill, all outstanding guides and mediums, experienced the sounds of children running on the stairs, a little boy laughing and the strong scent of roses.

The following weekend I brought a tour in and we took a group shot at the bar. There, passing through the top of the picture, were three self-illuminated orbs, moving in unison near the ceiling. When I showed it to Jeanette, she told me about the séance, and it all fell in place.

The séance and the three spirits

Another fun Pub Crawl at Bar Mon Cher.

Lefty Lucy calling Burlesque Bingo to passersby.

Your Hostess Jeanette (on left)

ANECDOTE: A LADY WITH HER HUSBAND IN AN URN

During the summer of 2019 I was conducting another Haunted Pub Tour and all twenty-eight of us were lining up to check into The Dungeon. Being the host, I stand at the door as my tour patrons check in to make sure there are no problems with IDs, etc. I happened to look down the line of my group and noticed a lady, perhaps mid-sixties, standing in the middle of my group, clutching and Urn. Yep. Like somebody's ashes inside, type urn. I promptly got her up to the front of our group, because we were going to be a while checking in.

She thanked me and asked Alan, the door guy for a favor. He nodded. She stated that the Dungeon was her and her husband's favorite bar for decades and decades. Every time they visited New Orleans; they would hang out here. Sadly, he had passed over the summer and his ashes were in that urn. She wanted to know if it was okay to dump her husband's ashes into the planter next to the entry door. It was his dying wish.

I was standing there wide-eyed and a little emotional, when Alan shrugged, very nonchalantly, in typical NOLA fashion, like people ask this type of thing every day, and said "Sure, I don't care, go ahead". I was kind of floored, but also thought it was very cool.

So, my tour group and I watched solemnly as this lady dumped her husband's ashes in that planter. It is my understanding that the ashes of three more departed souls have joined him at the time of this writing. God, I love this town.

17

MAY BAILY'S BAR
415 Dauphine Street

May Baily's is one of my absolute favorite stops on our Haunted Pub Crawl. The hotel bar for the Dauphine Orleans Hotel, this place is brimming with New Orleans brothel history and boasts of four very diverse and active spirits! This is a must stay location if you're looking to immerse yourself in the haunted lore of the city. Not surprising, I've also had more than a few ghostly encounters at this bar.

The first was in July of 2017. I had a full tour of 28 people and as we entered the bar, I recall one lady doing a Face Book live video, sharing the experience with her kids back home that they were entering a haunted bar. I thought it was cute. We finished the tour with no incidents and then a few days later I got a call from our front office that one of my weekend tour patrons had called and left a message asking for me to contact them right away, that they had something they wanted to share with me.

At first, I was worried that something bad had happened to them, so I did as instructed and called them right away. Turns out it was the lady from my tour who had taken the FB live video. She said once she posted it her kids kept messaging her asking who the man was in the mirror in the old timey costume. Recalling that there was no one in the bar fitting that description during our visit, I asked her to send me the picture.

She then related that the image appeared as the reflection of a person sitting at the bar. The clothes appeared to be from the mid to late 1800s. She said it was possible to run the video backwards and forwards and watch the apparition appear and disappear as she passed by the mirror in her video. As requested, she sent me both a still image and a snippet of the video, which played out exactly as she described. I'm including the still image for your examination.

Please note that the mirror is behind the main bar and reflects what is in front of it. There is a picture reflected in the mirror of a lady sitting on a chair. That is a famous E.J. Bellocq photograph of a Storyville prostitute. In the lower right-hand corner, just below the Bellocq picture, you'll notice a slightly blurry image of a man in a smoking jacket, with a cravat, sitting with his elbow resting on the bar. That man was not there during our visit.

Was this a ghost, or perhaps a time slip, revealing the lingering spirit of a bygone patron hoping for one last adventure? We're not sure. Come join us for a visit and see for yourself.

The Mysterious Man in the Mirror

The next great capture happened a few months later after just telling my group about the ghost known as the Dancing Girl. A little girl who dances around the pool in a white dress. There one second, gone the next. Moments later one of our patrons caught this iridescent orb next to the pool at one of her favorite spots.

Orb of the Dancing Girl by the Pool

Still, one of my favorite tour experiences, ever, took place in this bar. And it wasn't even paranormal. I believe it was in the spring of 2017, I had an older kind of grizzled looking couple in my Pub Crawl tour group of 6 people. Picture the couple from the painting American Gothic. I was thoroughly convinced by the second stop on the tour that these people absolutely hated me.

I mean, it was kind of hard to miss, especially in that small of a group. They didn't laugh at any of my corny jokes, did respond to any of my creepy details. Nothing. Just stared at me with this cold hard look that made me think they were imagining my death in various Rob Zombie-esque back woods scenarios.

Once we got in May Baily's people scattered to the bathroom, or for drinks and I was alone at the corner of the bar. I turned to find the wife of the couple standing about three feet behind me. Silently staring. Yikes! She said, "I want to ask you a question." And I thought, here it comes, she's going to tell me how much they hate the tour and ask for a refund. I said sure and she said "I need to tell you something about myself first. Then I'll ask." I said, okay.

Not sure what was coming next. She began to tell me about herself and how, as a much younger woman she had experienced a late term miscarriage. It was something that still haunted her. I felt everything in me soften at this point. She said that a few years after her miscarriage that a little girl in white, about maybe three or four years old, started showing up in her house. She was always laughing and smiling and playing. Then the lady stopped, looked me straight in the eye and asked, "Do you think that could be my daughter?" I was floored. And speechless for a second. The breath caught in my throat.

Once I could breathe, I responded with exactly what I felt and believe in my heart. "Ma'am, there are so many things that we don't know, or don't fully understand about this life. But from what I've seen and experienced, I think it's quite possible that she is your little girl. That she's showing you that she's okay, that you can let go of the guilt, and that you'll see each other again. I think it's important to her that you know that and that's why she lets you see her when she's happy."

She got teary eyed and hugged me. I got teary eyed, as well, and hugged her back. Then she pulled back, almost instantly composed and said "And here's the kicker. She even travels with us when we go to see relatives. I look up and there she is, in the corner of the living room or in our guest bedroom, where we're visiting. Ain't that the darndest thing?" I laughed and said, "It sure is. She's a part of the family and wants to be with you."

And that's when it hit me. For some people ghost stories are more than just fun tales and passing entertainment. For some, myself included, these are our stories. They speak to our essence, to our mortality and, also, to our hope for something after. So come for a visit to New Orleans and join us for an adventure. Who knows, one day we may just be telling people stories about you!

18

PIRATE'S ALLEY GHOST
622 Pirate's Alley

Pirate's Alley. Just the name alone conjures up images of swashbuckling sword fights, illicit treasure and adventure on the high seas. It's a well-known fact that Pirates played an integral part in New Orleans history and left behind a roguish legacy that is still celebrated today. In fact, when we moved to New Orleans in 2011, we asked several of our closest local friends to advise us on the essential items we needed to live and thrive in New Orleans. Number one was an alarm system, cause we got crime here. Number two was a generator, cause we got storms here. And number three? Number three was a pirate costume cause we got special pirate themed days to celebrate and lots of booty to be plundered. So, in this particular instance, the sobriquet of Pirate's Alley does not disappoint.

Allegedly named Pirate's Alley after the large numbers of pirates who would gather to hawk their wares and lobby for illicit smuggling jobs in the narrow alley between the looming foundational church and state buildings, where God apparently has no peripheral vision.

The big score was to land a job for one of the city fathers, whose offices were located in the Cabildo (French for The Council). They would come out and give these scalawags a job to go forth and gather up some illegal or illicit item for them, be it drugs, alcohol, prostitutes, or even illegal slaves (yes, even in the age of unbridled slavery in the U.S., that was a thing).

As you can guess, the competition for these plumb assignments was fierce, often resulting in bloodshed and death. Hence the origin of The Ghost of Pirate's Alley.

As the story goes, our ill-fated pirate was lobbying hard for one of those prize smuggling jobs when another pirate attempted to horn in on his action.

It escalated quickly from an argument to a fist fight, and then on from there to a brazen knife fight.

Our salty hero was gaining the upper hand until, surprise, his nemesis pulled out a pistol. Rut Roh! Realizing that he now literally has a knife in a gun fight, he turns to flee and only makes it a few feet away before the other pirate shoots him in the back and kills him. His blood running out along the drainage rivulets in between the pavers.

These final moments are what people claim to see during their ghostly encounters with him in that alley. A Pirate running in their direction, face filled with fear, there one moment, gone the next.

I've had people on my tours, walking down the alley way, chatting, when suddenly they felt like they were bumped by someone running up from behind them and pushing past.

Others have spoken to me about feeling a rush of wind come up on them as if someone had just run past. And these instances have all occurred with absolutely no prompting from me, as we were on our way up the alley for me to tell them the story. The bewildered looks on their faces speaking to the authenticity of their experience.

But one of my most pleasant surprises was learning that a couple close friends from our old Mardi Gras Krewe, Jeanie and Roy Linder, had their own encounter with the Ghost of Pirate's alley years before we met them. I'll let Jeanie and Roy relate their story for you in their own words.

Jeanie: "We were visiting New Orleans for Halloween in 2010 or 2011. So, it was me, Roy, our son Charles and his friends Jake and Larissa. It was early Sunday morning. I say early, but it was probably around nine o'clock, which is early for New Orleans. We were looking for a place for breakfast.

While we were discussing where to go, we were standing in Jackson Square in front of the Cabildo, by the entrance to Pirate's alley. There was an exhibit at the Cabildo, so I was looking at that while everyone else was discussing where to get breakfast. I was reading the signs and there was just nobody out. Like I said, it was early. Just a few people milling around the Square. The artists and tarot readers weren't even out yet.

So, I was reading the exhibit signs and I saw something on my left, out of my peripheral vision, and it was an eerie sort of sixth sense feeling, and at first, I didn't know what it was. But then I noticed that it was a man. A man running. I just sort of glanced over and saw he was dressed all in black. I went back to reading the signs, but then I noticed he was coming towards me. And when he came around behind me, he turned and ran up Pirate's Alley, and when he did, he brushed my shoulder. It was so weird because I turned to my right as he continued up Pirate's Alley and I remember thinking how strange it was, because it wasn't a thump, like somebody bumped into me, it was more like a woosh. And then I looked down the alley and there was nobody down there. No one at all. Like he just vanished. That's when I realized that I hadn't even heard footsteps running. It was just a woosh, a brush. It was so weird. I asked Roy, who was standing back behind me, "did ya'll see somebody run by here?".

Roy: I did. I caught a real quick glimpse of someone who had on boots, like a trench coat and a tricorn hat.

Jeanie: And he was all dressed in black. And it was just like the weirdest thing ever because there was so much room that there was no need to run into anyone. But he was running fast and hard.

Q: Like he was in a panic?

144

Jeanie: Yes. He kind of reminded me of a Captain Morgan pirate.

There you have it. In broad daylight, no less. And there wasn't even alcohol involved. At least not at that point.

So, if you're in town for a visit, don't forget to take a stroll down Pirate's Alley and walk in the bootsteps of pirates long past. And maybe even encounter a few in the present. Soak in the history, check out the Faulkner Bookstore below where William Faulkner wrote his first novel and grab a cocktail at the world-famous Pirate's Alley & Absinthe House. There's no telling what adventure you may find.

Jeanie & Roy Linder

Amazing Pirate Couple who poses for pics in Pirate's Alley. Stop by, grab a photo, and tip them well. That flintlock may be loaded.

ANECDOTE: **THANK YOU MR. DOUG**

If you've taken my tours, you've heard me say that New Orleans is, I believe, one of the few places left on Earth where magic still exists. Not just within the confines of our imaginations, because it definitely does reside there, but also within the fabric of every molecule that makes up this amazing city. It's real and it's tangible and it has existed here for thousands of years in what the indigenous Chitimacha tribe referred to as the "thin places". Add in what fellow guide and writer Emily Anne Smykal refers to as the "confluence of cultures" of people from Europe, Africa and Meso-America who came here in the 1700's to etch out this colony and port city and, as a result, you have this blended magical gumbo that resonates in every fiber of your being. It really is that substantial. And it still amazes me after all these years and fills me with awe and wonder.

Sometimes these magical moments are the result of a momentous occasion, a profound instance of epiphany where you suddenly just "get it" and it sparks an awakening deep in your soul.

Other times it is more subtle. A connectedness that taps you into the ebb and flow of energy that hums throughout the city in a very palpable way. You get a sense of knowing which gives you a glimpse beyond the barriers that separate us and revels the potential for an awareness that exists outside ourselves.

Sound like a bunch of magical "woo woo?" Maybe. But a recent experience on one of my tours has me seriously rethinking the extent of those possibilities.

I was on Esplanade Ave with my group doing the Dead Frenchmen Tour, talking about hauntings, mysterious underground tunnels and Pirates when I glimpsed a young man walking down the sidewalk in our direction. As a guide your head is always on a swivel, keeping an eye on your surroundings for signs of potential interruptions and danger. This guy was probably early to mid-twenties, ragged and dirty and mumbling to himself, his arms and hands flailing around in an agitated fashion. He was clearly disturbed by something, possibly a run in up near Check Point Charlies dive bar. His voice was raising and lowering in volume, increasing and decreasing in cadence, and peppered with profanity.

This is generally a warning sign for guides in the Quarter as oftentimes folks exhibiting this type of behavior are drawn to our groups like moths to a flame and the outcomes of these interactions can be very uncertain and sometimes dangerous. But I was certain of one thing; I had never seen this guy before in my life.

I continued with my story, keeping an eye on him, and noted that as he came up on our group, he got very quiet. He pulled his arms in by his sides and his hands close to his chest. He also averted his eyes and kept his head down as he passed silently behind my group.

He continued on past until he was about three doors down from where we were standing, where he quietly sat down on a stoop and cradled his head in his hands. My heart went out to him.

I could tell he was struggling, so as we passed him, heading up Esplanade, I reached in my pocket and pulled out a five-dollar bill. I handed it off to him as I passed. He took it, looked me right in the eyes, smiled and said, "Thank you Mr. Doug." I was floored. He stood up, smiled again and then headed off in the direction of a small food market up the street.

I just stood there for a moment, speechless because, as I stated before, I had never seen this guy before in my life. How did he know my name?

The only time I had spoken my name during the entire tour was when I introduced myself to my group in Santos Bar an hour earlier and at that point there was no one else in the bar but us.

So, this is still a mystery to me, and I haven't seen him since. But for that one brief moment in time, we had a connection that I believe reached across the conventional boundaries of personal interaction and touched my soul.

You may call it luck, coincidence or even bullshit.

I call it magic.

19

DANGER IN THE OLD QUARTER
Doug Bookout & Friends

New Orleans has a well-earned reputation as one of the most dangerous cities in the country. In a town where the famous Mardi Gras catchphrase is "Let the good times roll!" Sadly sometimes people come here looking for that good time and they're the ones who end up getting rolled. As one of my good friends, blues guitarist Mark Pentone is fond of saying, "The danger is part of the allure of the city." And, interestingly enough, he's right.

Some people who come here romanticize the violent aspects of the city, and its violent past. And while that may be enticing in theory, it's a whole different ballgame for those who experience it firsthand.

Another ironic aspect of the danger here is that many of the acts of violence in the Quarter are not thrust upon tourists by locals but are sometimes packed up in suitcases and brought in by the visitors themselves.

In this chapter we're going to explore what it's like to work in the Quarter and gain insight from the people on the front lines who live it day and night, the bartenders, bouncers, locals, and, of course, tour guides.

Personally, I've always believed that New Orleans tour guides should get hazardous duty pay for working in this city. Sometimes due to the threats you encounter from outside your tour group, and other times from those within.

I always start off my tours with a little safety briefing to ensure the safety of our patrons on our tours.

Little tips like stay on the sidewalks, cross at corners with your guide, and assume that that every driver in the Quarter is a drunk driver. No seriously. We have drive-through daquiri stands here, after all. Also, look both ways, especially when crossing one-way streets. Bike riders are notorious for cruising, in dark clothing, in the wrong direction and can take you out in the dark before you even see them coming. It happens.

We also establish a safe word, which I ask the patrons to select. I watch their backs and they watch mine. And it may sound funny, but it can also be very effective. Not surprising for a lot of visitors to this town, the most common choice is "pineapple". If you know, well, you know.

One evening I was standing in front of the locked iron entry gates to the Herman Grima House discussing American Horror Story and Madame LaLaurie, played by Kathy Bates in the show. Most people are not aware that the LaLaurie scenes were not filmed at the LaLaurie mansion, but rather at Herman Grima.

Anyway, I was deep into my story when a loud argument kicked off on the sidewalk to my left about fifteen feet away, towards Dauphine St. The argument intensified to include shouting and yelling "You fucking bitches better give me my fucking money!"

A girl in my tour group starts yelling our safe word for the day, "Pineapple! Pineapple! Pineapple!" at the top of her lungs. That's when

I saw the gun and the guy holding it yelling "I'm gonna shoot your fucking asses!" Then all hell broke loose.

The young couple, who were apparently trying to score some drugs off of this guy, fled from the armed dealer around my group, heading towards Bourbon St.

My group of twenty-eight people, now in the line of fire, freaked the fuck out and collapsed into me, pinning me against the wrought iron gates.

I caught a quick glimpse of the perpetrator running after the couple towards Bourbon and started pushing people off of me and trying to calm them down and move them away from the danger. Most were shaking, some were crying. About half just said "fuck this! This is too dangerous!" and just dropped off the tour. A few of them tipped me, which was appreciated, but kind of flabbergasted me. I think I was more surprised by that than the drug deal gone wrong.

The rest hung in there for one more story and I took them to the Dungeon to get them drinks and calm their nerves. Then I found a couple of police officers, reported the incident, and gave them a description of the armed perpetrator.

I doubt there was much they could do at that point, but at least they had a suspect description should they run in to him later in the evening.

I did avoid that area for quite a while afterwards. My main take away from this experience was this; please do not attempt to buy drugs from sketchy assholes on the street. It's just not safe. Buy them from the sketchy assholes in the bars like everyone else. I mean, seriously!

In July of 2021 tourism was starting to pick back up in the Quarter again, but as I and many of my colleagues noted, the streets felt decidedly different. Meaner, seemingly nursing a grudge and looking for some form of payback. People seemed edgy and coarse, and entitlement was off the charts, especially from the cheap seat tourists. Tipping was way down across the board and bad attitudes were waaaaaay up.

But most people, myself included, were just happy to be working again and doing what we love. Sharing this town and its twisted history.

So, one hot July Saturday evening I was cruising through my Dark History Cocktales tour with a fun small group of patrons, when we got to the location for my "Queen for a Day" picture which is featured on page 67.

But before we take the picture, I need to explain to my group why we're there as a prelude to our next bar stop, The Dungeon. That's when I noticed two young guys, about mid-twenties, stop on the sidewalk a few feet away. I hear one say to the other in a thick southern drawl, "Oh naw, naw naw, I ain't gonna let this happen."

Next thing I know he's launching himself between me and my group, pushing me back and falling to the ground right in front of us, obviously drunk off his ass. His slightly less drunk buddy runs over and pulls him up by his backpack, apologizing profusely and attempting to drag his drunk buddy away.

I have to admit, it was pretty comical at first, and it would have been okay if it had ended there. But sadly, this drunk little asshole just wouldn't let it go. He kept trying to come back and get in between me and my group, and his buddy kept pulling him away. I was really starting to lose my patience, but you know, stay professional in front of the tourists, right? So, I said "Look man, you're interfering with my tour and showing your ass and I can have you arrested. So, if you don't want to spend the rest of what will be a really unpleasant night in a New Orleans jail, listen to your buddy here and move on."

His response was, well, sadly what you'd expect from a member of today's seemingly bottomless Darwin Award winner gene pool. "Fuck you man! I ain't scared of no jail cell! I see what yer trying to do. What yer selling them!" I replied, "You mean the rock and roll history of the Dungeon?" And then it hit me, He was probably one of those crazy Qanon conspiracy nuts and thought that I was going to take these nice tourists somewhere to be eaten by lizard people. Sorry buddy, that only happens on my basement pizza parlor tour in DC.

At that point I pulled out my phone and said "Last warning. Move the fuck on or I'm calling the cops." His buddy tugged on his shoulder, and he reluctantly complied, and they turned and walked away. I watched them for about half a block as they moved down Royal toward Canal St. Problem solved. Or so I thought.

A few minutes later we're done taking pictures at our little landmark and getting ready to move on to the Dungeon, when I see my group recoil and gasp, eyes wide open in shock. I turn to see this asshole, yes, the same asshole I just shooed away, running up from behind me from across the street and trying to land a sucker punch on the side of my head. I tilted my head to the side, which was really all I had time to do, and he caught me on the right shoulder. Hard. And then it was on.

Now I was sixty at the time this happened, a month away from turning sixty-one, and I thought my fighting days were long over. I mean, unless I'm at the seafood buffet at Golden Corral, then it's every man and woman for themselves. Those coconut shrimp are killer. Am I rite?

Anyway, for an old dude I guess I can still throw a pretty solid right cross. I got a few good licks in and finally laid him out. His buddy scooped him up and away they went. Again.

Long story short, we called NOPD, and they never showed. My tour guests got a bonus good story out of the deal, and they tipped me well. Appreciation for drinks and a show, I suppose.

Since that happened, I have purchased both pepper spray and an extending metal baton. I am very aware that I was lucky this time and it could have quite easily gone the other way. But one thing I know for sure is that it's a very satisfying feeling when those silver skull rings we wear for ornamentation actually connect with someone's jaw. They make a really cool cracking sound.

Golden Corral, here I come!

To shed some additional light on to what we've been dealing with on our tours, post pandemic, my friend Charmaine Swan Rich also has a tale to tell.

"Tour guiding is not for the faint of heart. Most nights it makes for a fun job, you feel like you are on vacation with the tourists and sometimes make a friend or two. That's what we usually talk about. But we do work on the "streets" where anything can happen at a moment's notice. Those nights where something feels "off" can be life changing and instant life lessons that will always be remembered.

I had a crazy, terrifying night in the French Quarter. I was telling the last story of my tour on Royal street - had about 24 people and a car pulls up slowly alongside me. I moved out of the way so it would pass by - as usual. But this guy stops. Right by me. Demands to know what I am talking about. I said "It's a tour. I'm talking about witches." He demands that I tell him. He is smoking weed and drinking a beer. There is a teen girl in the front seat and about 3-4 seven-year-old boys screaming and laughing in the back. He then asks me if I am a witch. I said "Yea, sure." He jumps out the car, gets in my face and demands I put a curse on him because he WANTS to die. He looks like he wants to hit me. My entire tour group is frozen with fear. He is "daring" me to put a curse on him. So, I said "I just did, it's done." He said "what??? You just put a curse on me???" I said "yes". He then got even closer to me and said again in my ear "I WANT TO DIE!"

I was sensing this guy was pretty messed up and really did want to not be here anymore. At that moment, a guy on my tour steps in the street and says, "hey what you doing?" He turns away from me to the guy on my tour and curses him out. Then turns back to me, more pissed, and says "when is the curse going to happen?" I then say "well, that's up to the girl in the front seat. That's how it works". I look at the girl and poor girl looks terrified!!! The guy then says "that's my little sister - she can't tell me anything! You didn't know that - you are not a witch!" I then smiled and said "oh well, you are right! You got me there!" I gave him his "power" back by saying he was right. So, he got in the car and as he was driving away, he screamed at my group "you are all pussies and fags!!!" My poor group was still frozen and scared. I kept my composure and continued the story and ended the tour. When the guy jumped out the car, I did put my hand in my purse - have a taser flashlight in there - and mace. But it all happened so fast, and this time logic and a calm head saved me and my group.

A lady on my tour took this guy's picture and the manager of our company went to the police station to file a report. As it turns out this guy harassed 8 other tour guides that night. And this man is wanted by the police for sex trafficking. This shocked me and now my thoughts wander back to the scared teen girl in the front seat. Could I have helped her? I will know better next time - but I pray there isn't one".

Guy confronting Charmaine on her tour

Days after the above incident happened to Charmaine, another friend of mine, Ashlee Schmidt, suddenly found herself in the middle of a drive by shooting. She was kind enough, while still processing what occurred, to talk to me about it and allow me to share it with you.

Q: I just read your post. I'm so glad you're okay. What happened?

Ashlee: *I was taking a smoke break outside my bar at Chartres and Iberville with a few patrons around 4am. Suddenly someone fired 12-15 shots, rapid fire in front of the Ghost Bar next door. Bullets were hitting all around us.*

Q: Oh my god, that's terrifying. What did you do?

Ashlee: *I immediately shoved everyone in the bar and locked the doors. I literally shoved blind people into the bar. Left their walking sticks outside, cause fuck that, but, you know, please don't fall as I push you inside my establishment.*

Q: That's amazing that you had the presence of mind to do that and think of other people. Speaks to the kind of caring person you are. I read on Nola.com that they guy who was targeted is still alive.

Ashlee: *I heard he was shot multiple times, but later died. Also, first 3 rounds fired were the 3 that hit him, then the spray of bullets followed him and him alone down Iberville. It was definitely a targeted hit. The guy was standing in front of Ghost/Calegeros, white car pulls up, 15 rounds in seconds and they speed off. But they only targeted 1 person, not the crowd inside the bar.*

Q: Jesus. It's just staggering that no one else was hit. How are you holding up?

Ashlee: *Initially I was in one constant panic attack for about 5 hours. I mean, I was right there. Like feet away. Now, I'm super anxious and loud bangs/pops have really got me on edge.*

Q: I'm so sorry. Things like this seem to be happening all over the city.

Ashlee: *It's really gotten bad. I hate what's happening in the city right now.*

Bullet Holes in the Door Frame

Then sadly, mere days after Ashlee's horrifying experience, another bartender friend was almost robbed at gunpoint while getting into an Uber at the end of her shift. She screamed and fortunately it startled the robber enough that he ran away.

So, considering all this clear and present danger and all of the varied ways this place can take you out, the most logical question to ask is, if things are really that bad, then why do we stay?

I was discussing this with my good friend Rachel Lockett a few days ago and I think she summed it up perfectly.

"Louisiana is just not a great place to be when shit hits the fan. Never has been. Especially New Orleans. Times have been tough. Unexpectedly so, with Covid etc. That happens with every catastrophe in this city. Not just hurricanes. But any disaster. It comes back, just never the same. The city is hard. I hate when it goes through its metamorphosis...it really is the worst thing in the world to watch/endure. Then, one day, years later you come back to it and you're re-enamored (I know that's not a word) with it and see the sparkle again. And you forget about the bad and the ugly you witnessed......all for you to relax, get comfortable and allow it to do it to you all over again. So yeah, I get it. I'm in a messy break-up phase with the city right now, lol. Mad at it. Knowing it's not good for me but I want it sooooooo bad.

I still love it, refuse to give up on it or talk bad about it.... even still sell the hell out of it. Hypnotized with each new & crazy adventure, forgetting the previous beat down from even a day or a year ago. The city can do no wrong. It helps that people spend a lot of money to drink hard and forget their vacations and those that didn't choose to live here are living dangerously close to permanent blackout. The rest of us are crazy. And crazy people don't know they're crazy. New Orleans not only embraces crazy it encourages it. Gives you a tip bucket to put out front of your crazy and pays you for it.

This is no place for the faint-hearted. New Orleans is the abusive lover you'll never recover from. You might find someone else, but it will always be your soulmate. Till death do us part".

Amen sister! Preach!

ANECDOTE: **3 PACKS OF CIGARETTES** – *James Cheston McNeil*

I have this neighbor across the street. His name is Richard. I'd say he's about 65 years old. For the past three months that I've been living at my new place, he will come over and ask for a cigarette. Maybe 3-4 times a week. He's been living here since March because he's taking care of his immune compromised sister.

He doesn't just ask me for cigarettes when he sees me outside, either. He will come through the gate, knock on the door, or ring the doorbell to ask me for a cigarette. Needless to say, it was annoying, but I'd give him a cigarette because his sister didn't let him keep cigarettes because he was supposed to quit. Still, he would come over a bum a few each from me.

This continued until I set out my first carved pumpkin this October. He has not come to the door since I have been keeping carved pumpkins out at the front of my house. I didn't really notice it until I saw his sister this morning.

I asked her how Richard was doing from across the street. She looked confused at first and her eyes started welling up with tears, then she got angry. She asked me how I knew Richard. I didn't want to rat out Richard for sneaking cigarettes so I said "Oh, he would just come over and chew the fat with me. You know, just shooting the shit."

She said she knew I was lying because Richard passed away back in March. I laughed because by this point Richard owed me 3 packs of cigarettes. She didn't find this amusing and stormed off to church.

I'm an eternal skeptic tho, and Richard still owes me 3 packs of cigarettes.

20

BONE GANGS
Doug Bookout

"Wake up! Wake up! You may be next!" The ominous call rings out in the early morning hours of Fat Tuesday, just before the sun comes up. The North Side Skull and Bone Gang, the oldest and most enduring of the New Orleans bone gangs, is winding thru the historic Tremé neighborhood, continuing the centuries old tradition of reminding us that death is just around the corner, and we'd better take heed. It's time to wake up and grab life by the horns and live it to the fullest until that fateful day arrives. It's no coincidence that this exhortation comes on Fat Tuesday, the final day of Carnival, which literally means "farewell to the flesh".

When I'm asked by tourists what sets New Orleans apart from other southern cities with dark and tragic histories my answer is simple, the ability to acknowledge and embrace death. It is woven into the fabric of the black culture here and speaks to the resiliency of its people. Three hundred and four years of pain, suffering, death and inequity has not bowed the heads of the culture bearers here. Many of the traditions we have in the city came over with the enslaved people of color during the African diaspora and have endured for centuries. Bones gangs, Second Line Parades, Jazz Funerals and various burial traditions, all have their roots in African spiritualism and speak to the transitory nature of life and death as an integral part of our existence. They bravely and boldly face it head on.

The Second Line parade is a prime example. Most visitors to New Orleans associate them with weddings, because that is generally how they experienced it in the French Quarter. A booming brass playing upbeat dance music leads a bride and groom, who respectively hoist black and white umbrellas in the air, winds through the streets followed by the wedding party and attendees. They all wave white handkerchiefs in the air and sway to the music. It's a post ceremony celebration on parade and bystanders are encouraged to clap, sing and dance along to the festivities.

My wife Toni and I held one to celebrate our 25th wedding anniversary along with our good friends, Seth and Cheryl Cohen, who were celebrating their 15th. It was a joint celebration on New Year's Eve 2015 and was a night I will never forget. We started out with about 75 friends and family and encouraged others to join in as we snaked our way through the Quarter towards our end point at the intersection of Bourbon and Orleans. We ended up with well over 200 revelers dancing and partying in the street as the band played on. Epic! So, if you have the chance, do it!

It surprises most people to learn that it began as part of our funeral culture in neighborhoods of color going back centuries. And they are still held today. You see, the second line is the celebratory part of the funeral rite. It is proceeded by the first line, which is a slow, mournful, walk from the church to the neighborhood cemetery. During the First Line, the band plays slow funeral dirge music, like Just a Closer Walk with Thee, as the body of the deceased, and the group of mourners, make their way to the final resting place. And those handkerchiefs? The mourners are using them to dry their tears as they suffer their loss. And those umbrellas? Those are to keep the weather at bay, whether it be rain or the hot sun beating down on them.

Once they get the deceased to the cemetery, they place their body in their grave, crypt or tomb. They call this "cutting" or "setting their spirit free". Afterwards the upbeat music kicks in for the Second Line and the procession dances and sings their way back to the church in honor of the deceased. They're celebrating the fact that they got to share their lives with the person they love, who has now gone on to glory. Now some who lack understanding, as is always the case, have criticized this as somehow irreverent or disrespectful. Not at all. In fact, this is probably the healthiest way of dealing with life and death, and the acknowledgement of the transitory nature of our existence on the earthly plane, that I have ever seen. It also serves as a way for a group of people to collectively mourn their loss and share their grief all while celebrating the one they love. It is woven into the fabric of the culture down here and Bone Gangs act as a not-so-subtle reminder for us to prepare ourselves for that stark reality.

To expand on this, I just happen to be friends with the founder and Queen of an amazing all-female bone gang here known as Skinz N Bonez. Her name is Claudia, but she is widely known by her bone honorific as MardiClaw. On the Skinz N Bonez website she describes the origin of the Krewe and their mission, as such: "Skinz N Bonez is a female bone gang from New Orleans. Formed in 2011, with the assistance of our "soul sweepers," Skinz N Bonez is known for their tradition of waking up the neighborhood on Mardi Gras morning. This tradition dates as far back as 1819 with the original male bone gangs (see Northside Skull and Bone). Skinz N Bonez is part of the renaissance of Mardi Gras krewes, social aid & pleasure clubs, Mardi Gras Indians, and bone gangs that have risen since Hurricane Katrina. Bringing back a tradition long held only by male bone gangs in New Orleans, Skinz N Bonez wake up the living on Mardi Gras day, lending a feminine element to the morning with song and dance, chant and drum, and smiles on our faces. It is our goal not only to wake you up to greet the day, but to instill a sense of tradition and cultural significance to one of the oldest religious ceremonies in the world: Carnivale. In honor of that carnival spirit, we shed our flesh, down to bone, and remind you that we are all mortal. Echoing the Day of the Dead / Dia de Los Muertos traditions of the Mexican people, and the European traditions of the dead to the living, we remind ourselves - and everyone else - that life is short. Enjoy each moment, and each tradition and custom, and pass it from one generation to the next. We bring the spirits of the past to the streets on Mardi Gras day. Join us in our celebration of honoring our ancestors".

161

Pretty impressive, right? I was able to sit down with MardiClaw and ask about all things Skinz N Bonez and, as usual, meeting with her is always an education. I hope you enjoy.

Q: You started as an all-female krewe in 2011. How did that come about?

MardiClaw: The year before at Mardi Gras I had become friends with Wild Man John of the Wild Tchoupitoulas black masking Indian tribe. And he would ask me, every year, to walk with him at Mardi Gras. He asked me that year because it was just Queen Yolonda and him. They were the only Wild Tchoupitoulas left, no drummers, etc. So that year I carried his flag on Mardi Gras day. I walked the whole line with him. It was a beautiful experience. And after that I did St. Joseph's night and the parade on Super Sunday. Over the summer we talked jokingly about how cool it would be if he had a bunch of women behind him playing drums. So, John at the Hi Ho took an ad in the Hi Ho ads asking women drummers to come out and join Skull and Bones. It was actually Skinz N Bonez, but we thought women might balk at that. Skinz is the skin on the drum. The drum head.

Q: Oh, that's fantastic. I never knew that.

MardiClaw: Yeah. My husband came up with that. That summer we had our first meeting and Wild Man John was there, who is now Big Chief Ellis, and we were doing our version of Little Liza Jane, and everybody sucked (laughs). We were all in this circle, singing Little Liza Jane, and when it came your turn, you had to improvise and say your thing. The rule was, we're not gonna end this circle until everybody says something. We went around like thirty times until we were all really annoyed with the one person who was afraid and wouldn't sing. They were afraid to say something and eventually they said something, and we finished the drum circle and finally took a break.

Q: That's awesome. I remember how intimidating that could be when it got to be your turn when we did the Krewe of Boo parade with you guys one year. You feel the pressure (laughs). How did you release the actual name?

MardiClaw: I remember we were watching the HBO show Treme at the HiHo. And there were the guys who write on your hands. Dear New Orleans. They have a whole picture series on their website. We were out front, and we had them write on our arms. I have a photo and John had Wild Tchoupitoulas on his arms and I had Skinz N Bonez written on mine. And that's how we made the announcement of the name. We would meet every Sunday at the Hi Ho Lounge, and it took a long time, oh my god, to get where we are today.

Q: What, if any, challenges or pushback, did you face in creating the krewe?

MardiClaw: We faced a lot of obstacles. Because I think there was a point where we could say "we're invited", that was one hurdle. Then it was basically, then we had to learn the songs and the Indians were there and were like, "These are traditional songs and we're going to teach them to you". We didn't teach them to ourselves. They were our mentors and there was a weight of responsibility with that. To get them right. It evolved over time. I spent a lot of time with Ronald Lewis, this was very pivotal, and his stance was that women changed Mardi Gras. Post Katrina New Orleans was also when the Cherry Bombs also debuted. There was much to be said about women rising during that time, including Ye Ma Ya parade (Anne Marie Coviello), 6t9 also rose, bringing candy to kids in blighted neighborhoods (from the 6th to the 9th wards) and brass on Halloween. The city was much more activist then. Covid has certainly kept us inside, and politics and the rise of social media has made things harder. That's about to change, I believe.

Q: For those who don't know, who is Ronald Lewis?

MardiClaw: He was the Gatekeeper of the North Side Skull and Bones Gang and who owned House of Dance and Feathers. He passed during Covid. He was one of the first people we lost here in the city. It was very upsetting.

Q: I'm so sorry.

MardiClaw: Anyway, he and I talked a lot about how women changed the face of Mardi Gras. After Katrina, go back and you'll see that there were no brass bands. And then Muses raised the money and he *brought in outside bands to fill the empty slots during parades until we had brass back. He and I spent a lot of time talking about that. He was very..., let's just say that you didn't make a move without discussing things with him first. And I was like, step back, you don't own that yet. I wanted to bring a feminine element to it because I think women bring a little more joy it was kind of a reversal. I had lost my dad in 1990 and that's when I began embracing the Day of the Dead. So, the skeleton thing was not new for me. I would have a gathering and we would say the names of the ones we had lost. So again, this was not new to me. This was me evolving it over, well, since 1990. In fact, I was even a skeleton in my high school yearbook. That far back.*

Q: Was that in Seattle?

MardiClaw: *No. I actually grew up in Portland. I always say Seattle because that's when I really evolved. I was living in Seattle when my dad died, and I was very sad. And I would, you know, go to this Hispanic store and they would have all of the Day of the Dead skeletons to find joy and a kind of closure, I guess. I just adopted it and kept it because it helped me get passed it. And I've visited Day of the Dead in Mexico, where American views are very different. And they're like "Why aren't you painted? Don't you respect your dead elders? What's wrong with you?" Whereas here people kick back on it because we're all so busy fighting with each other these days instead of uniting.*

Q: Amen to that. So what's so interesting to me about what you just said, and a lot of this I didn't know, was that Indians and the Bone Gang guys were like your mentors.

MardiClaw: *I definitely consider John to be a mentor. He was the person who got us going.*

Q: This is a female led krewe, but men can also be a part, correct?

MardiClaw: *Yes. The men were originally considered Soul Sweepers, sweep the souls off the street after you're gone. Sweep the bad juju off the street. There was also a security aspect to it as well. But then we started getting a few guys who were really good at drumming. I wasn't opposed to it. I don't go out actively seeking guys for the krewe. We've also had a few guys come to the krewe thinking that they were*

164

gonna find dates, and they're not with us anymore. I'm very protective of that.

And then there's some who come in with a level of maturity and it's not an issue.

If they come in here and make people feel uncomfortable, well, then they'll be facing me, and I'll make them feel really uncomfortable. I didn't start this krewe for that, and it sends the wrong message.

Q: Your masking is always exceptional, but you're also known for supporting charities around town, especially of the four-legged variety. How do you develop your outreach? I think our first time out with you guys was in 2013 and it was a bulldog rescue.

MardiClaw: Yes! That's when we were doing Calacas y Maracas. I have a member who runs ARNO (Animal Rescue New Orleans) at this point, and we've done stuff for them. I'm a dog owner, so what I'd do, I'd pick a different dog rescue group every year. I wouldn't stick with just one, because I felt like everybody needs exposure. We kind of stepped away from Calacas y Maracas and started doing a thing with Ronald Lewis where we would do fundraisers to raise money to get students backpacks. He ran Big Nine Social Aid & Pleasure, and so in the fall, we would show up at his place with like twenty or thirty backpacks full of pencils, papers, and stuff, because that's what Big None focused on. We kind of moved around a little bit to also help schoolteachers. We all know that schoolteachers end up paying for their kids supplies. I would do fundraisers for the various teachers in the krewe so they wouldn't end up going out of pocket. The charity work, if I see something, I mean, we're not like the Pussyfooters and going to raise thousands of dollars and I don't want to be like that, because that's not our role. But if I can help with that's smaller, that needs attention, I'm gonna go for it.

Q: We need more like you, and I really love that about you guys. It speaks to your character and your love for the city. It's just one of the reasons I'm a perpetual fan and supporter. Okay, switching gears, I have to ask about your connection to Anne Rice and her famous Lestat Vampire balls. How did that happen?

MardiClaw: Sue Quiroz is a big fan of ours, and she approached me and asked if we would like to play at the Anne Rice Vampire Ball and I was like, Ah, Yeah!!!! (laughs)

Q: Who is Sue Quiroz?

MardiClaw: She was Anne Rice's right hand and ran the Vampire Lestat Fan Club Ball here in New Orleans for years. Mary Dugas runs it now, since Sue has retired, but Sue is still here in town. But yeah, she was very tight with Anne and when Anne left town, she gave Sue the key to her storage unit that had all of her dolls and things she's collected over the years. She invited us and said, "I choose you guys because of your connection to the Indians. Anne arrives in a limo and you guys and the Indians will 2nd Line her into the venue". Of course, I'm not saying no to that! We've actually improved a lot since that first time, you know. I thoroughly enjoyed it. I enjoyed meeting Anne. Actually, when we got the write up for the article I mentioned earlier, New Orleans Carnivalesque Day of the Dead, we found out that Anne Rice was pushing Skinz N Bonez online and we were like, oh, we're star quality now (laughs). We were blown away! And I got to meet her and give her a doll. It was beautiful.

Q: That's a wonderful segue to my next question about your amazing signature throws. You guys put together some of the best handmade, hand-crafted throws out there that showcase all your talent and artistry as a group. Especially the dolls. How did they come about?

MardiClaw: So, there was a woman named Cathy who used to run the Le Bon Enfants (Good Children) Parade, which was a parade for kids on Easter down in the in the Bywater. Cathy is no longer with us. She had a group, and this is before Skinz N Bonez, that had a cart. And you would go up to the cart and you would give them something. And then you went around to the back of the cart, and they had given you a fortune cookie telling you what to do, and you would get a toy. And I went to the back, and they handed me a painted skeleton doll. I still have it. I went, "what?!!!" And, of course, my brain went "What?!!!" So, I began experimenting with them. I brought them out for Petite Rex that year. Other people were doing Barbie dolls, but they weren't doing the skeleton ones like we were doing. And then Barb and I were hanging out and we were painting them, and we were just going to give them out painted, and I was like, what if we were to dress them? Four

166

hours later we were dressing them all and then it became a thing. And we would give them out and people were just astonished. And since then, the quality has gone way up over the years.

I used to get them really cheap and now I just go and buy real Barbies. I don't mess around. I go for Barbie, I go for Love of Monster High dolls, trolls, we don't care. Give us a little doll and we're gonna paint it and send it back a skeleton and it will be dressed.

Q: We have one in our glass display case with all our favorite Mardi Gras and parade mementos and the doll you gave me at the Krewe of Boo in 2015 is front and center in that collection. It's one of my favorite things ever.

MardiClaw: *I have had ladies from Muses come into Surrey's, where I used to work, where I had them up on the walls for sale at $30 a pop, and they would want to buy a bunch of them to put in their shoes.*

Q: Well, they are definitely works of art.

It took years to figure out what paint to use, what varnish. It was a process.

Q: How has the krewe evolved over the last decade?

MardiClaw: *We've had several different people handle the drumming. We had Katie Harvey, known as TinkerBone. She was our 2ⁿᵈ Queen. She was kind of our first person who organized us to drum. Then we had BeBop Robecheaux, who is no longer with us. He came up with the brilliant idea that if we all made your own drums, we would be more likely to play our drums. And he got us drums, and he was right. Then Barb was with us for a while and then Dhani came in. She's amazing. Indiana Bones!*

Q: I absolutely agree, she is amazing! So, with that, last question, what is your vision of the future for Skinz N Bonez?

MardiClaw: *I really like the performance ideas we've done where there's more talent under the surface other than just drumming. There's probably six or seven singers in the krewe, we've got guitar players, drummers, we've even have a standup bass. One year, at the*

Anne Rice Ball, we had an upright bass player. We got up and performed on the stage and did a song. We also do a thing in October, one of the many things we do in October (laughs), at one of the hotels, they hire us out, where we perform for their clientele. I also like the idea of the cabaret shows we've done to raise money. We're also developing a deck of tarot cards. I'd also like to see more music videos. We did one during the pandemic, and have one in the hole right now, we just haven't filmed it. I'd also like to see us go back to D.C. again. We've done that before. We were going to go for the protests for Summer of Rage, we just didn't have enough notice to get it all together in time.

I think my vision is for me to step back and let Dhani take over a little more, cause I'm getting up there in age (laughs). I'm not gonna stop doing the art, or the dolls, but I've reached a point physically where I may have to step back more in the coming year. I just want to see it evolve and to help keep women strong. Especially with what has just happened with Roe. I'm still very angry about that. We've also talked about going out to Jackson Square and performing. Putting together a series of protest songs, like we did before. We have our own versions of some Rage Against the Machine songs that we do. We're gonna pull that back up. I think it's important to stand with everyone. When I was a kid, at eight years old, when women weren't allowed to have their own bank accounts. I remember my mom took me with her to get her account and it was 1968. People don't realize. Then you move forward to 1974 and I watched my friends get a credit card. Then we got gay marriage, and now you're going to try take all that away? No. Not happening.

So "Wake up!" ya'll and live your lives to the fullest. As our famed New Orleans Trumpet Master, Kermit Ruffins, likes to sing. "Enjoy yourself! It's later than you think"!

All Hail The Bone Queen, MardiClaw!

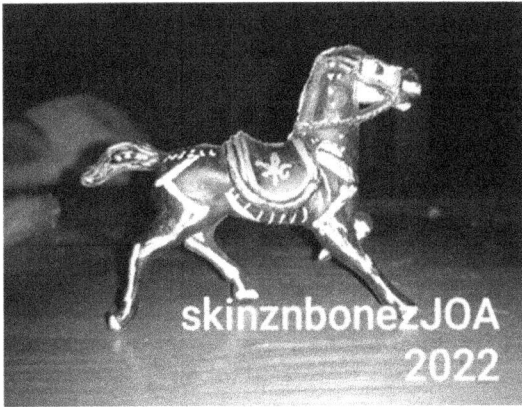

skinznbonezJOA
2022

Note: All Pictures used by permission

See Original Art at www.mardiclaw.com and also on Facebook & Instagram.

CELEBRITY SIGHTINGS

I once asked Blues guitarist Mark Penton why he didn't go on the road more often and he replied, "I don't need to go out on the road. The road comes here." After living here for a while, I understood what he meant. It does at times feel that all roads lead to New Orleans. Here's just a few of the celebrity encounters we've had since we moved here.

Arnold Schwarzenegger

Jayda Pinkett Smith & John Schneider

The Incomparable Amy Lee

Evanescence!

That time Queen Latifah's Dad played cowbell in our band across the street from where she was giving a balcony interview

The Queen waving down to us from The Bourbon Orleans balcony, telling her dad that we did a good job

Lacuna Coil! They promised that they would come to New Orleans, and we can't wait!

With Rock Goddess Cristina Scabbia

At the Jazz Fest Gospel Tent with music legend Allen Toussaint

Actor Extraordinaire Clarke Peters

Stoop sitting with Artist Craig Tracey at his gallery on Royal

Blues Icons & Great Friends, Big Al Carson & Mark Penton

The incredible Josh Gates!

James Franco at the Saints & Sinners Grand Opening

One of my all-time favorite actors, David Morse

Legendary Blues Guitarist Little Freddy King

Hanging with Kermit Ruffins & my drum mentor, Rodney Rollins, at the Mother-in-Law Lounge

Amazing singer, songwriter & performer, Mia Borders

Award winning Screenwriter George Pelcanos

Monster Funk and R&B Gentleman Jon Cleary

Acclaimed Actor & Super Nice Guy, Jon Seda

A True Force of Nature - Steve Zahn

Incredible talent - Troy "Trombone Shorty" Andrews

Stephen Moyer & Alexander Skarsgard filming True Blood on Bourbon Street!

Actor Rob Brown

The incredible Wendell Pierce

Beloved Treme Brass Band Legend – Uncle Lionel Batiste

Drummer extraordinaire for Avril Lavigne & the New York Theatre, and a really great guy – Rodney Howard

21

THE DRAGON'S DEN
435 Esplanade Ave

The Dragon's Den, and the building that houses it, has fascinated me
for many, many years. Not only does it have great bartenders, staff
and management, it boats a killer motif and plays host to some of the
best DJs and musical talent New Orleans has to offer. It also boasts a
robust and fascinating dark history, many aspects which are still
shrouded in mystery. In a town like New Orleans, where the ghosts
simply come with the buildings, the Dragon's Den stands in a category
all to itself.

Built in the late 1800's this building has played host to many different
"institutions" over the past century and change, brothels, opium dens,
prohibition bars and even a laundromat. But it's most notable guest in
1916 was none other than the notorious upper class English occult
priest, the man the British Press dubbed as "The wickedest man alive",

Aleister Crowley. Yes, that Mr. Crowley. The guy from the Ozzy Osbourne song, Mr. Crowley.

Always on the hunt for mystical, magical places and energy portals, Crowley landed here after spending thirteen years in Scotland at the Boleskine House overlooking Loch Ness, which he believed was also a mystical energy portal. If the Boleskine House sounds familiar to you, that's because Jimmy Page from Led Zeppelin, who was a student of Crowley's work, owned the house from 1970 until 1992 when it was destroyed in a mysterious fire. Page also has New Orleans ties and an association with another famous French Quarter bar known as The Dungeon on Toulouse Street (for more on that story see Chapter 2).

Once here Crowley fell in love with New Orleans and quickly dubbed it his "favorite American City", which inspired him to churn out two works of literature during the short time he was here. One is a fictional novel entitled Moon Child, about two wizards battling over the fate of an unborn child who will control the destiny of the universe, and the other is an epic poem entitled The Green Goddess, which is an ode to Absinthe and to the magical city in which he found it. Many believe it is one of his most acclaimed works, outside of his magical texts. But writing books wasn't the only thing he did while he was here. He also performed rituals, occult ceremonies, and his own special brand of what he referred to as "Sexual Magick". In other words, to him these were basically orgies with a higher purpose. It was all about the energy for him, whether structured and ceremonial, or raw and passionate. They were all part of the human experience on the pathway to enlightenment and opening up a higher consciousness. It is also strongly believed that he practiced some of those rites at the building that now houses The Dragon's Den.

In his song "Mr. Crowley", Ozzy Osbourne asks "Did you talk to the dead?" From the residual paranormal activity at the building one would have to say the answer is a resounding yes! Over the years reports of dark shadow figures, disembodied voices and strange activities within the mirrors all speaks to a residual psychic imprint at this location. From the macabre and mysterious Day of the Dead style painting that graces the downstairs bar to the various dragon themed works of art that crawl and perch all along the surfaces of the building, the staff have their own stories to tell.

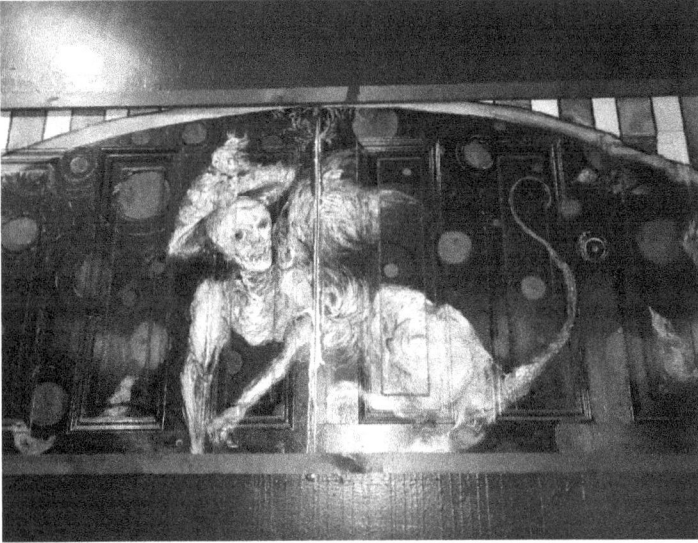

The mysterious "Colinda" painting found imbedded in the back wall of the old upstairs bar

The haunted mirror missing its twin

The Dragon on the downstairs bar

But don't take my word for it, go check it out for yourself. Grab a drink, imbibe and immerse yourself in a location that is unapologetically magical and unique, even by New Orleans standards.

One of my favorite people on the planet is Narisha Johnson, the manager of The Dragon's Den. I got to sit down with her and talk about the vision for the bar and their enduring contributions to the people and the culture of the city. Here's what she had to say.

Narisha: "We're located at the tip of the French Quarter and the end of Frenchmen Street, so our goal is to be a place where the locals are comfortable. We want them to walk in and feel like "this is my hangout; a home away from home feel." A place where locals can come and relax and not feel like they're a specimen under the watchful eyes of the tourists. But, with that being said, we're open to everybody. We want it to be as diverse as possible. That's why we are picky about each night we curate. We had a swing dance night on Mondays and a country night on Tuesdays. We have a reggae night Wednesdays, bounce night on Thursdays. We want every night to be different and unique, but open to all cultures of the city. Our DJs are the same - their own style, so unique and they curate a brand for their night. And actually, this diverse dynamic is also good for the staff. They enjoy working these different nights.

They don't feel like they're in a rut with the same thing every night and enjoy their shifts. The boss wants that diversity, if we can't find it, we just don't open that night. Right now, we're not open Monday &

Tuesday, not for lack of options - just not the right options for our mission. Peace, Love and Fun - That's our vibe.

[She points to their entry sign.]

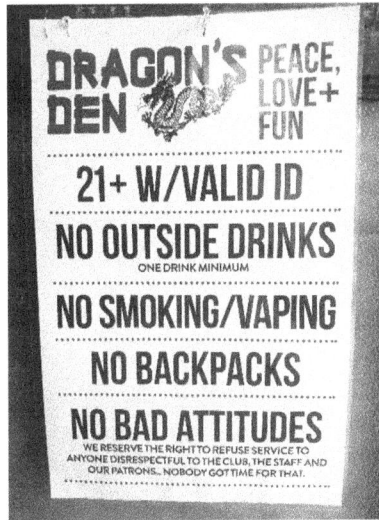

" See. No bad attitudes allowed. Everybody come and have a good time. That's the way the owner wants it to be. For us, it's all about NOLA community. We're about supporting our locals and our local talent. We're starting an Art Market on Wednesdays and Service Industry Sundays. A lot of our local artists, since the pandemic, have been struggling. They don't have money to spend on a tent to go to the other markets, you know? So we're going to support them by letting them come in, set up in our courtyard, make some sales, keep their cash and get some free marketing... why not, we got the space?"

Of course, we do get lots of tourists who come in, more so on Friday and Saturday. Some are looking for film sites. The first season of True Detective filmed some scenes here. The New Orleans based romantic comedy The Lovebirds also filmed here. So, people come in looking for the locations they saw in the movies or their favorite shows. All good, the staff is welcoming to all good attitudes.

We're open to all kinds of events, we've hosted Pride events, local Krewe parties, headliner Comedian tours, headliner DJs, up and coming NOLA musicians' showcases, community events. We are always about the community events.

Q: That's a breath of fresh air compared to what has been happening on Bourbon the last few years. People narrowing their clientele instead of expanding it and being inclusive.

Narisha: *Right. That goes back to the attitude thing we were discussing earlier. If you're visiting our home [the venue] you have to be respectful to everyone, the staff and everyone around you. We won't hesitate to call security on whoever is making anyone feel threatened or uncomfortable. We'll just tell them to have a nice time somewhere else for tonight, come back when they're more tolerant, or in a better mood.*

The culture here should be beautiful and embracing. You shouldn't feel age in here. You shouldn't feel color in here. There shouldn't be any "he" or "she" issues in here. That's the big vision and you should feel like you're in New Orleans. You should walk in here and feel accepted. Yes, it's a bit down and dirty. You walk upstairs late at night, and you see everyone just getting it and having a good time and it's like, YES!

Q: That's the way it's supposed to be.

Narisha: *Community activism: We have this beautiful art on our front door by Lionel Milton, showing our support for BLM. We gained national attention as the first bar to host the "Shot for a Shot" campaign during the pandemic to get vaccinations out to everyone, with the help of our longtime resident DJ RQAway and Crescent Care*

Genuine culture bearers are what keeps the culture alive. For instance, Hasizzle comes here and plays on bounce night. He's the king of bounce like Big Freeda is the Queen of bounce. Bounce was invented in New Orleans. It's New Orleans music. And he has Emmy nominations, jams with celebrity artists, etc., and still, he comes here every Thursday, like a normal person. No diva attitude, just true to his roots. This is where he started. This is where it's real.

Q: That's one thing that has always impressed me about New Orleans musicians, how genuine they are as human beings. No pretense. Very approachable. Unlike our past experiences in other places where we have lived.

Narisha: I call them shell people. They identify themselves by what car they drive, where they live, how much money they make. I lived there before. I moved to a city where I instantly felt at home and I thought, I should have actually been born here. This is my personality. I wear what I want to wear. Even if it's a white undershirt and jeans, that's what it is. You should like me for me. That's all, that's how it is here.

Q: People are definitely more real down here.

Narisha: I lived here for years, and nobody ever asked me what I did. They knew I was creative and that was enough. They don't give a shit. You cool, then you cool. You can be you. This is where you learn how to not care about judgment.

Q: Be cool or leave.

Narisha: Exactly.

Seriously. Who wouldn't love to hang out in a life changing place like this? I know I certainly do.

Narisha Johnson at the entrance to The Dragon's Den

ANECDOTE: **THE ONE THAT STICKS WITH ME**

Everyone loves a good ghost story. Sharing ghost stories has been a pastime of humans since time immemorial. Once the belief that our spirits exist separate from our bodies took flight, we have pondered what happens to our spirits after they depart. And if they can depart, can they come back? Or can they stay? Can they haunt us? As I write this, we're a little over a month away from Christmas 2021 and the annual viewing of one of most enduring Christmas classics, Charles Dickens, a Christmas Carol. Its original title was "A Christmas Carol in Pose – Being a Ghost Story of Christmas". Telling ghost stories at Christmas was a time-honored tradition in the Victorian era 1800's that has sadly fallen away over time. Unless you're a New Orleans Tour Guide, that is. I not only love telling them, I love hearing them as well, and always solicit stories from my tour patrons. Especially on bar breaks.

One, in particular, has stuck with me over the past few months with a profound imagery I just can't get out of my head. I had a wonderful family on my tour in October. A mother and father in their mid-50's to early 60's, and their 30 something daughter. She sadly had recently lost her husband to cancer and was still trying to find her footing as she dealt with her loss and grief. She admitted to me that she had always been sensitive to spirits, but since her husband's passing, had closed herself off. She said she just wasn't ready to deal with that quite yet, which is completely understandable. Her parents chimed in that they had always been aware of her gifts since the time she was a small child. It started in the house in which she grew up, in Connecticut. Apparently, the previous owner of the house, before her parents bought it, was an elderly man who was a very heavy smoker. Not only would the house continuously smell of fresh cigarette smoke, though none of them were smokers, but he would manifest throughout the property as he loved to wander at night. The young lady related to me that she had very distinct memories of sitting on her bed in the dead dark of night and watching the orange glow of a lit cigarette as it moved down the hallway, seemingly passing with purpose, across her doorway. Occasionally it would flare, as if someone had just taken a deep drag off of the other end, and then it would fade as it moved further down the corridor.

Night after night this continued to occur, for years, until she reached her teens and it mysteriously stopped. They sold the house and moved away some years later, but she still recalls those visitations. She believes he was making his rounds, checking on the house to ensure they were safe. I guess we'll never know. But I can't get the image out of my head of a little girl sitting on her bed, trembling, and quietly watching as the orange glow of a lit cigarette glided past her door, illuminating the hallway as it moved throughout the house. That image is going to stick with me for a very long time.

Phantom smells, disembodied whispers and ephemeral shadows are remnants of those who have occupied the spaces before us (Photo by Belinda Smith)

22

THE LALAURIE MANSION - REVISITED
1140 Royal Street

Earlier in the book, you'll remember that Chapter Nine covered the LaLaurie Mansion and the capture of one of the creepiest pictures ever taken on one of my tours. That incident occurred in the summer of 2016.

For the past five years I've continued to share that picture whenever I tell the story of the atrocities that took place there. And invariably I get asked the question "who do you think that is?" Up until this point all I really had were assumptions and somewhat educated guesses, with the most likely candidate being the Madame herself.

Now if I've learned one lesson in the past eight years of living in this city, it's that you do so on her terms, not yours. She can literally make or break you. But, if you come in with respect for the culture, history and traditions, are open and patient, there are times when she will reveal her secrets to you. This is one of those times.

As post pandemic fate would have it, I was very fortunate to come in contact with Christian Day, a Salem Warlock who owns the Hex and Omen shops on Decatur Street with his husband, Alexandrian Witch, Brian Cain.

Based on their outstanding reputation alone I have been sending my tour patrons to them for years for palm and tarot readings and witchcraft supplies.

After a few discussions I was honored for them to offer me a position to be a guide for the relaunch of their Spirits and Spells Tour. In studying their wonderful script, written by Emily Anne Smykal, I was intrigued to learn about a lady named Mary Oneida Toups. The With Queen of New Orleans.

Having heard her name before on American Horror Story, but not knowing much beyond that, I found her story fascinating. Divorced in her 40's, she came here from her home in Meridian Mississippi in 1969 looking for change and personal growth. Her quest of self-discovery was not unlike what was happening throughout the rest of the country at the time; Vietnam, civil rights, the Age of Aquarius, the rise of feminist movement, environmental reform, and the sexual revolution, to name a few. And if you're going to re-invent yourself, there is truly no place better in the world than New Orleans.

Naturally gifted as a sensitive she came here seeking answers. Possessing a voracious appetite for learning, she delved into the magical arts with an emphasis on Aleister Crowley and the Thelemic path of study and quickly established herself as a powerful force in the growing magical community. In 1972 she gained legal recognition and established The Religious Order of Witchcraft in Louisiana with the help of her husband, Albert "Boots" Toups and their good friend, a hard scrabble Voudon named Mac Rebennack Jr., also known as famed musician Dr. John, The Night Tripper. They were definitely in the right place at the right time. And her coven grew.

Now you may be wondering at this point what 70's French Quarter Witch has to do with a picture taken by one of my tour patrons in 2016. And that's the really cool part. It's all part of the interconnectedness, the magical gumbo, that makes this place so special.

In 1977 a young woman living at the LaLaurie Mansion, which was divided into apartments at that time, came to Mary Toups looking for help with what she believed to be a haunting in her apartment.

Toups visited the lady in her apartment one afternoon and quickly realized that the spirit activity was not just confined to her apartment but spread throughout the entire building. So, she decided the best course of action was to hold a séance in the courtyard at 3am with the most trusted members of her coven by her side.

It is said that she was able to help move over twenty earth bound spirits on to the afterlife that morning. But one spirit remained, either by choice or by cosmic mandate, that part is uncertain.

Mary Toups reportedly drew a sketch of this spirit, which I am desperately trying to get my hands upon. Until that happens, we'll just have to settle for the description of what she saw; "A dour older lady dressed and veiled all in black."

Thirty-nine years later a guest on my first private tour in 2016 gets this. The Madame herself; Delphine Marie McCarty LaLaurie.

Bachelorette Party Photo – July 10th, 2016

This is the city revealing her secrets to us. And I can't begin to adequately describe the bolt of excitement that shot through me when I learned about this incident. Why? Because I didn't learn about Mary Oneida Toups, and this incident at LaLaurie, until October of 2021 and I've been carrying that picture with me on my phone and showing it on my tours since 2016. Mind officially blown!

But there's more. On May 7th, 2022, the 304th birthday of the city of New Orleans, a young lady by the name of Hiedi Musselman, and her friends, took my Spirits and Spells Tour. At the LaLaurie Mansion she got the picture of a disembodied face floating in the center second floor window. A few days later a guide on one of our tour guide Facebook pages shared an interesting find in the form of a book by the name of Social Life in Old New Orleans, published in 1912 by Eliza Ripley. In it she describes stories about "the haunted house" and one related to her about a spirit possessing "eyes without sockets or sockets without eyes" that stares down from one of the upstairs windows. Once again, a perfect description of the activity at the mansion that continues to this day.

The face in the upstairs window! Photos by Hiedi Musselman

Also, sometimes they don't just linger in the mansion, but come out on the streets to greet you. Courtesy of Jonathan Weiss, here's a few pictures his tour patrons have taken during his tour of them doing just that. I think they want to know what we're saying about them, and I don't blame them one bit.

Tour apparition photos courtesy of Jonathan Weiss

VCV (Vieux Carre View) as recorded by Magic Nation
Lyrics by P. Mangum @2008
Music by D. Clinton, P. Mangum

French Quarter view shinin' in my rearview mirror
My direction couldn't be any clearer
Got you sellin' religion in the shops on Royal Street
Black water bayous under my feet

Well it's time to forget how you put me down,
twisted me 'round, took me high off the ground
Tellin' the world how you drove me insane, but I'm
drivin' back out again
I wanna see the world through the eyes of who I
used to be
Gotta get back what I gave away for free

Old woman ghost is staggerin' along at my side
Down to the river, it's so old and mean and wide
Thirty days of rain floodin' them downtown streets
Call me back luck lady, got Dallas leather on my feet

Well it's time to forget how you put me down,
twisted me 'round, took me high off the ground
Tellin' the world how you drove me insane, but I'm
drivin' back out again
I wanna see the world through the eyes of who I
used to be
Gotta get back what I gave away for free

Hoodoo voodoo statuette smoked my last cigarette,
but the ashes all fell down

Bottles in the gutter with pictures and dreams
I had to drink it all away is what I really mean
Steppin' to the corner where the streetlights shine

I'm tellin' you one more time

Well it's time to forget how you put me down,
twisted me 'round, took me high off the ground
Tellin' the world how you drove me insane, but I'm
drivin' back out again
I wanna see the world through the eyes of who I
used to be
Gotta get back what I gave away for free

To listen to this song on YouTube, please scan the QR Code below

23

PORTRAIT OF A CITY IN QUARANTINE
Claire Sargenti

May Baily's is one of my absolute favorite stops on our Haunted Pub Crawl. The hotel bar for the Dauphine Orleans Hotel, this place

March 2020

I went to see my city last night. It was 9pm on a Sunday. Late March. Busy season. Empty. Quiet. It's strange how the smell of piss gets so much stronger when there's no trace of beer and puke and sweat to wash it down. Even the panhandlers are gone. No one to panhandle to. I wonder where they've gone. The bars are boarded up- prepared for an invisible hurricane that's rushing through our streets and homes and in our veins. It's quiet here.

Even the ghosts have quarantined themselves tonight. The lights of neon signs and lantern flames glow bright tonight. It's a shame that no one will see them. I forget that I count as someone. I close my eyes and imagine a year ago last spring. It seems so far away. I think of all the times I spoke of Yellow Fever, Scurvy, Smallpox. The bodies on the streets. I think of just one month ago, Mardi Gras Day. The revelers on the streets. The glitter is still here. I open my eyes and continue on. And then some signs of life. An arrow. In chalk. In the middle of the street. More chalk. More arrows. "Hot Food This Way." A block away a beam of light streams out of the open door of NOLA Poboys and in that light stands a man with painted silver hands and a painted silver face. He wears blue jeans and a brown t-shirt. I used to see him every day on the corner of Bourbon and St. Peter Street until he moved to a different location. I've never seen him wearing clothes that didn't match his silver skin. I wonder if he halfway tried to earn some money in this empty town or the paint just stopped rubbing off.

On Royal there's a small gathering of people outside the Rouses. I wonder if they still have their jobs. I wonder if they qualify for unemployment or food stamps but knowing who they are they're probably just like me. Laid off without aid and wondering when the tourists will come back.

Down the street there's a recording of Louis Armstrong playing. A reminder of a New Orleans that existed long before I showed up here. I think about how many manifestations this city has gone through. And I wonder how long this particular one will last. And what's coming next.

Before the virus I'd be taking drunken tourists around the French Quarter, telling them of the histories and the hauntings that took place here at this address, over there on that corner… and now I feel like I'm the one who's doing the haunting. And my friends, my friends would be doing exactly the same thing. Our voices loud and strong keeping the spirits alive in the minds of those who choose to reside elsewhere. Our voices loud and strong blending into the cacophony of sounds of laughter and music and sirens and heated conversations, the tin-like reverberations of beer can tap shoes tapping out half-rhythms on the sidewalks and the jingle of change as the old timey cash registers open and close at the establishments that don't take credit cards.

And in the distance a figure appears. I know him by name. I meekly mumble a greeting and my words echo off the buildings. Nothing to absorb them and carry them away into the ether. A residual haunting. Over and over, it echoes- a repetition of right now- a time I'd rather forget. As he passes by, he says "I'm still here."

ANECDOTE: **THE POLITE GUNMAN – Jennifer Raven**

So, there was a parade in the French Quarter last night that just completely disrupted my usual tour route. No biggie. Rerouted to mostly Chartres Street. I'm on my third story, and we're on this little side street just before St. Peter Street. St. Peter is blocked off because there's a parade. Even people who don't live here know that. That's kind of important to this story.

All traffic coming up Chartres has to divert down Madison, which happens to be the street we're standing on. And I'm all into the story, talking about vampires and I'm kinda near the corner when an SUV turns the corner and stops. I noticed it was not moving so I looked behind me and there's no driver. I comment " well, idk why someone chose to park there but that's gonna suck for all those people who need to turn, right?"

We give a little chuckle and I continue with the story. I notice a taxi on Chartres and a guy is talking to the driver through the window. I assume that this is the missing driver and perhaps the taxi driver tapped him or something, they seem to be talking very intensely when it starts.

Some Karen lays on the horn and they're followed by a Kevin on the horn. Our guy yells at them to stop. Wait a second, he's almost done taking care of something important, just give him a minute. This reinforces my idea there was a fender bender. For the record, I think people who lay on the horn at a situation like this are complete trash.

They double down and now there's a chorus of these two twats laying on the horn. Dude. There's a parade. The street is blocked off with cones. Even if dude moves RIGHT THIS SECOND, you're not getting far. Chill. They do not chill. Dude is getting pissed. Fuck, I'm getting pissed. My people are getting pissed.

Dude goes over to the cunt laying on the horn and tries to talk her into stopping for two seconds so he can finish up. He tries to explain that he would be done by now if they hadn't kept at it.

The Kevin gets out of his car and screams something unintelligible at the guy. The guy says something like " oh, you wanna fuck with me like that? I can fuck around like that" as he stomps back to the car.

The Kevin screams something at Guy as he's walking away. Guy goes into his car, grabs a revolver, and, pointing it, walks back toward the Kevin while saying something like " you wanna go? Let's go!"

Now, at this point in my life, I have 29 people about to stampede. When a gun is brandished, you do not want to make yourself visible and that's what these ppl are about to do. I use my outside voice to tell them not to run, they're not in danger, do not engage, do not panic, do not run. I explain that a guy with a gun is like a TRex, he's in predator mode and if you run, he'll think you're running for a weapon and you'll become a target. I encourage everyone to stay together, and we'll slowly move down the block a bit and resume the tour, do not acknowledge or make eye contact.

Guy disappears around corner with gun, presumably to take care of Kevin and shut Karen up. My people are all freaked out, so I explain the psychology of what's going on, I tell a funny story, get them calm. Guy calmly gets back into his vehicle, drives right up to where we're standing and stops. Everyone freezes.

I turn, smiling to look at Gun Guy. He says "I want to apologize to all of you. I'm in the Army. I'm here to protect you." Some of my people interrupt him with a hearty and confused " thank you for your service." He continues " I'm sorry you had to see that. I had to teach those people a lesson. Y'all have a good night, stay safe and happy carnival!" He waves, smiling, and drives off. We all look at each other and we're like, uh ok.

I take the people to the square and on our way we see that our Karen has removed the cones from the road and has driven through, and all the fucking cars behind her follow, and now they're all laying on the horns at the parade, because stupid fucking people never fucking learn.

P.S. at the end of the tour, I had a lady tip me and she said," do you know what I do for A living? (i shook my head no) I'm a psychotherapist. Really. How you handled that situation with the gun? It was perfect. You did amazing. I couldn't have done it better myself. You did great!"

24.

MOTHER OF AN APPLE PICKER
Randy Walker

The first tour I took out after Hurricane Ida hit was a memorable one, to say the least. At that point it had been three weeks since that windy motherfucker had come and gone and the French Quarter, like the rest of the city, was still reeling. Most of the power had returned by now, but there was still the odd streetlight, cornerstone, or even entire half-block that remained dark. And these powerless blemishes peppered the quarter, creating a sort of patchwork quilt of dark and light that gave off the impression of a night full of danger.

There was also the disturbing chest-high stack of storm debris and black trash bag heaps that decorated a huge portion of the sidewalk curbs, to the point where many of my usual go-to tour stop spots were just not accessible, or if they were, they were right next to one of these giant reminders of the fury of mother nature, which had the unwelcomed effect of making a little ghost story seem incredibly irrelevant in such destructive times.

A good deal of the stores and businesses were still closed too. And more than a few of the doors and windows of various art galleries, souvenir shops, and tourist traps were completely boarded up, which seemed to hint at either an imminent zombie apocalypse or, perhaps even more disconcerting, a callback to the almighty quarantine shutdown from a year and a half ago.

Perhaps the most eerie element of all though was just how desolate the quarter streets were. You turned down any main street- Royal, Chartres, even most of Bourbon- only to find zero sign of human life for blocks and blocks. Instead, on these long stretches of empty street the only movement you would see were the bits of storm debris that had left their curb pile and were now frolicking up and down the pavement, dancing with a night wind that was just strong enough to give locals a hint of PTSD if they weren't careful.

Of course, I don't include myself in that last sentence. For one thing, I still cannot, and will never be able, to call myself a New Orleans local, as it's been explained to me a number of times that no matter how long you live here, or what familial connections you might have, unless you can rep an elementary, middle or high school in the Orleans (or a neighboring) parish you can never truly call yourself a local.

Dem the rules.

Also, the wind couldn't give me PTSD because I wasn't here during the storm. I didn't even have to evacuate either. By sheer luck I had been back home visiting my folks on the west coast when Ida hit. What had started out as a nice relaxing stay in my childhood home transformed into ten days of panic-watching the news and praying that this would not be "the big one" that would take us out. New Orleans folk know all about this prayer. Regardless of your religion or beliefs, it seems at least once every couple of years we have to get down on our knees and beg the sky above not to take our beloved city away from us.

I cannot imagine what it was like for those who stayed in the city during the storm and the awful AC-less weeks that followed. But I can tell you that for me, waiting out those days back in my childhood town was a surreal purgatory of convenient comfort and frantic handwringing. As lucky as I was to have a home with power, a fridge with food, and concerned friends with hugs (although being constantly asked, "So why do you still live there when this keeps happening?" got pretty old), one thing that became very apparent to me during that time was that I needed New Orleans to survive because I couldn't live anywhere else. I know that's practically a cliche for transplants to say at this point but trying to live in an "ordinary" town for those couple of weeks really cemented how true this was for me. I was beyond question a Nola-or-die guy who was terrified I'd be facing the latter of those options.

And so, every night back out west I found myself praying. Not just for the city, but for the tourists. New Orleans got its start as a sea-trading port and for a good long while that's how we thrived economically. But that was a long time ago. Now our entire economic survival depends on tourism. Without visitors, this "city of death" would die itself. I guess I had always known that, but on those sleepless nights during the worst of the storm and its aftermath, I found myself wide-awake, anxiety flowing through me, praying that the tourists who loved New Orleans loved it enough to come back no matter what.

And all the while, one undeniable fact running through my mind over and over again:

I work for tips and so does my city.

So yes, my atheist ass prayed and prayed and prayed for New Orleans to recover and for the tourists to return to their fun-loving, cash-spending ways.

I say all this to help you understand how eager I was to impress once I returned to the city and got my first tour since the storm hit. No matter what elements faced us that night in the semi-ravaged quarter, I was determined to give my group the best tour of their life and make them believe I was their best friend.

Anything for repeat business.

So, without further ado...

It's a small group, smaller than it should be, in fact. Originally, a family of five from Milwaukee had signed up for the eight o'clock tour, a

214

mother in her fifties and her grown children, but when I arrive, I find only three waiting for me.

"My oldest daughter and her husband decided not to come," the mother explains. "They just got married so they've been really busy and exhausted."

Before I can respond to this, the young lady standing next to the mom, who I later find out is the other, younger, daughter, cracked, "Don't worry you're not missing anything, both of them have their heads up their asses, especially my sister."

All three of them, the mother, the younger daughter, and the slightly younger son, laugh long and hard at this, to the point where I make a mental note that something's up between the oldest daughter and the rest of the family.

The mother must have seen me react to this because she touches my shoulder and says, "she's not wrong. My oldest is a bit of a bitch."

At this, they all laugh heartily again, and the other daughter shouts, "a bitch witch!"

"An apple-picking bitch witch!" the mom cackles.

Cue the third round of laughter, this one more raucous than the first two combined.

And of course, I laugh along. No, I don't understand what apple picking has to do with anything, or why the joke is so funny, but I'm determined to make them love me, for the sake of my ailing city and wallet, so I chuckle heartily, god help me.

The tour starts out well enough. They listen politely to my stories, laughing and gasping at all the right parts, and spare me comments about how messed up the city is right now.

I appreciate that.

And on my end, I make sure to engage with them at all times, enthusiastically answering any question they might have, laughing from the belly whenever they make a joke, and generally acting like everything they say is either impressive or witty.

215

I work for tips, and so does my city.

The mother engages with me the most. At first, she simply asks questions as we walk from one story to the next, while her grown children talk amongst themselves. But as the tour grows on, her line of questioning shifts from "hey do you know…" to "hey, I know this, but do you?". Basically, she starts quizzing me, trying to catch me not knowing something that she knows, because she wants me to know that she's not a typical tourist… which is pretty typical of tourists in my experience.

"I'm just saying we're not one of the 'bad ones'," she tells me, "We love this city and its history, more than most people even, especially my eldest daughter, and we're so happy to be here."

"Oh, get it," I assure her, "I could tell that instantly about you, and your family. I get it. You get it!"

And it's somewhere around here, as she's explaining to me how she's one of 'the good ones' and me nodding in agreement, that things take a turn towards trouble.

"Of course, my daughter loves this place even more than me. I know we were giving her a hard time before because she's been a bit of a brat with the wedding and everything. But she's honestly a unique spirit. She's into the dark realm of life, you know? She dabbles in the dark arts."

This is when I know I'm in trouble. Whenever a customer starts bringing up the 'dark arts' it almost never leads to anything good.

"Oh, cool." I tell her dispassionately.

"Yeah, she's a real dark spiritual person. That's why she loves it here. The culture. Remember when my other daughter called her a witch. That's because she is one."

"Oh, cool."

"Yeah, it is," she responds without missing a beat. "Hey, remember how I told you she got married yesterday? Well, she actually got married in a cemetery. At night! Her and her husband broke in, set up some quick lights and exchanged vows and vowed to stay together for life in the cemetery, isn't that amazing?"

I don't respond to this, but I hope my silence sends the obvious message. *Amazing* isn't the word I would use in this case. The whole thing sounds kinda shitty to me. But I also know that I can't judge her too harshly, because over the years me and my friends have absolutely had a wild night or two sneaking into cemeteries...

But still, the idea of tourists from Milwaukee breaking into a cemetery in a city they don't live in and getting married amongst dead strangers just rubs me the wrong way. Seems rather icky. But I don't say anything because part of me thinks that'd be kinda hypocritical, right?

And besides, *I work for tips and so does the city.*

My silence seems to irk the mother, and as we reach St. Phillips Street, she slows her pace so that she's now behind me and walking next to her other daughter. She then says, at a volume loud enough so there's no way I can't hear her, "I wonder what Julia is doing right now?"

"She's probably asleep back at the hotel," her other daughter offers.

"Maybe. But you never know with her. Maybe she's out apple picking again. You know how much she loves to pick apples, especially in this city."

I scratch my head in confusion at this. At the start of the tour, she had also called her daughter an apple picker. Clearly this is code for something, but for the life of me I couldn't figure out what.

As I'm going over this in my head, I felt a presence next to me. It's the mother, walking alongside me again, looking into my eyes.

"She really loves this city. We all do."

"It sure is a great city!" I smile with fake enthusiasm, my voice and tone returning back to its full eagerness as I address all three people on tour. "Good news guys! We've reached the bar break portion of the tour! It's the oldest bar in New Orleans and one of the few that's entirely lit by candlelight. What do you say we all get a drink?!"

Once inside, we find it to be empty save for a few lonely souls, and the mood is incredibly ominous with the flickering light of the candles barely illuminating the vacant tables, chairs and stools.

As my group orders drinks at the bar, I hear music coming from down at the far end of the famous establishment. I leave my group to investigate and find to my great surprise the piano player playing over in the corner.

What the hell? I think. *It's Tuesday, the piano player only comes on weekends, maybe the occasional Thursday, but never on a Tuesday.*

But there he is, playing to a grand total of two people. Normally, I imagine he'd be rather annoyed by the lack of music lovers around him, but after these last three weeks of nothing, he looks as relieved as I feel just to have work again.

Sensing a good opportunity, I quickly usher my group from the bar to the piano, and they're all beyond delighted to find this surprise waiting for them. We each take a seat at one of the stools that hover around the pianist and his instrument and happily sing along to the popular Billy Joel song "The Longest Time" which I know seems too perfect to be true but that's what's happening right now. For one beautiful moment, everything's great. I remember why I love this job, this city, this lifestyle I've created. I remember why I prayed all those nights for all of this to come back. Damn right it's fucking beautiful.

And then, with the others singing and laughing merrily, the mother turns back to me, mouth close to my ear, and whispers:

"These are the photos of her wedding. Look! How great is that!"

I hesitantly look down at the phone she's holding up to my face and sure enough, there's a picture of a bride and groom inside a cemetery at night holding hands among tombs.

"Very nice," I tell her, hoping that'll be the end of it.

But then, with a flick of her finger, a new photo appears. It's the same as the last one except now you could see that the bride and groom are no longer holding hands but rather holding something between them that's round and white, something that looked very much like a…

"That's a skull, a human skull!" she tells me in hushed excitement.

218

She immediately shows more pics from different angles that reveal that the bride and groom were, without question, holding what looks to be a human skull.

As I process this, she leans in even closer, and I watch the wavy light of candles splash over her face as she whispers:

"That's what I meant when I said she was an apple picker. That's what we call it. New Orleans is so amazing and special, it really fits the gift she has. That's why she got married here. She's great at it and it's great to apple pick here."

The world's longest pause occurs here, because… I have no words.

"That's really not cool," I finally hear myself reply.

Her expression switches to one of defensiveness before she tells me:

"No, you don't understand, she got permission beforehand."

I frown in confusion.

"You mean she knew the guy before he died and asked to use his head for their wedding?"

"No, of course not. Before she entered his tomb though, she summoned his spirit and asked if it was okay. Remember she's connected to the dark arts. She can talk to the dead. That's why she loves this city so much."

I feel a great fury rumble inside me. Jesus fucking Christ. What do I even say to this?

And while I'm trying to figure this out, she puts her phone back in her purse and turns her attention to the music, acting like nothing happened.

Then the people around us start clapping because the song is coming to an end, and they put more bread in the piano man's jar and demand he play that other Billy Joel song that every piano man gets asked to play every fucking day of their life. And some are rude about it, and some are not, because down here we have the 'good ones' and the 'bad ones' that come to visit, and it's easy to tell the difference. But we also got the apple pickers, who are more than willing to pick away at the culture 'they love so much' until there is nothing left. And they are much more difficult to spot.

But at the end of the day, it doesn't really matter. *Because we work for tips and so does the city...*

Note: I have a website, Randythestoryteller.com

Please don't come here and disrespect the living or the dead.

ANECDOTE: JULIE – THE OCTAROON MISTRESS

On our tours we tell a story at 734 Royal about a girl named Julie who was what they called an Octaroon mistress. These were girls of mixed race who rich creole gentlemen would hire to be their mistresses. Julie spent one frigid winter night on the roof of this property to prove her devotion to her lover, only to sadly die from exposure in the freezing cold. They say she still wanders the roof, pacing, wondering if he will ever come for her. A lady on my recent tour may have just captured that haunting occurrence. Note the cycle of orbs traversing the rooftop. ♥

Photo credit: Cathy LaBumbard

25

THE KIDS IN THE PARK – PART TWO
Charmaine Swan Rich

Hi ya'll – it's me, Charmaine, your spooky tour guide, popping out of the darkness of the night. How ya been? Since I last penned Chapter 6 in 2020, we survived the pandemic and are now on the recovery side – living and thriving. And so is the spirit world. We started doing tours again in the summer of 2020 – with face masks. What a challenge... But now back to normal and business is really starting to pick up. I know you came here to talk about our favorite little boy – George. George is the 12-year-old spirit we visit at City Park on my bus tour. A serial killer killed him and three other girls there in the 1920s. He still loves the tours and the people coming to visit. I recently started to bring out "equipment." As in ghost hunting equipment. He loves to play with the equipment and gives us a form of open communication to the spirit world. I usually bring my Rem-pod and sit it on the tree for George to play with.

The Rem-pod is a device that uses a telescopic antenna to radiate its own independent electromagnetic field around the instrument. This field is easily influenced by objects that manipulate electricity. Spirits can easily manipulate this field as we believe they are energy and as we learned in science class energy is not created or destroyed. The Rem-pod has different lights that light up when spirits are nearby, and it beeps. This past St. Patricks' day when I took a group out to visit George he decided to play with the Rem-pod. I thought it was cute that on this day George only lit the green light to celebrate St. Patrick's Day. I also bring out dowsing rods which are used to find underground water. They are also used to communicate with the spirit world. We use them by asking "yes" and "no" questions with the spirits. I have used them so often that the spirits now know that crossing them is the answer "yes" and pushing them out is the answer "no". They have also used the rods to point to a person in the group when asked. Finally, they use the rods to hit the shoulders of the person – that is a hug. George does like to hug.

One night I had a young man using the rods and he was very open with the spirit world. George was talking to him, and the rods were moving the entire time. The man had established a connection with the spirit world. When it came time to leave, he told George good-bye. At that moment the rods went to the man's shoulders and stayed there. They even pushed on the man's shoulder creating a mind-blowing amount of pressure. The man began to cry and looked at me and said he felt an enormous amount of pressure around his body, like a hug. He also didn't want to leave. He said he felt like he just couldn't move because the pressure of the hug was so warm and loving. It was a hug that felt so great you just don't want it to ever end.

Other times when people use the rods and ask the spirits to point to a certain person, they do it. One occasion was when a bridal party was on the tour. The girl using the rods asked George to point to the bride. George did. No one on the tour knew who the bride was except for the girls. They all began to scream! Then, George turned the rods around and gave the girl holding them a hug. She began to cry. And she revealed a secret that her friends didn't even know. But George did! What she didn't tell her friends was that before they took this bridal trip to New Orleans, her boyfriend had proposed to her! She was going to be a bride too! She didn't say anything because she didn't want to take the attention away from her friend's trip.

On another tour a very skeptical man asked George to point the rods to his wife. Of course, George did. I really love it when spooky experiences happen to skeptics. He began screaming "Honey, honey, look at this shit!" I can image George smirking at this point.

There was a week in October when George got very creative with the rods. At this time, he brought loved ones to interact with the living. It rarely happens and is a special moment when it does. One night a woman used the rods to ask if her parents could give her a sign that they were ok. Her mother responded with the rods right away. The rods moved answering questions correctly only her mother would know. Then, later in the session her father briefly came in and answered questions. The woman was in tears – happy tears. She told me she knew it was her parents because her mom would always answer right away, take care of things right away and her dad always took his time in responding to questions while he was alive. She said it was their typical behavior. It brought me joy that she had that experience on my tour.

Also, during that week, George helped another woman out. This time we got pictures. A woman was using the rods to talk to her father. She was very successful. As she was using the rods, another woman on the tour began to take pictures of her. They did not know each other. As you can see in the first picture as the woman is using the rods, you really can't see the woman. She is the "blob" of light – the spirit's energy encompassed the woman. In this picture, look at the man standing behind her, in a hat and casual shirt. It is the spirit she was talking to – her father. She told me her father died of a heart attack. But he was a fighter. The doctors brought him back 3 times, but the spirit world had other plans. He did pass due to the heart attack. As the rods were moving, he was there with her. What makes this story even better is what her father is wearing in the picture. And we do know this is her father because the next picture is her father while he was alive. What the spirit is wearing in the picture is what they buried him in! She told me he loved to wear that hat and a casual shirt and shorts. He wore it all the time, so that's what they buried him in.

Does this mean what you are buried in are your forever clothes? Or is your favorite outfit your forever clothes? Just another question we ponder until it is our turn.

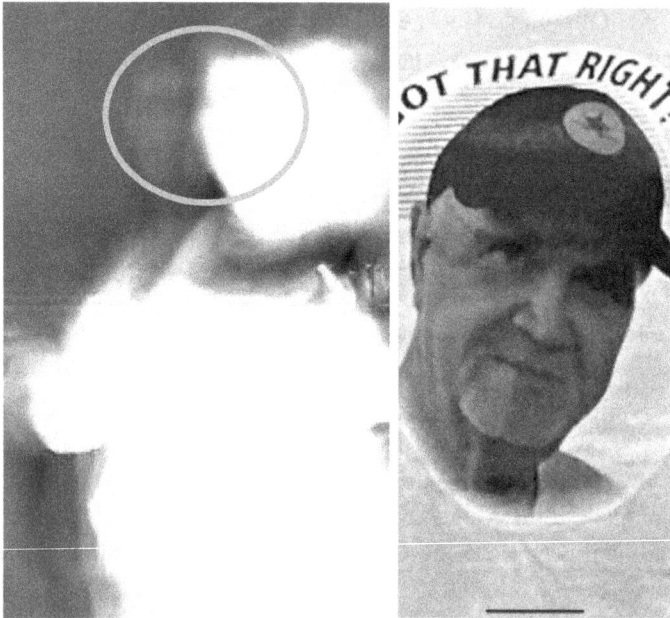

This past year George helped me out with a personal situation. In late April 2021 I had surgery. I have never had surgery before and was scared. One of the last bus tours I did was on April 6, 2021. On the 7pm tour I talked to George. I told him about my surgery, and I asked him if he could be by my side in the hospital, if he could take care of me and hold my hand. I told him if I knew he was there with me then I knew I would be ok. Well, I got my answer on the 9:30pm tour the same night. As I got off the bus, and the tour group followed me, a girl on the tour took this picture of me. I was walking by myself, making sure the area was secure for the group – gotta look out for the alligators. In the picture, George is next to me, holding my hand. When I saw the picture, I knew I would be ok with the surgery and George would take care of me in the hospital. I then felt like I was ready for the surgery. Which was successful. Could George be my guardian angel? I think he is probably one of them. I had a medium on my tour not too long after this and after the tour she told me George told her "I was his favorite." Well, the feeling is mutual and there are times it brings a calmness within my spirit to know George is on my side.

George is not the only spirit in the area… there are many more. You never know who is going to show up! One night in October there was a certain mischievous spirit that made his presence known. Most of the activity does happen in October, when the veil between our world and the spirit world thins. The increased energy makes me giddy! One night I was taking a group out and I dressed for the part. I had on a red top and black skirt with my lace up boots going for the steampunk look. To complete that look I had on a black top hat with a red sash. I do love that hat, but I learned that night, so does another spirit. I did my tour as usual, feeling rather spooky while telling George's story. A girl on the tour took pictures of me as I was talking. After I finished the story, the girl showed me the pictures she took of me. It is me in the picture, but not my face! The spirit decided to put his face on my face! Not the first time a spirit has decided to "distort" my face in a picture, but this time was mind blowing! The face on my body has white paint and is a man. But who did this? Luckily the tour guides I work with are extremely knowledgeable. I showed the picture to a fellow tour guide and right away he said, "Charmaine, that's Baron Samedi!" WOW! Baron Samedi is the head of the Ghede family and is the husband of Maman Brigitte (Haitian Voodoo). Together they are the guardians of the past, the cemeteries, history, and heritage. Baron is also known for his outrageous behavior, swearing, and making jokes. He is the one who is at the crossroads of death and life and can take your life or save you. Also, he does play jokes on the living and likes to chase after mortal women.

He is portrayed as a black man, wearing white makeup, a suit, a cane, and a black top hat. So that night, Baron picked me to play a joke on. He put his face on my face. Why? Not sure but it was Halloween time. And strange things always happen in New Orleans during Halloween.

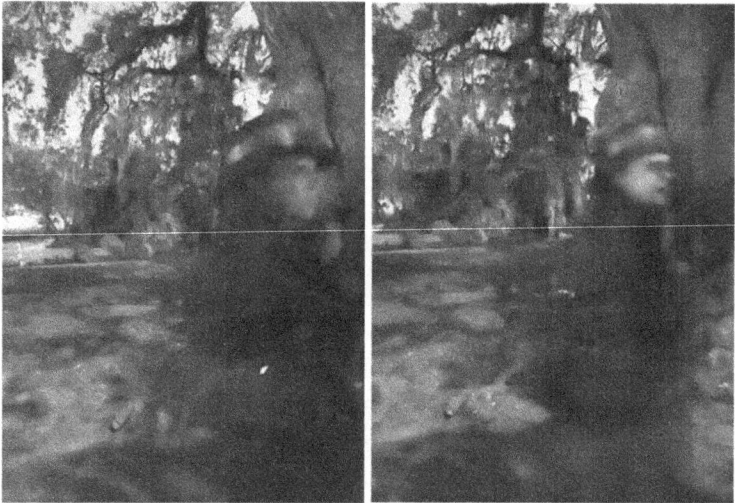

Another spooky early October night I had a very small group – about nine people. It was a "good" group… lots of positive energy. On this tour a wife of an elderly couple on the tour told me her husband could always "see" the spirits. A fellow empath on the tour always makes for great time. We get off the bus in City Park and the man starts to look around and says, "Man, she's not kidding! They are everywhere!" It really feels good when I get acknowledgement from another living person. After I told George's story, the group was walking around admiring the beautiful live oak and taking pictures, desperately seeking George. Right as I announced we were heading back to the bus, a person, a male, about 5'8" with pants on and a hoodie seemed to walk out of the live oak tree. He walked out of the tree, away from us towards the street. A couple of girls on my tour began to scream. I just stood frozen, not sure what I was seeing, but knowing he walked out of the tree, he continued to walk away from us and never looked back. For me, it was like time stood still. It seemed like hours had passed in those few minutes. As the man got closer to the street he disappeared. The fellow older empath was right next to me. Neither one of us moved and a word was not said the whole time. Not even when the younger girls screamed and ran to the bus. Finally, my brain snapped back to reality, and I again announced to the group to go back to the bus.

As I made my way back, logic and reality assured me it was the drunk guy on my tour going into the bushes to relieve himself. That's the explanation, and now I am going to have to wait for him to get back to the bus. But that assumption was dead wrong the minute I got on the bus. The drunk guy was already on the bus, and he was passed out. So, what just happened? As the right and left side of my brain were having an argument in my head, the older man, my fellow empath, who was visibly shaken, looked at me and said, "That man came out that tree!" "That man came out that tree!" He just kept saying it over and over. I looked at him and said, "You saw him too?" He said, "Yes". The hysterical girls refused to talk about it. The older man only said that sentence the rest of the tour and I just wondered who it was who came out the tree.

And, finally, spiritual memories made on my tours are sometimes not necessarily made with the spirits. Sometimes it is with living people who share a wonderful psychic connection you didn't know existed. I had two such experiences that I will treasure and remember forever. Of course, the first was on my first Halloween night as a tour guide. I was walking to the bus in a very busy French Quarter. The energy was crazy, the veil was gone, and Halloween night was upon us. The veil is the energetic and psychic barrier between the living and the dead. I was dressed up in a spooky costume, dodging the many drunk souls dressed up as different creatures of the quarter on my way to the buses. In the middle of chaos, I ran into a woman who came up to me face to face. She stopped me, grabbed my hand, and put a large ring in it. She squeezes my hand shut and disappeared. I got to the bus and luckily my fellow tour guide is a voodoo priestess. I told her what happened and asked her what to do? She asked for the ring. She then sprayed Florida water on it and my hand. She said "Now, you are ok, you can wear it." In Voodoo and dealing with the spirit world, Florida water is used as a cleansing tool. I never saw the woman again.

Another time, during October, (of course) a group of about 18 lifelong friends in their 70s-80s were taking my tour. They honestly did not act or look like they were that old. They were a fun group with an abundance of great energy. While in City Park, at George's stop the whole tour is walking around taking pictures and singing to George. During this time a couple from the older fun group would come up and talk to me about the spirits and life. A lady came to me and as she was talking to me, she took my hand in her hand. When she did this, both of us felt a spark or shock of electricity between us. It was that feeling when you shuffle your feet across a room and touch a metal doorknob in the wintertime. But we were outside, in the heat, and there was no shuffling. When we both felt it, we laughed. My laugh had excitement in it, hers was more of a gentle warmth. She looked at me and said "You are an empath! So am I!" She knew from the spark between us. The moment we shared is unforgettable. It was warmth, acceptance, and knowledge all rolled into one. I didn't want it to end. We shared a smile; she held my hands tight, and then she walked away. As she walked away, another member of the group came up to me and said, "She is the oldest of our group, she is 83 and the sweetest person in the world." I learned that whenever I have lost confidence in myself to think of that sweet 83-year-old woman and the warmth and spark she showed me, and we felt together. Treasure the small things.

As I end my chapter, remember the spirits are always with us, either giving us that one little hope we need in a desperate situation, to playing jokes on us, to supporting us, and taking care of us. We are all here, together. Let's make it the best life we can and the best after life too…. I loved chatting with you and hope to see you soon in our beautiful Crescent City. The haunting darkness of the city welcomes you and you never know who you will run into. And it's a good idea to look over your shoulder from time to time…

All photos courtesy of Charmaine Swan Rich

Sweet (as recorded by bnshkr)
Lyrics by P. Mangum @2015 - Music by R. Stamps

Dip your wings in tar and rust
Sleep the sleep of the just
If you lie down with the truth, see your tears, they
turn to dust
When my life was bought and sold
Did you ever feel the cold
From the ground under your feet as your time
grows old

I know what you told me
I know what she said
I know the confusion that lives in your head

Every way we turn, apart
Feel the beating of this heart
Locked inside a box of gold, for your fathers there to
old
When you see the open door
Will you dare to step through
Walk along the water's path, all the way to my side

I know what you told me
I know what she said
I know the religion that lives in your head
Sweet will go sour
Good will go bad
I'll burn down the walls of all the pious ideas you've
had

To listen to this song on YouTube, please scan the QR Code below

26

SANTOS BAR
1135 Decatur Street

One of the things we love about New Orleans is the diversity and the feeling of inclusion you get as you move around the different sections of the city. The love and care are obvious in every facet, in the food, in the music and in the culture, all just waiting for you to come and be a part of it. As long as you're cool, that is. So, if while you're here you get a little hankering to walk along the dark side I have just the place for you, Santos Bar. Nestled in amongst a few other local favorites, The Abbey, Hex, Omen and Aunt Tiki's, Santos has become the nexus for Goth rock and Metal music in the French Quarter. Boasting an amazing bar and floor space, an elevated stage dripping in red neon vampire fangs, super capable and chill bartenders, a second-floor balcony bar, and bands like Goat Whore, Fat Stupid Ugly People, Blood Drunk and Goddamn Gallows, this place is every goth and metal heads dream venue. Hell, even Phil Anselmo from Pantera comes by to play every once and a while and stamps the place with his no bullshit metal cred. They open at 4pm, but things get kicking much later than that in an area where most tourists fear to tread after dark. And that's why I chose it as the place to launch my Dead Frenchmen Tour. The looks on the faces of the tour patrons as they walk in is priceless. No Dorothy, we're not on Bourbon Street anymore.

The land and building itself has a fascinating history and dates back to the early 1700's when it was originally used as an armory before being turned over to the Ursuline Nuns as part of their convent property in the late 1720s. It is also said that the old child cemetery from the convent backs up to the property along that section of Decatur Street, which may play into the paranormal activity experienced in the building and all down the block, which includes Turtle Bay Bar and Restaurant just a few doors down. In the 1800's the area was guilty by association with the Gallatin Irish boarding house and brothel community right across the street. Those two seaport blocks, from Ursuline to Barracks, were known as the two most dangerous blocks in the world due to the violence and astronomical body count.

It is said that police officers would not patrol the area at night but would return each morning with a horse drawn cart to collect the bodies from the previous night's festivities, then get the hell out before it spooled back up again. Then, in the 1920's there were strong connections to mob and racketeering activities, prostitution, and opium distribution. The 1950's saw the building become the first incarnation of the Crystal Bar, which was later rebranded as the Blue Crystal, both of which had their run ins with the law. It has changed names many times since then, before turning into its current identity about 6 years ago as Santos Bar, which is my personal favorite. I have to admit, I had a huge musician's man crush on the stage the first I laid eyes on it in December of 2016. Those red neon vampire fangs just called out to me. And thanks to Jesse Tripp and her band, The Night Breed, I was able to realize that dream when my band opened for them on my birthday in 2019. A night I'll never forget.

To shed some light on the place I was fortunate enough to get a chance to interview Colin Decarufel, who is the manager and a working bartender at Santos

Q: I know you've worked here a while can you share with us one of your favorite experiences?

Colin: "Oh, that's tough, there have been so many. I guess one of my all-time favorites was right when we opened as Santos, maybe about five years ago. We had a thrash metal band in here. Guys in the pit throwing elbows, throwing kicks, it was pretty wild. So at some point, this guy takes a trash can and he just chucks it, trash everywhere. And one of the times he throws one he just nails this kid with it. He hits him in the head and trash goes everywhere, and shit. The kid that got hit gets pissed and calls the cops, crying that he was just assaulted. In a mosh pit. At Santos. I was like, "Dude, you're in there throwing elbows with these 300-pound dudes, you're going to get hit anyway". He was probably some out of town kid from across the water. So, the cops responded about a half an hour or forty-five minutes later. The kid waited around for the cops forever. There's actually a picture floating around somewhere of him outside with the cops and the cops are like shrugging (laughs) "Are you hurt? ("Fuckstick" was unspoken, but implied) What do you want us to do?"

Eventually it just fell apart and the cops left. I think they were almost ready to arrest him at one point because he got so belligerent about it.

Q: So, what did you guys do afterwards?

Colin: *Well, in typical New Orleans fashion, they made Trash Lord into a hardcore thrash Krewe. It became its own little inside joke. People turned it into a meme. Definitely some New Orleans shit ((laughs).*

Q: That's amazing, though I bet it was a bitch to clean up?

Colin: *Forever live the Trash Lord! (Laughs)*

Q: Switching topics, I used to talk to a former bartender when she worked here and she would tell me about a ghost who she called "The mysterious red-haired man", who would sit at one of the booths across from the downstairs bar and quietly stare as he watched her set up her bar for the evening. Has anything like that ever happened to you?

Colin: *"I know I've seen this, and it's pretty apparent that so has the staff and even so have some of our customers. Upstairs we have our second and third floors, some parts have been unfinished for decades. The section I'm taking about is over the back building where our dry storage is located. Has been for years. That's the creepy part. The staff says they see a big old white guy in overalls. They say they think he's wearing a white shirt, but I don't think he's wearing a shirt. You only see him for a split second. He's always in that back area. Always. That's how we close up the building. We turn off all the lights, run up these stairs and then go down the side stairs that leads to a little alleyway on the ground floor at the side of the building.*

Whenever you come down those stairs, you feel something looking at you back there. There's a wall and I've seen him like, Whoosh, and a glimpse of overalls."

Q: Like an arm with a strap?

Colin: *"Yeah. It's scary. And you can feel it. I've only seen him a couple of times, especially when I first started working here. But you know he's there".*

Q: Anything else?

Colin: *"There's a lady down here. She's generally by the ladies' bathroom. She's wearing some kind of white nightgown, or dress. She kind of looks like the girl from the Ring. Dark hair, dark features, but she doesn't look like a zombie, or anything. She just looks like a lady. So, what happens, if say you're in the men's bathroom, the door opens to the ladies room. It's a very specific creak and it only happens on that door. That's it. And it only happens when no one else is here. It's terrifying. It also happens if you're alone in one of the stalls in the ladies bathroom. You will hear it. It's very specific. I've had to stop using the men's bathroom to come out and find out what the fuck is down here. It happens when we're closing up. Almost all of the staff have seen her. Other people have said that they've heard noises in the bathroom, like someone was in there, and waited their turn, only to find out a short time later that no one was in there. It's pretty wild.*

I've never had any interactions with ghosts or spirits, for my entire life, until I came here. I closed a door, and now it's open. I locked a door and now it's open. Nothing really happens around the bar, it's always that back area. That area is older than the front.

Colin in front of the Lemmy picture at the bar in Santos

237

Jesse Tripp & the Nightbreed on the stage at Santos

Dead Frenchmen Tour patrons vamping it up!

The soundboard at Santos

The writing is on the wall! You must come to Santos!

Bachelorettes grabbing drinks and vamping out ahead of the Dead Frenchmen Tour

Sometimes the Vampire is your guide!

So, what are you waiting for? Book a tour now! The darkness awaits!

ANECDOTE: **UNREGISTERED GUESTS – Cathy Garger**

So, it was in the beginning of October. We were in New Orleans for a TripAdvisor meetup. There were probably about twenty of us. Several of us were staying at the Place d'Armes. We were coming in one night at about ten o'clock. We were walking in with another couple, chatting, and we walk into the courtyard where the pool is, and we see this lady from our group. She was single. And she was swimming in the pool with all her clothes on. Very odd. So, she gets out of the pool and we're talking to her, like, "what's up?" And she said, "I'm not going back in that room". And we were like, "why?" And she says she was in the room and the lights are going on, the lights are going off, the tv gets turned on, the toilet is flushing. So of course, she is drunk. And swimming in her clothes, so we were like, "yeah right". So, we're sitting there talking to her, facing her room, which was the first one on the bottom. And we see the lights go off. And we all look at each other and we're like, no. And I said to her, "your lights just went off". And she says, "Yeah, it's been doing that all night." Then we see the tv come on. The faint glow of tv filling the room. And we're like, "holy shit".

So, we walk into the room and we're looking all around. Everything looked fine. And the toilet flushes. So, we contacted the front desk and they said they would send maintenance over. As we're waiting, we see that the tv goes off. And the lady says, "Look, I know I'm a sloppy drunk, but I also have OCD. Come here, look at my bathroom". And, of course, everything is perfect. Organized by height, etc. Then she says, "Look at my dresser." Again, perfect. You looked at that stuff and you just knew that woman had OCD. Then she pointed to the second bed in her room and said, "Look at that cover over there. It's all messed up, like somebody has been sitting on it. I have OCD. I can't tolerate that. That happened while I was in the shower". So, by that time the maintenance guy shows up, and he looks around the room and says, "Well, I don't see anything wrong. I checked the fuses. But we sometimes have guests that don't register. They're usually not in this room, but they move." Now it's eleven o'clock at this point, and he says, "I have another room I can move you to. And we'll help you move."

And the lady responded, "No, that's okay. I'm just gonna have another drink and go to bed."

I saw her the next morning and I asked, "How was the rest of your night?' and she said, "The lights went on, the toilet flushed, the tv went on and off and finally I just got fed up, sat up in bed, and said Shut the fuck up! I have to get up early tomorrow!" She said the tv went off, the lights were already off, and she heard nothing else for the rest of the night. I guess in New Orleans that's how you handle unregistered guests.

The checking in, no problem. The checking out however...

27

MAGICAL PEOPLE
Doug Bookout

While taking our tours and hearing stories about magical people like Marie Leveau, our Voodoo Queen, Mary Oneida Toups, our Witch Queen, and various other characters such ZoZo LaBrique, Aunt Julia Brown, Doctor John Montenee, Betsy Tolendano and Jean St. Malo, to name a few, it's easy to think that our gifted and powerful mystical folk existed only in our past. But that's not the case at all.

New Orleans currently is, and always has been, populated by magical people. In this day and age, they're known by names such as Voodoo Priestess Miriam Chamani, Vodou Priestess Sally Ann Glassman; Warlock Christian Day; Brian Cain, High Priest of the New Orleans Coven: Alexandrian tradition of Witchcraft, Psychic Medium Reverend/Priestess Claudia Williams and Psychic and High Priestess Elie Barnes; Voodoo Priestess Lillith Dorsey; Uncle Birch aka Michael Correll. They are our torch bearers, our light bringers, and our sages, who carry forth the magical legacy of the city and who inform and enlighten our current age.

They literally stir the spoon in the giant pot of magical gumbo that keeps this city humming with a unique magical energy all its own. Their influence is felt far and wide and just being around them can affect you in deep and profound ways. And it's not just because of the mantle they carry and the ages old wisdom they impart, but also for the magical gifts they possess.

I had the occasion to experience those gifts in action for myself just recently. March of 2022 to be exact. It was a few weeks after Mardi Gras and about a week after I had been hit with the one two punch of strep throat and Covid and was down for about a week. Even though the Covid symptoms were relatively mild, because I was vaccinated, the strep throat really did a number on me. It was like swallowing handfuls of razor blades every time I swallowed. After about a week I was testing negative for Covid and was cleared by my doctor to return to work. So, I came back into that germ infested Petri dish known as The French Quarter to take out a tour. My first tour back was going great until something totally unexpected and terrifying happened to me at the halfway point; my vision split in two. Suddenly I was seeing two of everything and because the sun had already gone down, that just made it worse. Lamp posts, street signs, car headlights, people. My group of six tour patrons suddenly grew to twelve, though sadly the tips didn't manifest in the same way. It was a surreal experience. As I walked, leading my group, who had no idea what was going on, I found that if I looked straight down my vision would clear up. So that's how I finished my tour. I calmed myself, walked a little slower, pressed on and when we stopped, I looked up and spoke to six people and their doppelgangers. I was basically doing my tour by rote at this point. We joke about being able to do our tours blindfolded, but that was an experience I truly never want to have again.

When I returned to Hex after completing the tour, Elie Barnes stepped out from one of the privacy screens where the psychics do their readings and saw me at the front register. She was a good fifteen to twenty feet away. She looked at me and declared "Doug, your aura is split right down the middle. I can see it from here". I was floored. I also need to establish right here that Elie knew nothing of my illness or my condition. She just read it from across the room, like it was the most natural thing in the world. And for her, and people like her, it is.

She then came over and told me a natural way to remedy the situation, and of course it worked, because healing is also part of the magical equation. If that's not an example of practical magic in action, then I don't know what is.

Elie Barnes illustrates this point and describes the concepts that drive these encounters from a magic practitioner's perspective as such...

"From my point of view, I understand the Universe as a multi-dimensional structure that is in constant movement to contain the multiplicity of atoms and the structure the whole, so that it continues to function. The map of the Universe is a web of glistening strings, sparking on and off with each other in a perpetual dance. There are vortexes and back holes and white dwarfs and tesseracts. Places on Earth have wavelengths that differ. Maybe because of lay lines beneath the surface, maybe because of electromagnetic aspects to the rocks in the soil, maybe the amount of water in a place or maybe because spirits were planted in the place long ago by distant clans. In any event, as it is above, so it is below in accordance with the One thing.

New Orleans is one of those magic places that call to her sacred children, witches and priests, shamans and ghost hunters alike, we clamber to her banks and draw in her precious healing waters. The Mother Life of the Mississippi river merges underground with the bones of all our ancestors, European, African and Native. The bones of the people who settled on this part of the Mother. Life and Death together for ever in a place for pirates and priests.

I see it all every day, it has become so common place that I don't think much of it. Sometimes I see in black and white out of my left eye and it seems like prehistoric times, with mammoth ferns and palm shrubs and armadillos. I can see people's auras if they are very out of whack, or if they are really ill. And as my coven mate and Priestess Carie Ewers will say, we see skin crawlers, shape shifter's aliens, demons and fallen angels on occasion as well. There are a lot of elemental forms here and human ghosts in usually bad shape are here all over the place. Children and animals too. People have let their guards down and the living and the dead do mix in bars and clubs, late at night under the moon. It is a magician's paradise because there is such a variety of power to work with in this historic place. "

Come by Hex and experience the magic with Elie for yourself

After his visit here in 1916, Aleister Crowley encouraged magical people of all stripes to visit the city of New Orleans and experience the unique energy of the city for themselves for the very same reasons Elie Barnes described above.

One such person is Reverend/Priestess Claudia Williams who owns Starling Magickal Occult Shop on Royal Street with her husband Jan. She has a fascinating New Orleans story, which she has agreed to share with us.

Q: All magical people have an origin story on how they got here. Please tell me yours.

Claudia: My husband and I were both born and raised in Manhattan, New York City. We were both musicians and music geeks. And my mother-in-law had given us a trip to anywhere we wanted to go. And the time was running out to use the tickets, so we knew we wanted to come to New Orleans, because of the music, largely, and the history. So, we came here. And we came in the middle of August when everybody told it was going to be absolutely deadly, because of the heat, and it was actually 10 degrees hotter in New York when we left than it was when we got here. We were lucky in that regard. And yeah, we fell in love with it. We were both occultists. I was born into that, and my husband had become interested when he was fairly young. So that was another area where of great interest for us here. That's what we fell in love with. The whole environment. We had a house in Rhode Island, and we hadn't gone here in a year, and yet somehow, we managed to come here three times during that time period, so we just knew where our passion was and we and had an opportunity to move and to buy a house here and we decided to take it.

Q: So, what year was that, when you decided to make that change?

Claudia: *We had been coming here for several years, by that time. But we decided to make the move here in 1994. And we got our house. And the first week in 1995 we moved on to it.*

Q: That's amazing. Did you know you were going to open an occult shop right from the beginning? Was that part of the plan?

Claudia: *No. There were several occult shops right within just a few blocks of us and we didn't want to come from out of town and step on anyone's toes or insult anyone. These were people we respected. So, I did some artwork for them, and I sold some of my artwork. My husband deals in all kinds of rare and collectible books, so he was working with that. And what happened was that eventually people started to come to us asking for occult items. Asking me to mix oils for them. Asking us to find particularly occult books or to make them occult incense. And we would say, um, you know, so and so does that just a few blocks away and we know him really well, and he's been doing it for a long time, and they would say, Yeah, I know, but I really want them from you. And it was like, at the point, that the decision was being made for us. And, of course, that's what we really would have liked to have done from the start, but we would have never done it, just coming in and stepping over people. That's just not our way. So, we took a couple, maybe two or three years to go from a shop where we were selling books and other kinds of art and crafts items to fully occult.*

Q: I love that you came here and started from a place of respect. That's so important. And sadly, a lot of people don't do that and then they've just moved here and there's already bad blood. Not a good place to start. And once that happens, people don't usually succeed or last that long after that. Respect and acceptance is key to finding your way and becoming a part of the culture and society here.

Claudia: I wholeheartedly agree. In New York, and as big as New York is, if you really want to be taken seriously, and not as just another restaurant or another boutique that is corporate backed and is a tax loss if they don't do well, that's it. No one really cares. If you want to do well, you just don't go in and insult the people who have been there. And have been doing it for a long time. We had a lot of experience seeing that in others and that was just something we were not going to do.

Q: This is really just a big little, small town. It's not like six degrees of Kevin Bacon here, it's more like two or three degrees of separation. So, you have to be careful who you piss off, because people are extremely interconnected here and if you're not careful, you'll come to regret it.

Claudia: Sometimes it just one and you're done. You really have to get to know the players and decide if you care if they don't like you, or how they can affect you. Or, how you can affect them. Fortunately, because we go out of our way to not deal with too much drama, and to not create any ourselves, we really haven't had any problems. But it can always happen, and you're always aware of it.

Q: Well, you guys have a great reputation. I initially heard about you through Michael Bill as I became a tour guide, and then the more I grew in the community the more I heard about you and your reputation for being stand up and respectful people and that you really take your magical practices seriously.

Claudia: Yes, we do. And I'm very glad to hear that. That means a great deal to both of us.

Q: So that would mean you started the shop sometime in 1997?

Claudia: Probably late 96, early 97, yes. The amount of money that it takes to start an occult shop, the way we would have wanted to start it, is rather significant. This is because you have to have some of pretty much every oil you can think of. And oils can be really expensive. The same is true of herbs, botanicals and resins. Not to mention things like incense burners or atheme Ritual items. We basically started with what we had on hand that I had made mostly just for myself. And then ordering whatever we could and as much as we could, so we could order more. Now we have the largest selection of the highest quality oils of anybody around. It's very rare that someone comes in and looks for an oil and we don't have it. So, it started much smaller and built much more slowly than we would have loved to have done, but that's just how it turned out and how it had to be.

Q: So, on the practitioner side, New Orleans has the well-earned reputation for being the epicenter for spiritual growth and development. Not only in fulfilling your own needs, but in helping other people fulfill theirs. And having been here as long as you have, that's a legacy. And something to be proud of.

Claudia: *I was doing it in New York too, so my history with it goes back quite a way. But thank you. Having been here, and having the shop since 96, 97, it's really what we know and now it's second nature. I don't think we could do anything else full time at this point.*

Q: What has been the most rewarding or fulfilling part of being a magical practitioner here?

Claudia: *I would have to say that being a psychic here, that part has been the most fulfilling. This is because I do work that not everybody does, or likes, to do. Including helping find missing people, or bodies. Things of that nature that really have an impact on people. Sometimes it's a missing animal. And I've been able to find it and bring it back and put it in its owner's arms. Sometimes it's missing people and you know going in that they're not likely to be living. But at least if we can find them that will help the family if they want to bury this person properly and receive closure. That's really more rewarding to me than the totally magical stuff.*

Q: I didn't know this about you. Do you work with Law Enforcement on this?

Claudia: *I do sometimes. I've worked with a variety of different law enforcement agencies and sometimes I work with the families. A lot of times the families don't believe what they've been told by law enforcement and my job will be to tell them whether they had* *information withheld from them or if they've been given bogus information. And I'm happy to say that usually that's not the case. And I'm not a huge fan of law enforcement. At least not in New Orleans. They've generally been given the most truth that anyone could give under the circumstances. That's something that's nice to be able to tell someone because if they think they've been lied to it just makes the whole experience much worse.*

Q: I can imagine that would be terrible.

Claudia: Also, what is really rewarding about the magical part is that the magical part goes along with a spiritual journey / religious part. And with that, sometimes somebody, let's say, buys an oil to reunite them with their lover. And I tell them the history of the Cipriano oil, which is a fabulous oil for doing that, but I also tell them the story of St. Cipriano which they usually don't know, he's often a saint they've never heard of. So, that gets them interested in what other saints, or other gods, of different pantheons do and can do and they might want to connect with them. That's very rewarding because that helps them along on their own internal journey.

Q: Have you had any personal experiences that you'd like to share? Any epiphanies or events that have confirmed to you that this is where you were meant to be?

Claudia: I'd have to say that I've had so many I couldn't even point to a single one and say that was THE defining moment. There have been many, many defining moments over the years now. Oh yeah. I've had many, many situations from buying the house and discovering that it was actually built by an ancestor of mine, which we didn't know when we bought it. And what would happen back in the 90's there were still a lot of people around who were in their late 80's and 90's and they would come by the shop and they'd sort of look at us kind of strangely. And it turned out there had been a family here who had been so terrified by the haunting of the house that they ran leaving everything they owned behind and never came back.

So, the older people would ask me, have you had any problems with the hauntings and we'd be like, well, it's a French Quarter house and we assumed it would probably have some kind of spirit in it, or spirits.

And we would hear more and more about these people who just abandoned the house. Finally, I got a copy of the police report of the night that they left the house, and the police saying that they were hearing all these strange and horrible sounds, but they couldn't figure out where they were coming from. Just all this really terrifying stuff that these people were having inflicted on them. And then we also found out that the house had often been used by other occultists and they did all kinds of practice here. So that was interesting. And some of these old people would ask, "So it really hasn't terrified you?" And we'd say no. And then eventually they heard that my ancestors had actually built the house and they would use this term, that I thought was kind of weird, and a little creepy at the time. They would say "You know, it's been haunted so long and you haven't had any problems since you've been here with it. I have to say, I think the house wanted its blood back."

Q: Whoa!

Claudia: *Yeah. And I do kind of feel that my blood is in the walls of this house. I can feel the ancestors I had here. Sometimes I hear them or see them. Sometimes other people hear them or see them. So that right there, that was just a major confirmation. I was in a place that I had a connection to and I didn't even know it. Now I'm very deeply connected to it. And I understand more of the reason why. The minute I saw it, I fell in love with it.*

Q: It was meant to be, huh?

Claudia: *Yeah.*

Q: That just gave me cold chills. But yeah, that's the serendipity that so many people talk about in this town. If you know, you know.

Claudia: *That was pretty amazing to us too. My husband fell in love with it too. It wasn't like I loved it and he didn't, and we had to argue over whether to get it. We both just fell in love with it and this is just where we wanted to be. And still to this day.*

Q: Last question to cap this off. Do you have any advice for newcomers or people who are thinking of moving here because they too have felt the call and believe in their hearts that this is where they are supposed to be on the next step of their magical journey? How do the find connections and get rooted and grounded?

Claudia: Being rooted and grounded in New Orleans can be a tricky request (laughs). New Orleans is a very hard place for some people to feel grounded. But certainly, I would say that whatever you want to do, learn your area and what people are doing in your area of interest and who the major players are. And why they're in those positions and why people respect them. Continue to go to their shop, or their restaurant, or their service, whatever it is. And I would also say that it's very important to respect the people who are already doing what you want to do here. There's always a lot to learn here and hopefully, if you're lucky, that continues on until the day you die. New Orleans has lots and lots it can teach, in so many ways, so be open to that. And also, be open to the fact that what you think, or do, or practice, may change a bit while you're here. Not that it will get stronger or less strong, it might just...alter. And be prepared for that.

New Orleans will either, in about six months, really take you in and you'll be making friends and you'll be settling in and feeling like it's really gonna be home. Or, I've seen it chew people up and spit them out and if they're lucky enough to survive that, then they just leave and never return. It can be a very rough city in as much as it's beautiful and it's wonderful, and all the great things about it. So I think that if you come with the right attitude and are open to it, and let it teach you some stuff, you'll be a whole lot better off than if you come in thinking you're going to teach New Orleans.

Q: You're so right. I've either seen or experienced everything you just described firsthand. It really humbles you in some many ways.

Claudia: Absolutely. But it's also okay to be proud of and confident in your talents. Just don't let that go to your head and think you're going to come in here and change the city. Cause that's just not gonna happen. The city doesn't care for it, nor do the people who really live here.

Q: In my experience there is a process to all of this. The city will test you, try you and sometimes beat you up a bit. But if you hang in there, and your heart and intentions are true, she'll reveal her secrets to you.

Claudia: *Absolutely true. And some people just don't have the stomach for all of that. It's definitely a place for older souls.*

The Reverend/ Priestess Claudia Williams at Starling Magickal

The famous "oil wall" & the Altar

It's all true. So, if you're the type of person who likes their encounters to be more of the paranormal variety, there is truly no better place than New Orleans to practice ghost hunting skills, check on your own psychic eye abilities and hear tales from the people who are currently existing as ghosts now. It is the perfect "target rich environment" for people who wish to hone or expand their magical gifts and do so with likeminded brothers or sisters in arms. That quest for a connection can be life changing and was most certainly what brought pioneers like Mary Oneida Toups and Voodoo practitioner Frank Staten, The Chicken Man, here in the late nineteen-sixties to soak in the age-old wisdom that seeps up through the pores of this magical city.

The Altar of the Dead at Hex Olde World Witchery

Fortunately for us there is a person in New Orleans who embodies all of those aforementioned characteristics and talents, gifted psychic medium and ghost hunter, Carie Ewers.

254

Carie Ewers: Psychic/Medium, Witch, Ghost Hunter

Q: I've always known you as a very talented and gifted psychic medium and was extremely thrilled to learn that you were teaching classes on paranormal investigations at HexFest. I mean, I've seen shows where a psychic medium is brought in to consult with the investigators, during the investigation, but to have someone with psychic abilities, who is also a practicing witch, leading an investigation? That's just amazing and incredibly rare! How did you come to be involved with that aspect of the magical community?

Carie: My first experience with the paranormal was at about 4, and I started practicing witchcraft at about 10. I'm 50 now, so it's been a while (laughs). I grew up in the Blue Ridge Mountains of Virginia, so it's very steeped in traditions there, especially with spirits. And, as a child, I would see these people in everyday situations, whether we were grocery shopping, or whatever, and I never understood why everyone seemed to be ignoring all these people that I was seeing. You see, I was born with a caul, which is a veiled membrane.

When you're born with a caul covering you, it's believed that you're special and can see into the spirit world and have heightened paranormal abilities.

My first experience was when I was barely 4. I was at my great grandmother's house, and I had gotten in trouble. I had pulled a

255

bunch of pots and pans out from under the counter and was being kind of a nuisance and she, my great grandmother Rose, I remember she sent me upstairs to one of the rooms to kind of sit. You know, when you're a kid and you have to be put in the corner when you're bad, it was that kind of thing. And I remember a lady coming in the room, and I was so excited, because I love my great grandma so much and I was so upset that I had upset her. And this woman came in, with this very heavy Irish accent. Hair up in a bun, high necked dress, and I remember her telling me not to cry and she had this white dove in her hand. It was a white ceramic dove, and I remember this like it was yesterday. It had its little head tucked under its wing. She handed it to me. And I will always remember the weight of it in my hand. I went down the stairs and my great grandmother had this old Victorian house, and it had a switchback staircase. I remember going there. I remember going through her parlor room into the kitchen and she turned around. She was so sweet, but she was like "You're supposed to be upstairs. You're being punished." And I remember handing her this ceramic dove that the lady upstairs gave me. And she looked at it, and I remember all the color draining out of her face because that was the dove that had been buried with her mother back in Ireland. My great grandmother would have been well into her 80s at this time. And I remember she asked me "Where did you get this?" And I was like, "The lady upstairs…" and she was like, "Don't fib. There's nobody else in the house." And I said, "I'm not", and I described her mother, but it would have been her mother when she was younger. I will never forget it and I remember it like it was yesterday.

So, I guess that kind of started my journey of seeing things and experiencing things that other people didn't. Even when I was little, even before I wanted to investigate, or anything like that, I always approached it from a place of compassion and always wanting to go and maybe talk to that little girl in the corner or that man that nobody wants to talk to or that nobody can see. It was a while before I started fully understanding what ghosts were. That took place a few years later.

Q: Wow! That just blew me away! And what an amazing memory to have as a keepsake of your Great Grandmother. I would believe that being a psychic medium would give you a unique ability to connect with spirits that most investigators do not possess. How does that affect your approach and methodology?

256

Carie: Being a psychic and a medium definitely affects the way I approach an investigation. I always ground myself. Always, always, always, make sure I'm grounded. And, in the best headspace possible before I go into any investigation. There is a protection spell that I will do, and not just for myself, but for whoever is investigating with me. And then, whoever is on the team with me, I put the first letter of everybody's name into a sigil. And then I make the sigil on the spot and draw the sigil on all the team members with a protection oil that I make before I go in.

Q: Okay, I have never heard of anyone doing that before. That's very unique and cool and proactive. You're incorporating magic into your paranormal investigation and that just takes it to a whole other level.

Carie: I always think with energy, even if it's not a paranormal energy, to me, energy has a pitch. Even just walking around New Orleans, I feel like we live in a necropolis anyway, like the dead are everywhere, intermingled with the living. You and I are corporeal, and we also have those people around us who are ethereal. And I always think, in my mind, when I think about spirits I think about real people. We definitely have spirits here who have once been human and New Orleans also has a few spirits who have never been human. I think that's when I think about doing any type of protection work, even if somebody doesn't identify as human, I think it's so important. I also think it's very important to always approach it with compassion.

When you're going into an investigation, if I'm going into someone's home, and they are trying to specially get in touch with someone, I always tell people, especially if I'm walking them through it to do it themselves, to be very clear and concise about who they want to talk to. Especially in that situation. Let's say you want to talk to a grandparent or a loved one and I'm with you, I always ask their name and introduce myself. "I have so and so with me, and we would like to talk to you."

I'm always able to pull someone through but sometimes if you're in a place like, you know, we go to an old hospital or an abandoned place, there's a lot of energy that is negative and that's why I think that protection magic and putting the sigil on everyone is so important. Because we do have spirits around us who are very dangerous. For example, let's say we're investigating an old asylum, like Pennhurst asylum, or something like that. There's so much residual energy in places like that. People who have died under violent circumstances, whether it's by their own hand or someone else's, when they pass. If they were mentally unstable, they don't suddenly gain a certain type of discernment once they pass. That's why you need to be protected and as grounded as possible when you're going on these investigations.

One of my favorite things to use, to get everybody protected, is to use the sigil and also burn Palo Santo. I'm more of a Palo Santo user than sage in these situations. The word Palo Santo literally translates to "holy wood." It comes from Peru, and I think there are parts of Ecuador where you can get it. It just cleanses the space and recalibrates the energy in the space.

It's something I always take with me on an investigation.

Q: Let's talk about gadgets because I know you taught a class on them at HexFest, and I'm fascinated with them as well. You're on an investigation and you've opened yourself psychically, how do you augment that gift with the tools of the trade?

Carie: This is where I'm just going to nerd out (laughs)! I love the K2, the EMF detectors. EMF means Electromagnetic Frequency. So, what these can do, they help with other energies and shifts of energies that change in the room. I think they're incredibly easy to work with. People ask me what they can use where they don't have to spend a ton of money, so this is one I recommend because you can usually get them for under $50. But what an EMF reader does is it gives people a way to communicate with you. With the corporeal person.

I also love laser grids. They are awesome to set up at the end of a little hallway. Especially if I, as a psychic am trying to connect or during the process of connecting with someone who is in there, my eyes may be closed, I'm going to be grounded and focused, but another member of my team could be looking toward the direction that I'm facing. Especially if you have that laser grid set up a lot of times that will help you see when something is physically trying to manifest. Those are great. You can get the big ones, or you can also get the smaller ones that fit in your pocket. I always bring a couple of those.

Q: What about EVP (Electronic Voice Phenomenon) equipment?

Carie: EVP stuff is amazing! I love digital tape recorders. I love regular tape recorders. Those are really good, especially to just have one running in the background. Because, as you talk, sometimes spirit voices will come up and come through, and we don't hear them at the time.

And one of the things I like to do when you're going to do something like a double blind, say you have your EMF going and you have a psychic working with you. They're doing their thing. Somebody else could have a pen and paper, which I also very much recommend. When they start to feel something. Even if it doesn't make any sense, or if they smell something, hear something, they can write it down. And write down the time that it occurred. And later when everyone is going through the footage, everyone can combine input and somebody says they could have heard something and it might come up on the EVP equipment when nobody else heard it, but it's all happening at the same time.

REM Pods are great too. They are really good for detecting vibrations and different shifts in things. There are also stones that I like everybody on the team to have on them.

Q: Stones?

Carie: Yes. Some of my favorite for protection are hematite, black obsidian, Tourmaline, and Jet. I have a huge leather cuff, that has a piece of Jet imbedded in it, that I always wear whenever I'm going on an investigation, or I feel like I'm going to be around more spirit energy than usual. Rose quartz is another one that I like to have on me and to give people to wear or have on them during an investigation. Rose quartz is very good for helping us tap in to love and tap into compassion. I think that we forget this sometimes, it is scary too, if you're home alone, and you suddenly hear these voices, or see things move,

and it's scary to hear these things. I find that just a little bit of rose quartz is really grounding for me, and it opens up an aspect of keeping an open mind and staying as emotionally calibrated as I can.

The thing with spirits that I think we forget is that they're still people. I've gone and done investigations where I've helped spirits pass and *they've been elderly, or like, the little ones. It's very hard, but it's also very sweet. Because, say we pass at home, well, you may not haunt where you die. You may pass in a cornfield in Iowa in an accident, and yet you may go back and haunt your grade school. And how time passes for us, a year might feel like two hundred for them. It's always heartbreaking to me when someone passes in their home, and they stay. Sometimes they want to stay and they're fine. And sometimes depending on the conditions of their mental state, how they were physically when they passed, that can cause some serious issues and they become trapped. It's gotta be terrifying when your family is suddenly gone and here are some people coming in and knocking walls down and changing your furniture. Even though Beetlejuice is a comedy, as far as paranormal research and how to work with the dead, there is so much that is 100% spot on with that movie. They based the Handbook for the Recently Deceased on Egyptian Book of the Dead.*

Q: Interesting. I didn't know that.

Carie: *With ghost hunting, I think the biggest thing is to keep yourself protected and always make sure that wherever you're going, you have permission and you're not trespassing, because if something happens, especially if you're in an old house or something, and the floor collapses, it's not gonna be great. Never go alone. It's a safety issue. So always have permission and that covers the legal part. And I always try to educate myself as much as possible about a place before I go. This helps eliminate urban legends. I want to read other people's experiences, if I can, because they can pass off information to you. That creak in this place on the floor, it's not a spirit. And everybody has been able to debunk that it's just a creaky window, or something.*

I always double check my equipment before I go out. I always want to be as respectful as possible to the spirits that are in that space, because I feel like I get better results.

Q: This must all translate into some incredible experiences. Would you be willing to share any that were special to you?

Carie: *Oh my god, there's been so much! One of my favorites, and I haven't seen him in a very long time, but there was an older gentleman that I used to see on the streetcar. I would hop on the streetcar to go into the Quarter, and I would always see him. Finally, one day I asked* *one of the streetcar drivers about him. I told them that I would see this little gentleman all the time and he was always in the same seat, and it didn't occur to me that he was passed because I never felt anything cold. One of the drivers told me that he had been a streetcar driver and he had, in fact, passed. He had been retired, but had passed, and the streetcar he was on he was apparently the conductor for, and he loved to ride on that car.*

Q: Was it the St. Charles line?

Carie: *Uh huh! And, I've definitely had some creepy ones. This one is kind of the same story, but it happens in three different aspects of time here in New Orleans. And, of course, they all revolve around the Quarter, as most spooky things do. Right there by the Cathedral in Jackson Square, the first time I saw this particular woman, I was here with my dad after my parents divorced. I was five.*

Then, a couple days after that, it was dusk, and I remember seeing a lady in a really long, very beautiful dark greenish grey dress. And she never fully formed. And I was very fascinated. She was really pretty. She had dark hair. She had a really high neckline. Maybe something like a choker that she had put around her neck. She was between the Pontalba building and the Cathedral, near Pirate's Alley. There were still a lot of people out walking around. We went back to our hotel, which I can't remember where we stayed because this would have been in 1977 when I was five. I do remember the place we stayed had a little courtyard. The door to our room went out to this little courtyard. I remember hearing a knock and waking up. My dad was asleep. I got out of my bed and pulled the curtain back, and this lady was knocking at our door! I pulled the curtains back closed really quick, was freaking out, and I got my dad up. He got up and opened the door and there was nobody in the courtyard.

So, the first time I came down here with friends in college, I probably would have been about nineteen or twenty. We ended up coming for spring break and were walking around the Quarter and I saw that same lady again. I know it was her. She looked right at me. This was during the day, and we were turning from Decatur across from Café Du Monde on the St. Ann side of the Square. Then I didn't see her again until about two years ago. Just talking about this is going to make the hair stand up on the back of my neck again. I'll never forget it.

I was reading at one of the shops, either Hex or Omen, and I had just gotten off of work and I went to meet some friends for dinner at Muriel's. And I was parked over by work on Gov. Nichols. I walked back to my car after dinner, and I kept feeling somebody behind me. It was about nine o'clock at night. I'm very cautious when I walk to my car, like everybody is, and I turned, and I saw a woman step off into a doorway. And I heard the swish of a long skirt. And the first thing that popped in my head was that this was that lady from all those years ago. And then I was like, no. No way. I started walking again and I heard the sound of very low heels on the sidewalk. The sound was close enough that I could tell it was within the block. It made me feel like all the air was coming out of my lungs. And so, I got in the car and locked doors, started it. I went to turn toward Esplanade. I get about a block and a half up, and she's on the corner at the end of the block, on the left side of my car. The driver's side. The dress was the same green, grey color. The neckline was low, but not vulgar. My psychic sense tells me that she was a Madame in one of the Storyville brothels. And the reason that I think she has that high thing around her neck is that I think her throat was cut. It's a light color, but it does have almost like a faintish pink hue. I've never gotten that close to her. But the way she was following me to my car, I definitely got the feeling that she was trying to tell me something. I also felt that there was some energy that was following her. It makes me wonder if it was the person who killed her, and they are also trapped here too.

The veil is very thin for me, everywhere I go. To me it's almost like cellophane (laughs). It's almost weirder for me to go into a space and not feel some energy than it is for me to sense it. I always want to approach spirits with compassion, first.

Q: I always stress that on my tours as well. Ghosts are people too and if you respect them in their spaces, they will respect you. Disrespect them and there may be consequences.

Carie: *Absolutely.*

Q: Speaking of tours, I'm often asked by my tour patrons if there are any ghost hunting opportunities they can participate in during their visit. Same goes for people who have recently moved here and are looking for a reputable group to connect with. Do you have any recommendations?

Carie: Funny you should ask (laughs). It's always funny to me how the universe brings like-minded people together. I've been working for the past few days on my domain name for my paranormal investigation's website, to connect with and take people around New Orleans on paranormal investigations. Also, to meet up with likeminded people and form up a team. For paranormal investigations and private consultations, you can contact me here:

wanderingwitchparanormal@gmail.com

Q: That's amazing! Sign me up! Any parting warnings or advice for those looking to interact with the spirits of New Orleans?

Carie: Absolutely! It is so much fun in the city, and don't get me wrong, I love a good cocktail as much as the next girl, but please do not go into these situations wasted. It is so dangerous. Because your logic is impaired and it's just, it can be dangerous on a few different levels, spiritually, psychically, even physically. It's just not a good idea. I'm not talking about having a glass of wine on a ghost tour. I mean when you're going on an investigation. And if you're in any situation where something does not feel right, your gut feels off... you know that situation where the hair stands up on the back of your neck, listen to it and trust it. Anytime you're in a situation where you feel uncomfortable, it's okay to stop. It's okay to leave an investigation. It's okay. It's okay to stop it, leave and then maybe come back later. Or do something different altogether. The biggest thing is to just trust your instincts and trust your common sense.

Even if you're trying to investigate a specific thing in New Orleans, for example, and you might not get any energy in the place. Don't get discouraged. Just like sometimes when you're in a situation and you don't want to talk to people, well, spirits are the same. But, if you keep yourself open and you keep yourself grounded, here in New Orleans, you absolutely will make contact.

Q: Awesome. Amazing information. And speaking to that, I've had people on my tours who have reported back to me that they left the tour with an attachment and took it back with them to their hotel room. The incident I relate in Chapter 13 is a great and terrifying example of that. So, what I'm asking is, if a person finds themselves in that situation, where can they go to get help? What do you recommend?

Carie: Honestly, I would have them contact somebody like me. I've helped a lot of people do that. One of things I recommend for people to do, when you get home from that investigation or location, take a shower immediately. Not a bath, a shower. I always like to put sea salt on the top of my head and rinse it all the way down. Just to purify that energy. I've had people call me and I've gone to places in person because you just need that energy taken off. The sea salt shower is the biggest thing I would recommend, right away.

It's imperative that you respect the dead, in their spaces. Otherwise, you may pay the price.

Sound like a bunch of "mumbo jumbo'? I personally believe it's very important to keep an open mind about these types of things, as we're all going to take part in "The Grand Mystery" at some point on our journey. Our collective fascination with magic and the paranormal speaks to our innate desire to understand our origins, the nature of life and death and the possibility of an afterlife. These are the questions that have plagued humankind since the dawn of time.

I often have doctors and scientists on my tours, and we talk between stops, or on bar breaks, about the intangibles. The things in the human experience that can't be measured or quantified. The realm of the spirit and the soul. And they'll admit, especially after a few Cocktales, that there are times when they're just as baffled as the rest of us when it comes to this subject. I recently had a group of young medical residents on my Spirits and Spells Tour who were going through their ER rotation. They spoke very candidly about watching the spark of life leave a dying patient and the unshakable feeling that something had departed. The intangibles. Ether. Gossamer. Diaphanous. Magic.

The Altar of the Dead at Hex

In front of the Altar of the Dead at Hex on the Spirits and Spells Tour – Photo by Shelby Quave

Casting spells in the courtyard! – Photo by Shelby Quave

Shelby Quave, Warlock. Find him on YouTube at ShadeWarlock25

ANECDOTE: **THE GHOST OF CARROLL STREET –**
Jaime Loebner

I used to live in a house constructed in 1855 in Mandeville, Louisiana near the shore of Lake Pontchartrain. I didn't know it was haunted when I bought it. I loved the little Creole cottage with its sturdy bargeboard walls and beautiful view of the Causeway Bridge. I spent a lot of time reading about the history of the house and land and was pleasantly surprised to discover that the original owner of the lot was a free woman of color, Josephine Olivella.

I was able to obtain copies of the original handwritten deed, in French, signed by Ms. Olivella and Bernard de Marigny. I petitioned the Old Mandeville Historic Association to create a nameplate for the house that included Ms. Olivella's name as well as the last name of the person who constructed the home, Roy, along with my name. I wanted to honor Josephine Olivella and give her the credit she deserved for being so far ahead of her time.

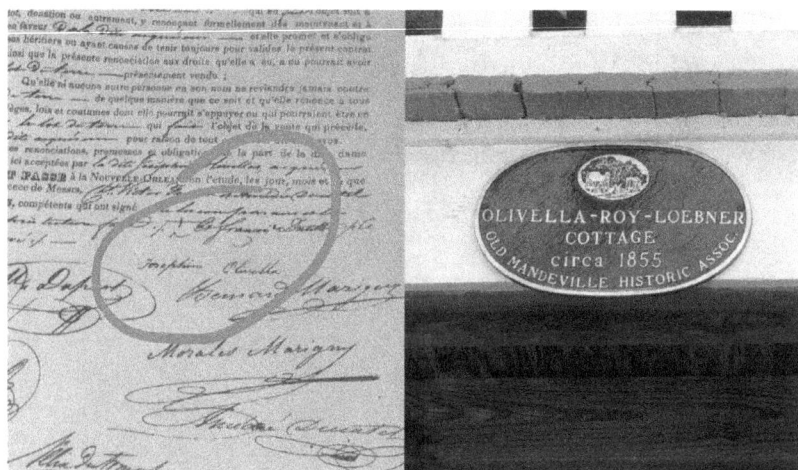

Early in the pandemic, I was very sick with the Covid-19 virus, before any testing or treatments were available. Although I had been in good physical condition, I thought that virus would kill me during the night. Little did I know my guardian ghost, who I think was Josephine, was looking out for me. On my sickest nights, when I thought I might not make it to sunrise, the light would suddenly come on in my bedroom closet.

It would flash on and off several times to awaken me, then stay on. This light had a switch located behind a shelf, so it was something I had a difficult time turning on even when I wanted to. I had to slide a metal ruler behind the shelf and carefully push the switch up or down. Now it was coming on for no reason, other than to startle me awake and make sure I was still breathing. It got me through several weeks of illness and then never happened again for the rest of the time I lived there.

28

NEW ORLEANS VOODOO

Doug Bookout with Brionne Bagneris & High Priest
Robi Gilmore

If you've ever had the experience of walking into a Voodoo shop in New
Orleans, you'll fully comprehend the term "sensory overload." I'm not
talking about knock off gift shops that borrow the name. I'm talking
about actual Voodoo cultural centers run by ardent practitioners of the
religion. They're colorful, eclectic, earthy, and, to the uninitiated, a tad
bit scary. These mystical spaces are filled to the brim with African style
masks and totems, colorful dolls, ornate sculptures, glass bottles filled
with strange liquids, altars, candles, gris gris bags and Catholic pictures
and statuary. Your eyes are drawn to every corner, wall and surface
trying to take it in and make sense of the mystery of it all. In the final
chapter of this book, which is my love letter to all things New Orleans,
I feel I would be extremely remiss if I didn't cover this important
religion and its lasting impact upon this city. Even if it falls short as a
fledgling attempt on my part, I am here to pay my respect in awe and
wonder with a humble and open heart.

**Mambo Brandi at the Gris Gris Counter in Voodoo Authentica of
New Orleans Cultural Center & Collection
(Photo Credit: Lily Evangeline Bull)**

But really, what is New Orleans Voodoo? At its roots, it is African spiritualism practiced by the West African and Haitian people who were enslaved during the diaspora and brought here to New Orleans starting in 1718. Once Bienville enacted the European Code Noir, or Black Code, here in 1724, enslaved people were explicitly forbidden from practicing the religion of their motherland: Voodoo. They were forcibly baptized as Catholics and severely punished if they were caught lapsing back into their old "heretical" beliefs. They could even be executed for multiple offenses as it could be seen as blasphemous by those who held the reins of power.

In addition, it was even illegal to teach enslaved people how to read and write. They were quite literally "owned" at every level: physically, mentally and spiritually. It's not surprising that this law stayed in effect in Louisiana until the Confederate south lost the civil war in 1865 and the enslaved people finally gained their freedom. It was then that the hidden truths behind the wretched institution of slavery became widely known, as did the truths about Voodoo.

But how did Voodoo survive and even thrive during that long period of brutal prohibition? What were the influences that shaped and molded the practice over time into what we see practiced in the city today?

To answer those questions, and more, I'm honored to have been granted interviews with two experts: one, a fellow historian and tour guide who has been giving Voodoo Tours for over 11 years. The other, a seventh-generation Voodoo practitioner, 3 form Voodoo Priest, historian and guide as well. So, with that, I'm going to dutifully step aside, ask the burning questions, and allow them to answer and provide their insights, expertise and experience.

To begin, we start with New Orleans' own Tour Guide extraordinaire Brionne Bagneris.

Q: *You know you've always been one of my favorite people in the city. Your big smile and big laugh always warm my heart and lift my spirits. Tell us a little about yourself.*

Brionne: I go by Brie, like the cheese. Mostly because people have such a hard time pronouncing Brionne. Born and raised here. Grew up in Mid City. Been a tour guide for 11 years. I graduated from the University of New Orleans where I studied Business Administration, Spanish and Hotel, Restaurant & Tourism. I specialize in Ghost tours, Voodoo Tours, Cemetery Tours and City Tours. When I'm not doing tours, I'm probably doing stand-up comedy somewhere. I like making people laugh. A day without laughter is a day wasted. Everything is so messed up in the world right now, sometimes you just have to laugh to keep from crying.

Q: *Preach. I understand that you were not raised practicing Voodoo, so how did you start doing Voodoo Tours?*

I learned about Voodoo when I was in college. I discovered through my experience that the people who weren't religious were generally the nicest people I've ever met. Not judgmental. Not gossipy or divisive. So, I started to study religions, and I learned a lot. It shocked me. I'm looking at all of these religions and how similar they all are. Different gods, same devil. A lot of it was driven by fear and peer pressure to conform. I found that all of the religions have a version of the ten commandments. They all have a golden rule, which is basically treat others as you want to be treated.

Now, I had been afraid of Voodoo my whole life. It's depictions on TV and the warnings I got from the people at church to stay away from that. So much so that I even refused to eat at Voodoo BBQ, because Voodoo was in the title (laughs). And I had no idea how much I was missing out, because it is really good. Same goes for Voodoo as well.

When I was in college I had a roommate, she was from Monroe LA. One day she had a Voodoo doll posted up on her side of the dorm room. I was so afraid of that thing. It got to the point where I just avoided communicating with her and stayed out of her way. I wouldn't even go to her side of the room to adjust the thermostat.

But one day it was so hot I had no choice but to communicate with her, so I said "Hey, I hate to bother you, but what's up with that doll?" And she said "Oh, that little thing? That was a birthday present. My brother got that for me for my birthday." And I was like, what? It just seemed so creepy to me, and I had never seen one up close and personal. She went on to explain that it was a good luck doll and was basically one of the best gifts she had ever received and since receiving it, her sleep was better, her grades were better, she had lost weight, and she saw it as positive. And I was like, oh wait, so that's a good thing? You don't use it for bad? And she was like, "Oh no, no way. I don't want that kind of karma." So, after that I went to the thermostat and turned the air down to 60 degrees (laughs).

I mean come on; it could have been me losing all that weight (laughs). That's when I looked at it against all the other religions and I realized how beautiful Voodoo actually is. Through my studies I came to realize that when it was created in Benin by the Dahomey tribe in West Africa, it wasn't created just as a religion; it was created as a way of life. The term "Vodun" is derived from the Fon language and means "God" or "Spirit." It was created so that people could unite, come together and become better people for themselves and their community.

So, when I started doing cemetery tours, we would always stop at Marie Laveau's tomb and once I learned about her story, that's when I decided that I wanted to enlighten people the way I was enlightened. I felt so stupid, all those years I was afraid of something that I come from.

That was our religion, Voodoo. And they beat us into Christianity, so we believed in it, we taught it to our kids, to the point where today there are still black families who have a picture of a white Jesus up on their walls. I mean, my god, the brainwashing and the control through slavery. And you look at Haiti, they freed themselves from slavery. And the reason was Voodoo. They never converted them to any other religion, so they kept their sense of identity. You cannot enslave anyone with a religion like Voodoo because it's huge on the people coming together to create a better situation. Treating people equally and becoming a better person than who you were yesterday. Voodoo was for the people. You can't oppress anybody who believes that. They overthrew their oppressors, and they've been a free country ever since. The Haitian revolution.

The iconic Madame Cinnamon Black with a large doll outside of the Historic Voodoo Museum (Photo Credit: Christine Breau)

Q: *And after that a lot of those people came here as free people of color, correct?*

Brionne: Yes. And that's when the establishment started making Voodoo look evil in the media and from their pulpits.

Q: *Yes. That freedom became a threat to a society built upon enslaving people. And people are sadly still perpetuating those divisive myths in order to keep power and control for themselves. I recently had two ladies on my Dark History tour from St. Louis. When they flew here, they had a stewardess on their flight approach them and tell them not to go into Voodoo shops because it was of the devil. Can you imagine that? Being that bold and entitled?*

Brionne: I deal with that all the time. They have programmed us to be afraid of this because they know if everyone came together and tapped into their spirituality, we would have everything we want, a better way of life in every way. It pays for them to keep us divided and afraid.

Q: *Same centuries old playbook, but sadly it works. It's effective. I don't know if you've experienced this but lately, as a tour guide here, I feel like I'm arguing history with some really ignorant people. And it never used to be that way before. They only want their skewed version of history validated and if anything contradicts that, they rage against it. When I talk about enslaved people using the Code Noir system to gain their freedom, I've actually had people step up and argue on behalf of the enslavers. It is mind boggling.*

Brionne: Yep. On my tours people are real-time fact-checking me to ensure I'm telling the truth. And my thing is, first of all, I'm Virgo and we're not good liars. We're not. At all, like, some of the historic truth is really easy and you mean to tell me you think I'm going to lie to you for two hours straight on the two-hour tour. Like, come on people. When I realized I had been so lost all those years, and I think about how my life would have been different if I grew up knowing what the religion really was. All I want to do is give people the same chance that I had, to learn the facts and see it as it really is, then decide for themselves.

Q: *Right. At least dispel all the myths and propaganda so they won't be so afraid. You made a statement before that really intrigued me; it's that people practice Voodoo every day, and they don't even know that they're doing it. Can you speak to that a little bit and give us some examples?*

Brionne: So, all Voodoo is, in a nutshell, communicating with the spirits and asking them to guide and protect you as you go through life. The word Voodoo means spirit. The root comes from the word Vodun, which means "of light." Which is why I said, you know, it's great as a way of life. So basically, it would be practical for use every day. Here's one example, if you have ever taken an Epsom salt bath? That is Voodoo spiritual bath. Any type of salt bath cleanses people's bad energy off of you.

**Spiritual Altars at Voodoo Authentica of New Orleans
(Photo Credit: Brandi C. Kelley)**

Ever have a friend who calls you and every time they call, they just need to vent? They're just spewing negativity. A lot of their energy stays on you. Then you wonder afterwards why you suddenly got an attitude or feel anxious. That's their energy staying on you. So, when you do that bath to cleanse that off of you, you'll feel better. Lighter. I learned that spiritual baths are most effective if you do it on the day of the week you were born. I was born on a Tuesday, so my spiritual bath is most effective on Tuesdays. Not that it's not going to work any other day. It's just most effective on the day of the week you were born.

Q: *I should start doing that after my tours now (laughs).*

Brionne: (Laughs) Yeah, definitely. As a person who works amongst a lot of different spirits, and because people can steal your energy and they can also put on their bad energy onto you. We've worked around a lot of toxic people, so it's important to do that salt bath at least once a month. Interesting, right? Another way to practice Voodoo, have you seen someone drink something and then pour some out for dead people?

Q: *Sure.*

Brionne: They say, "pour one out for the homies." That's practicing Voodoo. That is an offering to the dead. Same as leaving flowers at a grave. It's an offering for the dead.

Q: *Wow. What else?*

Brionne: Oh, yeah. If you talk to dead people, you definitely practice Voodoo. For example. I lost my grandmother 7 years ago from Alzheimer's and Dementia. It was tough. Really tough because I was like, just watching her forget me and forget everything, it's just so tough. So, when she finally checked out of the world, it just, man, it was bad. And it wasn't just bad for me, but for our whole family. She meant that much to us. But I talk to her all the time. Like, a song comes on, she loved Sam Cooke. Loved him. And Johhny Taylor. So, if one of their songs comes on, I just start talking to her, like, "Oh, grandma, this is your jam right here." I also miss her sweet potato pie. She made the best sweet potato pie ever. And every time during the holiday season, I'll be like, "Oh, man, Grandma, I could really use a slice of that sweet potato pie," you know. I don't see her. I don't hear anything back. I'm not hallucinating, but I still communicate with her. That is considered practicing Voodoo because they're not physically right there, but you're still speaking with them. But it's the same thing when you're saying your grace or your prayers. You ain't talking to yourself, right? All of that is considered practicing Voodoo. So that's just a few examples of how most of us are really practicing.

Brionne with her beloved Grandmother Juanita Taylor

Q: *You talked about the origins of Voodoo with the Dahomey tribe from Benin West Africa and the focus on the community. I recently read a wonderful book by Kim Marie Vaz entitled The Baby Dolls: Breaking the Race and Gender Barriers of the New Orleans Mardi Gras Tradition. In it she discussed black masking traditions and their importance to the strength of culture and community of New Orleans. Black Masking Indians, Skull and Bone Gangs, Baby Dolls and Second Line Parades, all have that spirit of inclusion and taking the artistry and creativity out into the streets where it can be shared by everyone. It all seems very spiritual and beautifully connected to me, even viewing it as an outsider.*

2nd Line Parade Brass Band Statue at Armstrong Park

Brionne: You know, I always tell people this; New Orleans is the most African city, the most spiritual city in the country, you know? We're very tapped into our spirituality. And somebody once asked me on a tour, "Why are y'all, so obsessed with the Indians?" I said, this is not an obsession, we just like to honor people who helped us and helped our ancestors. Indians helped us in so many ways. They taught a lot of us Hoodoo, number one. I'll get to that when we discuss root workers. But the Indians helped us. You know, slavery was very different here in Louisiana. On our only day off, which was on Sunday, they would share with us, they would trade with us. They introduced us to their Native American spices. We used it in our dishes. A lot of our dishes were basically African dishes with influence from the Spanish and French, and the secret ingredient was Native American spices and BOOM, just like that, Creole food was born.

They also helped a lot of our ancestors free themselves and become free people. You know, they helped us a lot. We honestly can't thank them enough for the impact they had on the black community and some of them are us. Some of them just as dark as us. Some of us are descendants of them. So, we just honor them at Mardi Gras, honor them on Sundays and in our second line parades. We do their chants and stuff. We're not going to let their culture die. So, we keep their energy. We keep their spirit alive as well, because they just did so much for us. It's an honorific and a tribute.

Big Chief Tootie Montana statue in Armstrong Park

Q: *Please explain the Hoodoo connection your mentioned, because another question that I get a lot is; "So, Voodoo is African spiritualism brought over during the diaspora, what is Hoodoo and how does that come into play?"*

Brionne: Like I said, Hoodoo is basically indigenous Native American influence on Voodoo. That's all it is. Our beliefs were almost the same in a lot of ways, so Hoodoo was just adding their little differences. For instance, they're bigger on speaking and manifesting their wants into existence. Just say it, you know? Affirmation. So, they're big on just being vocal about what they want, and, you know, again, they're huge with spiritual baths as well. The people who practice Hoodoo, there are a lot of people who refer to themselves as root workers. Those people, oh, my God. I always tell people, if you ever meet a root worker, you might as well make them your best friend. They can change your life.

These people know the science of every plant. They know what's good for you and what can kill you. Like, you can call someone, like, right now, you call right now, your friends. "Hey, hey, girl, I'm feeling really anxious today." They're gonna give you some herbs. They're gonna make you smoke it, drink it as a tea. or use it in your spiritual bath. You will immediately feel better.

Madame Cinnamon Black at the Historic Voodoo Museum
(Used by Permission – Historic Voodoo Museum)

I don't care what it is, whether you say you got the flu, etc. Bad headaches, they got stuff for that. Oh, I've been really depressed. There's something for that. Like, when I tell you these people are doing the Lord's work, I'm not lying. There will be people who will say, "there's no cure for this, there's no cure for that." There's a cure for everything. Seriously. There's a cure for everything. You know, the pharmaceutical companies, I mean, it's a billion-dollar industry. It's a sickness industry not a healing industry. You know what I'm saying? You know, so you got all these things that cure. God has pretty much already given us everything we need.

Q: *Agreed. So, can anyone practice Voodoo?*

Brionne: Voodoo is not just a black thing or African thing, anyone practice it, as long as they have positive intentions. Can there be circumstances where it feels and smells like appropriation? Sure. But that's a small percentage. Voodoo doesn't have a race on it. As long as they not out here trying to, you know, conjure evil spirits I mean, why not? Let them have that it. I'm not bothered by it. As long as they're not out here trying to misuse Voodoo, I mean, hey, because again, Voodoo is 95% positive. If you use it for bad, just be warned, it does come back 10 times.

Q: *Oh, 10 times? Okay, because I know witchcraft has a 3-fold rule. Whatever you put out comes back to you, 3-fold. So, 10. That's a hefty price.*

Brionne: Yeah, you cannot be out here misusing Voodoo. In New Orleans we have over 40,000 practitioners. Just in New Orleans. That's not even the whole state, just the city. That's like people who are overtly practicing. So, the most common way we can misuse Voodoo is for love. We never recommend you use Voodoo for love unless you're married and have been together for a long time. Because the cases like that it helps your love grow stronger for one another. But if you like them and they don't like you, nothing good is going to come out of it. It creates something called graveyard love. You know, if I can't have you no one will. Don't try it, I'm telling you. You don't want that. But it's very real.

Q: *We have a lot of visitors here that come to New Orleans, and a lot of people are intrigued by Voodoo, but they're a little afraid to go into these stores, these cultural centers, the museum. What would you tell them to* *help assuage those fears so that they will go and experience this for themselves?*

Brionne: You are more likely to be an evil Christian, or religious person, than you are to be an evil person who practices Voodoo. We've got so many people out here who misuse religion, right? And the most common misused religion is Christianity. And, you know, a bunch of other religions as well. It's just more common with Christianity, especially in this country. But when you actually walk into the Voodoo shops, you will see when you read everything, and when you read the all of the labels, everything you pick up, oh, this is for a protection. This is for traveling grace. This is for happiness. Some are for multiple purposes. If you actually go in and read, because reading is fundamental (laughs). You will see, oh, wow, this stuff is actually for something positive. No one is trying to hurt anyone. All you have got to do is go in and explore and see.

Family, Culture & Community being celebrated at Voodoo Authentica's Free Annual VOODOOFEST on October 31st (Photo Credit: Brandi C. Kelley)

The only thing I'm gonna say, don't get no Voodoo dolls that's made in China (laughs). That ain't no real Voodoo doll.

Q: *Speaking of Voodoo dolls, I understand that there was a period in New Orleans history when Voodoo was still being practiced in secret, that Voodoo dolls were used almost like medical records to keep track of cures the Voodoo practitioner had given to a person. They would put a colored pin or piece of cloth on the head, stomach, etc., of the doll to correspond to the treatment they used for that person.*

Brionne: Yeah, especially for pain relief. They would use them to keep up with their patients so they could remember which area of their body they were treating. But now, today, it's more of a manifestation thing, you know? Like the doll represents you, they put your name on it, you put something of yours on it, and you stick the pin in it to manifest it. This pin represents love, this one health, happiness, fertility, healing, energy, strength, etc. Just like my roommate did in college. Got a teenager with a terrible attitude. Get a doll (laughs). Treat it the way you want them to treat you. Hug it, kiss it, be kind to it. So, this is actually how the dolls work, but of course, yes, the media and the propogandists demonize it. Sure. They'll show you stabbing a doll and then someone's begging for mercy thousands of miles away. It does not work like that, unfortunately (laughs).

Q: *Yeah, sign me up. I have a long list (laughs).*

Brionne: Right? But just don't overdo it. Some people do way too much. Oh, this doll's for money. This one is for patience. This is for happiness. This is for fertility. This is for good health. You don't need no Voodoo Doll Toy Story going on in your house, right? Three tops if you want more than one. One for you, one for your family, one for that Facebook friend that's always asking for prayers but never say what it's for (laughs). Yeah, so just go, read, learn. You're going to see a lot of things that are going to surprise you because there are a lot of catholic people who practice Voodoo.

Q: *Yeah, the synchronization. That's how Voodoo survived, right?*

Brionne: Exactly. Disguising Voodoo practice. For instance, the Orishas and the Catholic saints are so similar that they would pray out loud to a Catholic saint, but in their hearts and minds they were actually praying to the Voodoo orisha that was close to that saint. That's how they were able to keep their religion and pass it on from generation to generation. Louisiana is top three in Voodoo in the world right behind Africa and Haiti. But because the Code Noir laws that mandated Catholicism were so strict, they had to find a way to make it work while they lived here.

Catholic Statues and Iconography at the Historic Voodoo Museum (Used by permission)

Q: *That's why they're so interconnected. They literally had no choice.*

Brionne: Yeah, that's why there's no such thing as Voodoo Church. There's a Voodoo spiritual temple, which is totally different. There's totally different vibe, you know? They go to Catholic church when they want to go to church. Also, there's no such thing as a Voodoo cemetery.

When they die, they get buried in the Catholic cemetery. Because people are always asking me, how is the Voodoo Queen (Marie Leveau) is buried in the Catholic cemetery? She was a Catholic woman who practiced Voodoo.

They're so similar, like, it's ridiculous. One God, God's helpers, all of their helpers, you know. Again, Voodoo is Orishas or Loas and in Catholicism they're saints, but they all represent the exact same thing, and they all send message to God on your behalf. They have different names. They look different. Both burn candles. They both have rituals. They both give up things for Lent. They both go to mass. They're not that different except maybe in the use of the dolls and the rituals. In Voodoo you might see a campfire, a drum circle, somebody butt necked dancing with a snake (laughs). And for the record, in Voodoo snakes represent wisdom, reincarnation and growth. Just like in Voodoo black cats represent good luck and protection. A black cat that crosses your path is actually good luck. It's made to seem that it's bad luck because it's associated with Voodoo, so it has to be evil. Right? Just a lot of things for us to unlearn once we get older.

Honestly, anything, black, you know? Like Voodoo, the Black Panther Party, Black Wall Street, etc. The media establishment has given them all bad reputations. The Black Panthers were out there teaching children how to read, feeding the homeless. They're the reason so many people, of all races and backgrounds, have food stamps today. They created that. You know, Black Lives Matter. That was something to raise awareness against racial injustice and police brutality. And they found a way to make that look bad. It's just like everything with black unity somehow equates to something negative. Historically they always find a way to do that. And again, it's the same thing with Voodoo.

Q: *Sadly, the more things change, right? I recently learned that Marie Leveau's Voodoo-related arrest records started changing in the press as it got closer to the Civil War to make it more sensationalistic. Oh look, they're having orgies, they're doing these sinful, terrible things, you know, that kind of thing, to make it fit the propaganda narrative that they were trying to sell in the newspapers to enrage people.*

286

Marie Laveau Painting by Charles Gondolpho
(Used by Permission – Historic Voodoo Museum)

Brionne: It's so ridiculous. Marie Leveau, first of all, is a fellow Virgo. She was born on September 10th, okay. Virgo women are huge on doing the right thing. Literally, we can't sleep while people are out here messing over people. We're just huge on what's morally correct. She was out here helping people, caring for people, mostly kids, with yellow fever. Especially orphans at the Ursuline convent. This lady got 87 people buried in her oven tomb and only 25 of them are family members. She would let people be buried in her family's tombs who didn't have family. That's who she was.

Q: *Oh, I didn't even know about that. That's amazing.*

Brionne: Right. Like the lady did a lot, and every time, every time, they make a movie about New Orleans or something with Voodoo, they always drag her in it, and they always make her look evil. It's just exhausting. Your heart has to be in the right place to practice Voodoo. When you see those altars in those Voodoo shops, or if you have one in your home, and it's very easy to make one, just get a small table, photos of your deceased loved ones, you know, the ones you actually liked (laughs).

Spiritual Altar at Voodoo Authentica of New Orleans
(Photo Credit: Brandi C. Kelley)

Leave things for them, a cup of coffee in the morning because they like to drink coffee. A shot glass full of their favorite liquor, their favorite snacks, their favorite cigarettes, cigars, you know. Basically, you take care of the spirits, and they take care of you. When you do that, it's a transfer of energy. I always tell people; when you got saved from that car accident, who do you think that was? Oh, that'd be God be looking out for me. Yes, God is looking out. However, God got so many people to look behind all at once, so he's using your ancestors to help protect you. Think about it. These are the same people who believe in guardian angels but don't believe in Voodoo. You think your guardian angel is some random Hispanic looking over you? (Laughs) No. It's your dead loved ones.

Q: *Oh, that's fascinating and beautiful.*

Brionne: So, when you do that transfer of energy, you want to leave something on your altar pertaining to yourself, it has to be relevant and specific. Like, if you want more money, you leave money. You want more business? Leave a business card. You know, something you're manifesting. I see a lot of people leaving cigarettes because they wish to stop smoking. Sometimes you see diabetics leave pieces of candy. People leave pain pills when they're wishing for better health. Now and then I see tiny bottles of alcohol, for people wishing to stop drinking, or possibly wishing for more alcohol, this is New Orleans after all (laughs). I always let people feel free to leave things on the altar, but word of caution, never remove anything from the altar because you don't know if the person's intent was pure when they placed it on there and it could be bad juju for you.

Q: *So, Juju is just Voodoo karma.*

Brionne: Yeah, all in all Voodoo is a very positive religion but a word of caution; Voodoo is very powerful but also dangerous if misused, such as using to harm/hex others or using it for love when the other person doesn't love you back. Just don't do it.

Q: *Warning heeded. Thank you for sharing with us it has been very enlightening.*

Next on my journey I was honored to take a semi-private tour with Voodoo Priest and Historian Robi Gilmore on the sacred ground of Congo Square, the birthplace of Jazz.

Q: Hi Robi, for those who don't know you, please tell us a little bit about yourself and how you became a Voodoo Priest.

Robi: My grandmother is a born and raised high priestess in traditional Louisiana plantation Voodoo. I grew up in the religion. Seventh generation. When I turned 18, right before I went into the Navy, I took my vows, and I went through the rights and rituals, and I became a high priest in plantation Voodoo. I now own the land that her grandparents picked cotton on. That was on my Daddy's side. Then, after I got out the Navy, I was around 27 or 28 years old, at the urging of my Mama, I went home to Haiti, and at the age of 28 became a priest apprentice in Haitian Voodoo. A year later, at 29, I got initiated into African Voodoo. Then, at the age of 30, went back home to Haiti and became a high priest in Haitian Voodoo, so now I'm a double priest, Louisiana Voodoo, and Haitian Voodoo, right? And then the family in Africa was going, 'um, oh, yeah, come on back.' So, I had to do seven years there. At age of 37, I became a high priest in African Voodoo. I am now in my 40s, and I'm a documented historian by the Smithsonian Institute and the New Orleans historical Society. So, you got the real deal.

Q: *That's amazing and I'm honored for your time. We're getting ready to enter the gates to Armstrong Park and you've already pointed out something that to most people would go unnoticed.*

Robi: Right. Voodoo is always hiding in plain sight. Down here, you'll see a whole bunch of mixed beans left as offering, and also tobacco. I didn't leave this. You'll see my family, who was out here every Sunday doing rituals, leaving this by the gate. The mixed beans in the offering are a representation of our lineage.

Mixed Beans offering

We all come from different lineages. I myself am Irish, Native American, and African and a whole bunch of other stuff. I'm also French. How do you represent all those lineages? When you leave your offerings throw a hand full of mixed beans down there, and each mixed bean would be a representation of your lineage. Remember, we pray to our ancestors in the religion of Voodoo. You have two parents, four grandparents, eight great grandparents. All those parents who have parents, who have parents, who have parents. How do you represent all of them? You throw a handful of white rice down there first, then put the mixed beans on top, and then you also have your food to eat as well.

Now, you'll also notice the tobacco specifically left to the spirit who resides at the gate, and yes, we are by the giant gate of Armstrong Park, but the offering is not left for Louis Armstrong, it just so happens that he spread jazz and blues and stuff like that around the world. He didn't grow up in this neighborhood that used to be here. He grew up in Uptown, but they named a park after him because this is the birthplace of jazz.

Louis Armstrong Statue in Armstrong Park

The gatekeeper, every religion has a gatekeeper. So, the spirit that stands at the gates, his name is Papa Legba, and y'all, I'm so sick of TV. American Horror Story Coven turned this man into a baby eating cocaine snorting Jamaican with a white face, red eyes and dreadlocks (shakes his head). But in real life he comes in three forms. He represents your past, your present, and your future. And the three forms make one. I know that sounds familiar, but that's not a Christian reference. Don't forget, they stole that concept from paganism during the Crusades.

His first form is Papa Eshu. So, he represents the little kid running around playing Tricks on ya, untying your shoelaces, and we always got to throw candy and peanuts on the ground to get his attention. Then you have the middle age form known as Papa Ellegua, so he's around my age with the two dogs on either side carrying a cane. He's standing at the gates going, "I wish him motherfucker would." And then you have Papa Legba the old man. He represents the sweet old man that protects all the children on the planet. He takes care of them. Sweet old man that sits in his rocking chair smoking a cigar and drinking rum all damn day. So, his element is time, cause time is an element. And so, the offerings are left down here because he's the opportunist. You pray to him to open doors to get a new job, maybe buy a new house, maybe you lost something, so you need a door to open to go find it. He's basically like St. Anthony in Christianity where they say they prayed to him whenever you lose something. So, think of him combined with St. Peter and then you have the gatekeeper.

Papa Legba altar at the Historic Voodoo Museum
(Used by Permission)

But first, let's debunk some stereotypes real quick, okay? I'm so sick of this damn Voodoo doll over here inside this French quarter. So, let's get down to the nitty gritty. Now, here's the truth. The idea of stabbing needles and dolls to hurt people doesn't come from Africa, Haiti or New Orleans. It comes from England. Yes, witches in England use a small doll made out of wax, known as a poppet. They would take these wax dolls and take the hair of the people that hurt them, put them in these wax dolls and take these long ass needles, and start stabbing these dolls with these needles, but not to hurt that person, let me defend witchcraft. I'm so sick of witchcraft getting a bad name, too. They did it to relieve their anger. Pagans back then were being persecuted, too. Don't forget that. St. Patrick is proof.

Q: *Gotta drive out them "snakes." Right?*

Robi: Right. Now, back in the 1700s and the 1800s, as a person of color, you know, it's illegal for me to go to the hospitals back then. It's illegal for me to go to the marketplaces, but the most important thing is it's illegal for me to learn how to read or write. Yeah, back then, we couldn't do nothing. There was nothing that I could have done except either be enslaved or a free person of color, where they also weren't gonna treat us right in the city, baby, I promise you that. Now, all these restrictions, but you know I'm the Voodoo priest, so that forced me to learn herbology from the Native Americans. That is not Voodoo. That's Hoodoo, which is what we practice. You practice Hoodoo, knowing that chamomile will help your stomach and make your skin feel good. Ginger will also cure some sicknesses and also help your stomach. That's the practice of knowing what herbs do. That's Hoodoo while being in the religion of Voodoo, you are practicing Hoodoo.

Q: *Got it. And that includes the use of Voodoo dolls as medical records as well?*

Robi: Voodoo dolls are Hoodoo not Voodoo. That's why it's inaccurate to call them Voodoo dolls. We just call them dolls in Voodoo. So, you come over to me, you say, Robi, I got a headache, and this headache will not go away. Gotcha. Dab a little lavender all right under your nose, rub some peppermint oil on your forehead and make you drink a full cup of chamomile tea. That should solve the problem. But while you're doing that, I'll make a doll that looks exactly like you to the best of my ability. You'll even help me make this doll. We'll work on the doll together. You know your face better than anybody on the planet. Once we're done, I'll take a needle, put it in the head, the forehead of that doll, and I'm going to take that doll and put it up there on the shelf cause I got doll of you up there and your family, too, have come to see me, and they got needles around the places. You go home. So, the next week, when you come back to visit me, you like, Robi, that's my doll up there. That's the doll we made together last week. I take the doll off the shelf and I'm like, "Oh, yeah, this is your doll." And I notice there's a needle in the head of the doll, so I'm gonna ask you. I see how I worked on your head the last time you came to visit me, is your head feeling better. If he says his head is feeling better, remove the needle. I ain't got to worry about them headaches no more. But if you say no, I'm gonna leave the needle in the head of the doll.

The Voodoo doll is a record keeping device. It's a medical chart. Remember, it's illegal for black people to read or write. So, they use the dolls to keep track of what they're working on, with their clients. That's it. Nowadays, the dolls are used for prayer, depending on the color. So, if the doll is blue, you pray for knowledge. Orange, inspiration, white for healing, black to break evil, purple, for lust, because we all need orgasms in our life now and then (laughs). Remember, Voodoo teaches sex positivity. And also, we believe in science. So, we color green for money, all that kind of stuff. They're just prayer devices.

There's no such thing as a negative or evil version of Voodoo. We don't have it. Right, okay. There's no black magic. Let me prove it to you. If we had the power to hex and curse or cast black magic, y'all realized Trump would have been dead a long time ago, right? Every rapist would be in jail, every pedophile would be 12 feet in the ground cause I'm gonna stomp them down an extra six feet, we don't have these magical powers. You know, most of these rumors about us casting black magic and summoning demons was all created because of toxic Christianity, and also because of black people being not Christian, they believed back then that if you're not Christian, it's devil worship. If it's not in the Bible, it's black magic. That's what they believe.

So, anything that was indigenous or not Christian was labeled black magic. And that's where all those rumors come from.

We don't have any evil or black magic in Voodoo, and I've been an advocate for the past 15 years of watching this stuff on TV of them going, "we'll put a little Hex on you in Voodoo." I'm going, Stop this, I'm tired of this bullshit. I'm getting too old to be seeing this shit when y'all got free information out here to show y'all, we do not cast black magic. And every time you depict us casting black magic, you give the slave owner exactly what he wanted. The world that he wanted y'all to live in. Right. There's no way around that.

Q: *I understand, too, that the depictions of Voodoo got more racist, more orgiastic, and more 'black magic', in the press leading up to the Civil War.*

Robi: Yes.

Q: *And Marie Laveau was used as a scapegoat for that.*

Robi: Yes. There is someone else who was bastardized in history, and I'm sick of all the lies on her. We'll speak more about her in a little while. Now that you're by my family's altar. Look at my face and you see the family resemblance up there as proof of it. There's a reason for that. So, the artist who came from Benin and handmade this, he did it because my family is over here every Sunday at 3:00 p.m. doing rituals, he met dad while he was out here, actually. And he was so impressed that the family was still keeping the African heritage alive in July 2008, he handmade this and presented it to the park in 2010 as a gift. And then my family started using this as an ancestral altar.

Voodoo Priest & Historian Robi Gilmore at the Congo Square Heritage Statue

And you'll see the family ancestry; my actual bloodline is here. Notice them dancing on top of the chains. The chains are not shackled to the slave's feet. That's a symbol of freedom. They're dancing on top of the chains because of this Native American woman right there in the background. What's going on with that?

The indigenous connection

The tribe that was here, there's more than one tribe. The Tchoupitoulas tribe, which is the how you pronounce that street. Tchoupitoulas. That's the name of the river people that live there. The Houma, Native Americans, my adopted son. That's his tribe. You also have the Chitimacha who would frequent here every now and then back and forth. But the Houma is the main one. Now, they're there, and they see these French people enslaving these Africans over here. The French tried to enslave them first already, but the natives know the area, as my Uncle Mandela said, who's a Mardi Gras Indian. The natives are waking up and slicing the enslavers throats, and the French couldn't take it. So, they went and got the Africans, and the natives were going, "We still gonna get our revenge."

Well, the Africans had off on Sunday because they were forced to go to Catholic Mass as part of the code noir laws. So, they would run from the French Quarter, hop the wall on Rampart and come over here and keep their culture alive. So, while they over here drumming and dancing, 'cause they can't escape, they're surrounded by four bodies of water, Gulf of Mexico, Lake Pontchartrain the Mississippi River, and Lake Bourne right here. Where are they going? The average size of an alligator 10 to 12 feet versus the size of a human so what would that make them if they tried to escape…alligator bait.

So, they' be over here getting it and the natives are going, okay, we see the French over there. Y'all Africans over here? Okay. Hmmm. And as an African started dancing, a native would get close to an African, take off a headdress, boom, throw it on that one, keep on dancing. Find another African slave, take off a shirt, throw it on that one, keep on dancing. Now at this point you got all these Africans dressed as Native Americans. Now the slaves got to be back at the slave cabins before the sunset, that's the law. So, as the sun was setting, the natives would be like, "Look at that, the sun's setting! That means we got to go back to our village and these Africans got to go back to the slave cabins." They take a look around. "I see no Africans here! Come on, let's go home." Yes, they walked them right away from slavery. The area where they went is known today as Lake Bourne, also known as Manchac Swamp, it has many names. They integrated and they had children, and my family is still out there.

Now we got the Mardi Gras Indians, half African, half Native American men. Y'all see them every Mardi Gras, you know about them. Huge feather outfits. My Uncle Mandela is the head chief of the Broken Arrow tribe. Half African, half Native American. That's my dad's brother.

Q: *Wow! I have never heard that before, the enslaved people just walking away with the natives to freedom from this spot.*

Robi: Yes, it was happening just that way. Right here. It was, right here.

Q: *That is fascinating. So, I have to ask, with all this real history you're laying out here, have you had any problems with people arguing on your tours against this history? Because I have, and it's getting worse.*

Robi: Man, I've been called a "nigger" this year like eight times already on my tour.

Q: *Unbelievable. I'm so sorry. (shakes head)*

Robi: Yeah. MAGA hat wearing types, like, come on the tour, start arguing. And then I go all ham on them, because I'm an actual historian. I just start citing sources to disprove their hate. Then I debunk Christianity within five minutes just to get them to leave the tour.

Q: *Those types are so easily triggered. I've had them cuss, argue, storm off. One guy even started breaking branches off a tree he got so upset. They write me one-star reviews. I wear those proudly. Occupational hazard, now, I guess. Anyway, in the Heritage statue who is the woman front and center of the group? Could you please speak about that?*

Robi: This is going to transition to us to what we believe in and what we do as far as our setup, as far as like God and the spirits and all that kind of stuff, because, as you noticed, there is a woman dead center of this statue. Women are dominant in our culture. Women rule the religion, the relationships, and the marriages. Also, to us, God is a woman. Now, why do we believe that God is a woman? Well, I mentioned I told y'all we believe in science, right? So, as we develop in our mom's body, you know, we were female first before we were a male. It takes a woman's body to start producing testosterone through her umbilical cord to our fetus to make this thing we love touching so much (laughs), turn inside out into a penis, but this is also how we found out that men are the mutation. God is a woman. There's no way for God to be a man. That is a whole woman up there giving birth to all this beautifulness. And we still believe that in Voodoo. Her name is Mama Oldumare. Mama Oldumare, or Mama Oudumare. She has two names, depending on which Creole is used to speak. And she is the Almighty to us. Olu is a Nigerian word. It means monarch. It means royalty de highest above.

Q: *Fascinating. Could you explain the Voodoo Hierarchy?*

Robi: So, yeah, so we have God. Now, under God, you have something known as the Loa/ Orisha, above man below God. Regular humans, some of them. Different colors, different textures, different sizes. These people are like that. Born and raised down here on Earth in the biblical days. Some of these people were born way before that time. Some of these people were born after that time, but the main seven African powers have always existed. They're the elemental spirits. But because of the good deeds and the miracles they performed in the name of God, whenever they died, God elevated them to that middle position above man and below God, known as Loa/ Orisha, patted them on the back and said, "You did a marvelous job down there on Earth. Here's the spiritual job and a spiritual domain. Now, go back down there and help man, because they keep starting wars and killing children. Now, man prays to the Loa before they pray to God. And that's how we got like Papa Legba, Yemoja. I'm about to introduce the spirits that are above men, and below God. So traditionally in west Africa you would leave offerings under your most fertile tree. When the offerings grow and create food, you use them to feed all your homeless kids and neighbors in your tribe. 75% will go back to the tribe and 25% will go back around the tree in order to make more food for your tribe. That's why we leave offerings. Remember, your religion must always keep up with the times of your people and the technology. If it can't keep up with the times it becomes a cult.

So the black beans were planted out here for Yemoja, the ocean spirit, also known as La Sirene, the siren, the mermaid. You'll see tobacco that is left out here as well. Normally, we don't leave her tobacco, but if people are not born and raised in a religion like me, they're allowed to leave whatever they want. So, you'll find some people who leave tobacco out here. There's also money left out here as offerings as well. We leave the money for two reasons. So homeless people can come and take the money. Remember, our religion is based around helping the tribe. So, the homeless already know, oh, come over here and whenever the Voodoo people leave and shit, take it. I specifically, in the wintertime, I'll leave, like blankets and pillows and socks, thermal socks and stuff like that. Those hand warmers, I'll leave them out here as an offering because they know, like, oh, High Priest Robi is leaving offerings. We need to go take the offerings. And I'll even go get them, because sometimes I'll be like, "Can y'all go over and take this shit before they throw it away? The money is out here for that reason. Also, money tastes like copper, which tastes like blood to represent your blood.

After Hours Blessing Ceremony at Voodoo Authentica of New Orleans (Photo Credit: Brandi C. Kelley)

We've never been a faith-based religion. Even 10,000 years before Christianity, we were trying to figure out how to survive and not worrying about a damn spirit. We've always been a practical based religion, based on evidence and scientific review, not faith. The only reason people believe that is because black people had to use Catholicism to survive, not combine with it.

Now, let me be clear on something. We have a huge crush on the story of Jesus. And notice I'm saying these words very precisely. On the story of Jesus. Remember, we've had 11 people in history named Christ, none named Jesus. So, the story of acceptance, the story of love, that's what we love about Jesus. But we also don't just have Jesus in there. We also have Buddha in the religion of Buddhism. We also have Shiva from the religion of Hindu as well. We also have all these deities from different religions that represent love and acceptance or the combination of chaos and stability. We have all that in the religion of voodoo, because any religion that requires you to leave your home and convince total strangers in the world that who they are is wrong and your way is right, and they don't convert to your side they'll be eternally damned, you're no longer in a religion, you're in a cult.

Speaking of cults, there's the Catholic Church, and there's a path that leads up Orleans Avenue from the Catholic Church directly to where we're standing. A path ain't always been there. It's there right now. The slaves took whatever route they could to leave Catholic mass and come over here. France, enacted a document here in the new city of New Orleans known as the Black Code, also known as the Code Noir. It was a list of laws and how to treat to slaves. One of those laws says that all slaves must be converted to Roman Catholicism, all slaves must attend Catholic mass. So, the slaves started adjusting their religion out of fear in order to make it seem like they're Catholic, so the slave owner could be like, "they converted", and we actually didn't. So, this is why you see statues of St. Peter, St. Mary, St. Barbara, St. Philomena, all in these Voodoo altars, and then you think, "oh, they're combining Catholicism with the African religion." We never did. That's what we want y'all to believe. We're actually using Roman Catholicism as a face to hide the fact that we're praying to our African spirit. So, the reason why today, you'll hear us singing the Catholic prayer and also singing to the saints at the beginning of a Voodoo ritual is to thank them for allowing us to hide behind them and remember, we're not the only one that's right. So, we thank the saints for allowing us to hide behind them in order for us to survive.

So now you have all this culture happening in Congo Square, and the natives with the Africans are going, "kay, y'all still here? show us your culture, show us your music." Africans are like, "You ain't say nothing but a word." So, the African men and women get up and dance. The natives are looking at the Africans going, "We do the same damn thing. Then the native men and native women join in, and from that union, I know this sounds funny, but this is how it actually happened. Jazz music was born from that marriage. No joke! That gave birth to most of the music we like to listen to today. Pop, rock and roll, Neo Soul, even country music.

All right, so now you got the Africans and the natives and they're getting it. They're getting it and the French are freaking out a little bit. You know, the Africans and the natives outnumber them three to one. So, they passed the law over here in the French quarter that says that no more than two to three people of color are allowed to gather in the Quarter. They got so damn scared, Africans ain't stop hopping this wall and coming over here on Sunday, though. So now you have them integrated with the Native Americans, and they're migrating in this direction.

Around the 1830s, you got a sprinkling of some new people right here along the wall that the French have hired as indentured servants to watch the Africans and the natives over here. And the French referred to them as Passe Blanc. They're passing for white. Now, their holiday has been stolen and still stolen to this day. They were raped, they were beaten, and they were not considered to be white until, if I'm not mistaken, 1901. Anybody want to guess? The Irish. So, the Irish hear this music, see this dancing, and actually join in. That's right. You cannot have Voodoo in Haiti or here, and if you ask any mambo in Haiti, if you go ask a priestess in Haiti, they'll tell you flat out, you can't have Voodoo here or in Louisiana, unless you include our Irish brothers and sisters. No way around it. We'd be ready to fight you over there. Here's two pieces of proof. The Irish gave us a gift, and people keep forgetting. Maman Brigette. Maman Brigitte is red headed, blue eyed, pale, white, Irish woman that cussed like a sailor. She was given to us by the Irish because the Irish were also helping us escape to our freedom. And we still have her in the religion. Here's the second piece of proof. My last name is Gilmore. Hi, I'm Irish. And we still commune with the Houma native Americans every Sunday. Some of the elders come out sometimes, and they sit with us and get on the drums. They leave offerings as well.

Q: *Amazing and so inspiring. Centuries of history and not the stuff you're going to get in the majority of school textbooks.*

The Mom Tree - 300 to 400 years old. This tree listened to the first jazz. Voodoo teaches that all living things, both flora & fauna, have a spirit. This imbues the religion with respect and gratitude, not arrogant dominion.

Robi: Now, we're over here for one main reason, and you're gonna be surprised about this. Marie Laveau, why are we over here, not over there at her house on St. Anne? Well, first of all, that's not her house. I'm so sick of people saying that. Even the plaque on the wall says that it's not her house. The city of New Orleans "accidentally" tore down her house in the early 1900s. How do you accidentally tear down somebody's house? Which means I don't know. Black women living in racist America at the peak of slavery? Yeah, they gonna tear her house down when she passes away.

Q: *Bingo. A blatant attempt at tearing down her legacy and silencing her throughout history. It didn't work too well, did it?*

The house Marie Laveau didn't build

Robi: It did not. Marie was famous for one thing, though. She would hop the wall and come over here. Remember, she's part black. These are her relatives over here, and she's part Native American. Now, this is where people started getting the stories from. Her and her sister, they always leave her out, and her mom, they always leave her out, too. And that's how the family, we're over here every Sunday, too. And just like every other black person that was enslaved, there were three people of color helping those black people escape. The problem was, Marie was a lot louder about it. She was very boisterous, and the story goes that she became a hairdresser. Most black women did hair back then. That was a common thing for black women to do, is illegal for them to get regular jobs, any woman back then. So, they did each other's hair, and what do we know about women getting their hair done?

Q: *They gossip and share personal information.*

Robi: (Nods) So, the story is that she would use the stories that she would hear from the slave owners, or their wives, while doing their hair to blackmail the slave owners. Now, in reality, what we do know is that she was technically using whatever undercover means that she could to smuggle slaves from down here up north to their freedom, and with the help of her influence, see people were scared of Voodoo back then, a lot of white people got involved in help her, too, not because they wanted to, but because they were scared she was gonna curse them.

Q: *Or reveal the secret skeletons they had in their own closets. That's the thing that triggers people. If I say that Marie Laveau used people's superstitions and beliefs against them to gain the freedom of enslaved people, that's when they'll go off and say she was breaking the law and was a criminal.*

Robi: And that's when you go, oh, so you're condoning slavery, right? You're condoning this act of a black woman freeing innocent people who have been beaten and raped. And had their children stolen from them, you're condoning that by saying these people are breaking the law. So, they should stay being raped, being controlled, and being hurt and beaten because you feel a certain way. Yeah. Wow, thank you for showing me exactly who you are.

Q: *Exactly. This is a hero story, plain and simple. These are enslaved people gaining their freedom from inhumanity. If we're going to debate that, we're not even in the same ballpark as far as morals, values and integrity goes. It's mind boggling.*

To complete the tour High Priest Robi conducted a short cleansing ritual using Florida Water and positive affirmation. It was a moving experience. I walked away feeling much lighter than I had felt when I arrived and also properly educated, as if a wide door had been opened to a place that I couldn't wait to visit and explore again and again. My journey wasn't over, it was just beginning. Depth, complexity, history and mystery coupled with positivity, respect, love and light. The world could really use a lot more of this right now.

A Veve is a detailed symbol representing a specific Lwa that acts as a conduit to facilitate communication between the living and the spirit. (Used by permission – Historic Voodoo Museum)

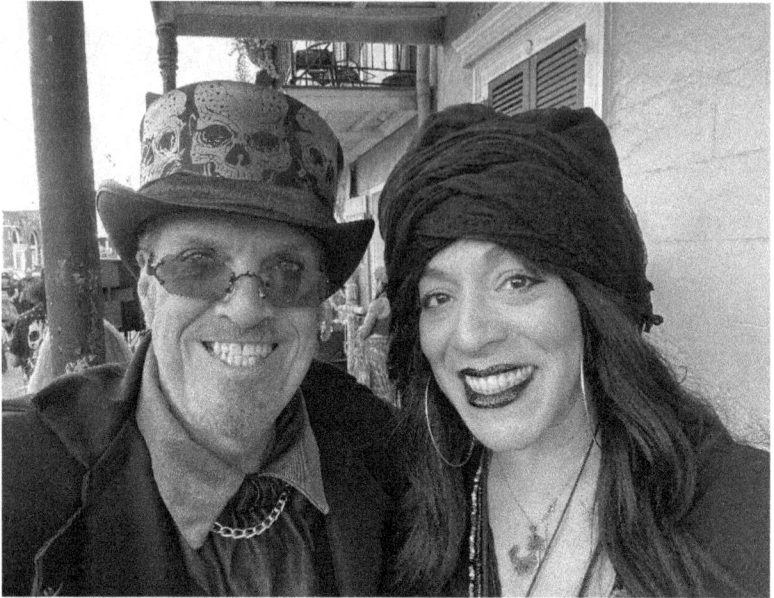

With my amazing friend Mam'Zelle Kamille Voodouisant at Voodoo Authentica's VOODOOFEST 2025

Dancing in the streets at VOODOOFEST 2025 at Voodoo Authentica of New Orleans

Special thanks & gratitude for the following folks who also helped make this chapter a reality:

- Brionne Bagneris
- High Priest Robi Gilmore
- Mambo Brandi C. Kelley & Houngan Juneaux Mayfaire Voodoo Authentica Cultural Center (612 rue Dumaine)
- Dane Gandolpho, Madame Cinnamon Black, & Madame M, from The New Orleans Historic Voodoo Museum (724 rue Dumaine)

RECOMMENDED READING:

Here's a list of a few of my favorite books to continue your quest.

- *Witch Queens, Voodoo Spirits & Hoodoo Saints* – Denise Alvarado (Weiser Books)
- *The Magic of Marie Laveau* – Denise Alvarado (Weiser Books)
- *Voodoo and African Traditional Religion* – Lilith Dorsey (Warlocks Press)
- *Haunted City* – Joy Dickinson (Citadel Press)
- *Fear Dat New Orleans* – Michael Murphy (The Countryman Press)
- *The Witches Book of the Dead* – Christian Day (Warlocks Press)
- *Initiation into Witchcraft* – Brian Cain (Warlocks Press)
- *The Cemeteries of New Orleans* – Peter B. Dedek (Louisiana State University Press)
- *Sage Advice Concerning Paranormal Events* – Claudia Williams (Left Hand Press)
- *Ash Tuesday Novel* – Ariadne Blayde (April Gloaming)
- *This Crimson Debt Novel* – Rose Sinister (Iron and Salt Press)
- *The Deep, Dark, River Novel* – Hannah Kate Stallo
- *The Free People of Color of New Orleans* – Mary Gehman
- *The Baby Dolls: Breaking Race & Gender Barriers* – Kim Marie Vaz

MAGICAL RESOURCES

Bottom of the Cup Tea Room – 327 Chartres St.
A quaint tea shop with psychic readings, tarot decks and more.
1-800-729-7148, www.bottomofthecup.com

Cottage Magick – 601 Elysian Fields Ave.
Occult gift shop.
504-402-6288, www.nolacottagemagick.com

Crescent City Conjure – 2402 Royal St.
Full service conjure shop.
504-421-3189, www.crescentcityconjure.us

Dark Matter – 822 Chartres St.
Oddities & Artisan Collective
www.darkmatteroddities.com

Earth Odyssey – 306 Chartres St.
Jewelry Store
504-581-1348, earthodysseynola.com

Erzulie's Voodoo Online Shop – www.erzulies.com
Boutique offering religious products.
504-525-2055

Esoterica Occult Goods – 541 Dumaine St.
Occult goods for Witchcraft and Magick.
504-581-7711, www.onewitch.com

Haus of Hoodoo – 1716 St. Charles Ave.
Metaphysical supply store
504-302-2042, www.hausofhoodoo.com

Hex Old World Witchery – 1219 Decatur St.
Metaphysical supply store.
504-613-0558, www.hexwitch.com

Island of Salvation Botanica – 2372 St. Claude Ave.
Metaphysical supply store.
504-948-9961, www.islandofsalvationbotanica.com

Marie Laveau's House of Voodoo – 628 Bourbon St.
Religious goods. www.voodooneworleans.com

New Orleans Historic Voodoo Museum – 724 Dumaine St.
Voodoo History & Cultural Center.
504-680-0128, www.voodoomuseum.com

Omen New Orleans – 1205 Decatur St.
Psychic Parlor & Witchcraft Emporium.
504-322-7440, www.omensalem.com

Path of Awakenings – 121 N. Rampart St.
Metaphysical Supply Store
504-327-7175, www.pathofawakenings.com

Pharaoh's Cave – 1241 Royal St.
Egyptian Import Store, 504-412-8868

Reverend Zombie's Voodoo – 725 St. Peter St.
Voodoo shop & spiritual readings.
504-486-6366, www.voodooneworleans.com

Starling Magickal Occult Shop – 1022 Royal St.
Metaphysical supply shop & psychic readings.
504-595-6777

Voodoo Authentica – 612 Dumaine St.
Spiritual arts and crafts. Psychic readings.
504-522-2111, www.voodooshop.com

Voodoo Spiritual Temple – 1428 N. Rampart St.
Spiritual Temple & Cultural Center.
504-943-9795, www.voodoospiritualtemple.com

LOCAL HAUNTS

So now you've read our experiences, and we've loved sharing them with you. Now it's time to come out and have some of your own. To aid you in this quest we've put together a list of our favorite paranormal hot spots for you to check out. Happy hauntings!

<u>BARS:</u>

The Dragon's Den (435 Esplanade Ave.)

Reportedly the New Orleans home of occult priest Aleister Crowley in the early 1900's, this lovely dark corner of the city always seems to be exercising its demons. Great drinks and live music. And beware of the mirror on the second floor. It's said to be a portal to the other side.

The Dungeon (738 Toulouse St.)

My personal favorite in the French Quarter. Ashes of the dead in the courtyard planters, dark ambience and signature drinks. They even carry Marilyn Manson's own brand of Absinthe called Mansinthe. Distilled to 66.6 ABV, of course. Dance with spirits in the cage in the Sound Bar upstairs, hold captives at the Venus Bar or tempt fate by playing Zeppelin on the juke box downstairs. You never know who you may run into, living or dead.

Lafitte's Blacksmith Shop (941 Bourbon)

Purple Voodoo frozen daiquiris, pirate ghosts and candle lit interiors in the oldest existing bar in the United States hailing back to the late 1700's. What's not to love?

May Baily's (415 Dauphine St.)

A cornerstone of brothel history in the French Quarter with four active ghosts. Beautiful bar, live music and quite possibly the best Pimm's Cup in town. Get a courtyard room at the Dauphine Orleans for your best chance at a haunted encounter and tell Jen the bartender I said hello.

MRB (532 St. Phillip St.)

Wonderful bar with great drinks, an expansive courtyard and the ghost of a star-crossed and heartbroken prostitute who committed suicide in the late 1880's.

Pirate's Alley Café & Absinthe House (622 Pirate's Alley)

This lovely and inviting little corner of Pirate's Alley is brimming with atmosphere and history. The bartenders are experts on absinthe, and you'll feel like you are being transported back to a time where anything was possible in this bustling old port city. For a price, of course. Pirate ghosts lurk in the alley by the Faulkner bookstore and echoes of the old jail whisper from the walls. The perfect place to wind down after a busy night of partying in the Quarter.

Santos (1135 Decatur St.)

High octane Goth rock metal bar on Lower Decatur with good drinks, live music and monthly Goth events. Even Phil Anselmo (Pantera) is known to show up with his band from time to time.

HOTELS:

Andrew Jackson Hotel (919 Royal St.)

Classic townhouse hotel with child ghosts and beautiful courtyard where they like to play.

Bourbon Orleans (717 Orleans Ave)

Situated smack in the middle of the French Quarter, this was our home base for all our visits. Nice accommodations, good food and a nice bar with live music. And, of course, several ghosts. Make sure you behave or else the Nun will get you.

The Dauphine Orleans Hotel (415 Dauphine St.)

Beautiful hotel set on an old brothel property from the late 1800's. Boasts four active spirits, especially in the pool and courtyard area by May Baily's, the hotel bar.

Lafitte Hotel & Bar (1003 Bourbon St.)

Located across from Lafitte's Blacksmith Shop Bar, this nicely appointed hotel is said to host the ghost of a grieving mother.

Lafitte Guest House (613 Esplanade Ave.)

Located on historic Esplanade Ave, which the Indians believed was a sacred path to the water, this quaint hotel is built upon mysterious tunnels that ran through the property in the 1800's and the ghost of a Lady in White, who inhabits room 6.

Lamothe House (621 Esplanade Ave.)

Built as a lavish residence in the 1800's by a wealthy sugar cane plantation owner, this property is occupied by the ghosts of a mother and her children along with a mysterious Lady in Red, who is believed to be one of the victims of a murder-suicide in the mid 1800's.

Hotel Monteleone (214 Royal St.)

A lavish family-owned hotel that boasts its own spinning Carousel Bar, phantom children playing in the upper hallways and the ghost of a former employee, so dedicated, he refuses to leave. But you, you can check out any time you like.

Place D'Armes Hotel (625 St. Ann St.)

A very charming and welcoming hotel, centrally located near the original Place D'Armes (Jackson Square). Active spirits on the property include a chatty older gentleman with a beard who is believed to have been the headmaster at an old school formerly on the property.

Hotel Provincial (1024 Chartres St.)

Posh, family owned, boutique hotel located by the old Ursuline Convent. The ghosts of Confederate soldiers and hospital personnel are a few of the reported sightings on the property.

Villa Convento (621 Ursuline St.)

A lovely guest house with individually appointed rooms. Built in the 1830's it is rumored to have been a mid-19th century brothel, with active spirits seemingly from that era.

RESTAURANTS:

The Cornet Bar & Restaurant (700 Bourbon St.)

Creole cuisine with balconies overlooking Bourbon St. Named Cornet because the owning family, the Karnos, gave Louis Armstrong the money to purchase his first Cornet. Active hauntings include a mother and her two children who are believed to have perished in the devastating 1788 fire.

The Creole Cookery (514 Toulouse St.)

Classic creole and Cajun dishes with live jazz music in the courtyard, said to be the haunted end to a tragic love triangle in the early 1800's.

Muriel's Jackson Square (801 Chartres St.)

Fine dining in an exquisite location haunted by the ghost of a former owner who committed suicide after losing the property gambling. Ask to see the table they set out for him each evening and also the séance room upstairs. The crawfish and goat cheese crepes are a must!

Tableau (616 St. Peter)

With active ghosts from the Civil war era, a ghost cat and Psychic Medium dinner events this is a must attend haunted location. They even have a video on You Tube of wine bottles flying off the racks. Elegant dining in a historic building connected to the also haunted Le Petit Theatre on St. Peter St.

Tujague's (New Location - 429 Decatur St.)

Legend has it that the original proprietors of this historic New Orleans restaurant, the Begues, were the folks credited with creating brunch. Serving traditional creole fare, it is a must for the discerning visitor and locals alike. The Sazeracs and Grasshoppers at the bar are outstanding.

Several ghosts inhabit the property, including the still bickering Begues. The spirit of Julian Eltinge, a cross dressing actor from the silent film era, and frequent patron of the restaurant before he passed, is still believed to inhabit the building. For fun Goggle "Tujague's Ghost" to check out the images captured by patrons.

Turtle Bay (1119 Decatur St.)

A personal favorite. Fantastic burgers, steaks and a nice beer selection, in a casual setting. Their weekend crawfish boils, in season, are not to be missed. Active haunting on the property of a servant girl who died of yellow fever in the mid 1800's and the back courtyard was once the child cemetery off the back of the Ursuline Convent. Bon appetite!

MUSICAL ARTIST PROFILES

ERYN

Singer ERYN is on a quest to establish her voice, both literally and figuratively. As an award-winning emerging artist, she's been hard to categorize – often described as a mixture of blues, soul, jazz, pop, rock and country. Now she's figured out that puzzle and seeks to lay claim to the RetroPop genre with her latest release from 2018, "Lady E". Eryn combines an old school sound that evokes rhythms and recording techniques of the past with a modern pop mindset and powerhouse live performances. She's looking for something authentic commenting, "The music industry always goes through waves of the bubble gum and the raw, and I feel like the public is starting to tire of the bubblegum that has been on the scene for the last decade".

In 2016 she became the youngest-ever inductee into the New Jersey Blues Hall of fame. Born and raised in Maryland and now living in New Jersey, Eryn began singing professionally at the age of 13 and hasn't looked back. She has performed with or opened for such luminaries as Buddy Guy, Doctor John, Robert Cray, Don McClean, Johnny Winter, Billy Corrigan, The Gin Blossoms, Bernard Purdie and the Little River Band, to name a few.

Changing her name has been a crucial part of her new, self-empowered perspective, as she sheds her last name, "Shewell" to perform simply as "Eryn". "This EP represents a new chapter in my book of life, and for me as an artist. There have been many changes for me since I released my last record four years ago.

Not only did I get married to the man of my dreams, but I was also able to cut out a lot of negativity and find a new self-worth. It's almost as if changing my name represented letting go of my past and heartbreak. We will always go through tough times, but now I feel more prepared to tackle them. Loving and understanding myself is the key to all of this. It feels as if all my previous works were me as a girl, and now I have become a woman".

Part of that cathartic journey is chronicled in the song she shared for the Guiding Spirits book.

"The song Stranger in my House hits really close to home for me. I wrote this lyric after getting into an argument with the person I was living with at the time. It just flowed out onto the paper like my muse was writing it for me. I turned around one day and realized that this person I was living with was a complete stranger, and although we had been in a relationship for a long time, I didn't know who he was. I think a lot of people have gone through this in their relationship and marriages can relate to this sense of desolation".

Follow Eryn at:

www.erynofficial.com

www.mattoreeband.com

JAMIE LYNN VESSELS

Jamie creates original New Orleans Roots Rock for the Wanderers, the Dreamers, the Fighters – with hard-hitting guitar riffs and lyrics that don't shy away from the hard and hopeful experiences that make us human. Jamie's voice and her unabashed honesty consistently create a community out of a room full of strangers.

The melting pot that is the New Orleans music scene had primed her to thrive in spaces that center on shared human experience, also leading Jamie to write even more about trauma, recovery, disordered eating, neurodivergence, depression and anxiety. Even her newest album's forthright political offerings are born from a protectiveness, standing against anything that would erode our sense of common humanity. Summing up her approach to songwriting and performing, Jamie says simply, "I want everyone to feel seen and included."

You can learn more about Jamie Lynn Vessels and her latest full album release, "If I'm Being Honest," including the single "Eulogy at Joshua Tree," by following her on Facebook, Instagram, Twitter, YouTube, Spotify, iTunes, and Apple Music.

In the haunting "Eulogy at Joshua Tree," Jamie steps into the legacy of legends past as she recounts the ill-conceived Joshua Tree cremation of country music icon Gram Parsons.

Jamie recalls, "Buried to this day just outside of the Crescent City, the connection to Parsons was a pull that I couldn't ignore. I wanted to, as humbly as possible, tell the story of the prolific and influential songwriter's untimely death. From the pact he and his friends made to be buried at Joshua Tree, to his stepfather forcing his body to come back to Louisiana because he wanted a piece of his inheritance, all the way to the friends stealing the casket from the airport and setting it ablaze at Cap Rock, the events add yet another layer to the young songwriter's legacy."

Keep up with all the latest at **jamielynnvessels.com**

LEXI LEW

Lexi is a seasoned performer and a beloved staple on Nashville's Lower Broadway live music scene with her perfect pairing of personality and versatility. By adding her own depth and texture to the mix, she effortlessly switches genres and is an expert at creating her own versions of all the crowd pleasing, sing-along hits in classic rock, country, pop and today's top charted songs. Her stylistic approach to the arrangement and vocalizing of familiar songs, paves the way for memorable, original, performances each night.

In August of 2012, with her entire hometown of Douglasville, GA, cheering her on, Lexi Lew took a huge leap of faith and moved to Nashville to pursue her dream. Following in the footsteps Trisha Yearwood and Brad Paisley, she graduated with a BA in Audio Engineering. She credits her time as an intern with Grammy Award winning Producer/Engineer Jaime Tate, at the Rukkus Room as being the highlight of her college career.

As an up-and-coming songwriter on Music Row, Lexi penned and released a bone-chilling country ballad called "Roses" in 2015. It is a story rooted in personal experience of a friend struggling with depression and thoughts of suicide. The music video is beautifully executed and superbly directed by Atlanta-based videographer, Dustin Blake. Along with her single, "back Home", an upbeat, carefree tribute to her hometown roots, "Roses" went number one on Georgia's 94.9 The Bull Backyard Country.

Lexi reunited with her former boss, Jaime Tate, in December 2021 to record four sings, including the first single "Ghost Town" that was released on February 25th, 2022, and debuted on Devon O'Day's Show, Main Street Today in Nashville. The song tells an eerie story about ghosts and spirits in New Orleans while featuring some amazing percussion that captures the essence of the city. It was written with the duo, Carvin Walls after they took a ghost tour with Doug while visiting the city in 2019. Lexi is proud to have the song featured as part of the release of this book, Guiding Spirits.

Follow Lexi at **lexilew.com** and on Tik Tok at **lexilewmusic**

PAULA MANGUM

Paula Mangum is a singer/musician/songwriter living in New Orleans.
Before moving here from Atlanta, she fronted multiple original and
cover bands, including 'bnshkr' (boneshaker) and MagicNation, both
of whom have songs featured in this book. She is currently rebuilding
'boneshaker' as an acoustic guitar/drum/percussion trio with fellow
members of Skinz N Bonez, of which she has been a member since the
krewe was founded in 2011. In her most treasured musical endeavor,
she is honored to drum in support of Queen Mary Kay Stevenson and
the Original Wild Tchoupitoulas Indians. When she doesn't have a
musical outlet, her creativity goes to the kitchen, where she is working
on creating a vending pop-up called Boneshakers Galley that will offer
specialty treats like candied jalapenos, fried walnuts, and spicy dark
chocolate peanut butter cups. A quote from Paula: "People used to ask
me why I spent so much time in New Orleans (before I moved here). I
told them that it was because my heart lives here and I had to come
visit it often."

STORY CONTRIBUTORS ~ YOUR GUIDES

DOUG BOOKOUT

A transplant to the city, I fell hard for this place during my first visit in 2004 and have never looked back. I sincerely believe that this is one of the few remaining places on earth where magic still exists and I have loved every moment of basking in that magic and living out my retirement dream bucket list in the city that, thankfully, adopted me. After 36 years of a military and Defense Industry career and family responsibilities, my wife and I decided to fast track our retirements while we were still young enough to enjoy everything this crazy town has to offer. My all-time absolute joy is sharing this city, her history and her stories with people who get it and want to know more.

We are currently living out the next phase of our bucket list in the place where the Crescent City began; Orléans, France. Between touring museums and contemplating life & death in Parisian cemeteries I'm also working on a series of paranormal based novels set in the mystical namesake city of Nouvelle-Orléans.

When I'm not doing that, I'm hanging with my wife and best friend, Toni, and talking to the spirit of our beloved Chloe, the cutest and most spoiled little puppy ever. We miss her every day and look for her in the spaces in between us, where she snuggled for over fifteen years.

This book has truly been a labor of love and I sincerely hope you've enjoyed reading it as much as I have putting it together.

ARIADNE BLAYDE

Photo by Louis Maistros

Ariadne Blayde is a playwright and novelist. Her plays have been finalists for The Arts and Letters Prize, the Tennessee Williams Playwriting Contest, Lark Playwrights Week, and more. Her play "The Other Room" won the VSA Playwright Discovery Award and has had more than 300 productions around the world. An excerpt from her recently published novel, **ASH TUESDAY**, was recently announced as a finalist for the 2020 Tennessee Williams Saints and Sinners Fiction Contest. Ariadne writes about New Orleans, social justice, and (at the moment) quantum physics. She moonlights as a ghost tour guide in the French Quarter.

More at **www.ariadneblayde.com**

CLAIRE CHRISTINE SARGENTI

Claire Christine Sargenti Pi'kssíí Aakíí (she/they/fae) is an award-winning interdisciplinary author and artist. Her work has been seen at the New Orleans Museum of Art, Ogden Museum of Southern Art, as well as in galleries, theaters, digital spaces, and print publications throughout America and Europe. She is the author of Noble Moon Tarot Deck & Grimoire, Vagina Book, and Interludes: A New (Orleans) Play and has published in Rougarou Journal, The Weaver Literary Magazine, San Diego Poetry Annual, among others. Her work has raised funds for various charities including The Nature Conservancy, Sexual Trauma Awareness and Response, Multidisciplinary Association for Psychedelic Studies, and Doctors Without Borders.

@clairevoyantspirit

Website: --
www.ClaireChristineSargenti.com

DREW COTHERN

Drew Cothern is a New Orleans actor, entertainer and all-around raconteur. You can catch him starring in Down's "Conjure" music video as well as other projects throughout the city.

Check out his artwork and his online store at:

Instagram.com@werewolvesofnola

www.redbubble.com/people/theunbeheld

CHARMAINE SWAN RICH

Charmaine was born and raised in New Orleans, LA. Her parents traced their French ancestry to the very beginnings of the city of New Orleans. The family tree includes a Major in the French army, Major Jean Fayard, who was assigned to New Orleans, and a "casket girl," named Angelique Girad – both arrived in New Orleans in the early 1720s.

Charmaine grew up in the Gentilly area of the city and the family moved across Lake Pontchartrain to Slidell, LA in the early 1980s. Attended Pope John Paul II High School and the University of New Orleans, graduating with a B.A. in Psychology and Sociology.

After graduation, she married her college sweetheart, a USMC officer. For the next 21 years they lived in ten different cities, too many deployments, a war, 2 children, 3 cats and 1 dog. Over the years and many different cities, she held jobs such as a schoolteacher, an athletic director, a coach, a financial advisor, a director of a at risk program for children, director of a childcare center, a merchandiser for Macys, and substitute teacher.

Finally, retirement came for her husband, and home was calling. The family moved back to New Orleans in 2016. She became a tour guide in 2018. Currently the kids are in college and Charmaine has more time pursing her hobbies such as photography, jewelry making, flipping old furniture and, of course, ghost hunting. She loves being back in her hometown, and her favorite holiday is Mardi Gras. She is currently a member of the Casket Girls, the Krewe of Morpheus and the Irish-Italian Club.

STELLA SALMEN

Stella is a Jersey Girl (now old lady) living in New Orleans since 2006. Always looking for the odd side of life, she has found it in the Crescent City working as a Bourbon Street Bartender, a musician, and least favorite - a legal secretary. With each position she learned more about the city and the people who so proudly call it home.

With her love for interesting people, music, and history, it was only a matter of time before she became a Tour Guide, so that she could share her tales with the many visitors that descend upon the city every year.

SIDNEY SMITH

Sidney Smith is the owner of **Haunted History Tours,** New Orleans oldest and most popular tour company. *"My vision was to create a tour company in which tour guides possess enough acting ability and stage presence for their stories to leave each tour guest with a 'WOW!' experience."* Today Haunted History Tours employs over 40 tour guides offering several amazingly different tour options focusing mainly on the paranormal aspects of New Orleans intriguing past (and present).

Prior to creating *Haunted History,* Sidney was an active performer of singing telegrams and stripper grams for *Merry Minstrel Singing Telegrams*, an entertainment company he created in the late 1970's and sold in the early 1990's.

However, what put the owner of Haunted History Tours on the map early on, were his skills as a photographer of major rock stars. Sidney has worked directly with musicians such as Paul McCartney, the Rolling Stones, Led Zeppelin, Bruce Springsteen, Rod Stewart, Dr. John, and the Allman Brothers Band just to name a few. In 2019, for its 50th anniversary, he published a 256-page, hard cover, coffee table book, '70 - '74...Plus A Little Bit More / A Photographic Memoir On The Early Years of the Allman Brothers Band. To learn more, visit **www.AllmanBrothersBookBySidneySmith.com** or **www.RockStarPhotos.net**

Book Tours at: www.hauntedhistorytours.com

ROSE SINISTER

Like most creatively-inclined persons forced by necessity to work to eat and to steal time for making art in the moments that exist between waking toil and dreaming, Rose Sinister has performed many jobs, and lived many lives. She's worked at call centers and grocery stores, been a hotel concierge and a milliner's assistant. She's been a tour guide, a jewelry designer, and produced the internationally renowned podcast, "Rose Sinister: Vampires."

The tour guide job was the best of all of them, until a series of unfortunate events beginning with the Pandemic and ending with a catastrophic car accident that left her back broken in three places, forced Rose to come to terms with her mortality and physical limitations in a viscerally transformative manner. During her long and often boring convalescence, she decided to turn her attention away from analyzing the cultural significance of vampire stories and toward creating a narrative of her own.

"This Crimson Debt," the first novel in the new "Community of Blood" series, was published in January 2023 by Iron and Salt Press, her very own imprint. Now, Rose still works the occasional odd job to pay the bills, but she is also an author, a publisher, content contributor for Vampyre Magazine, and a podcaster. The "Rose Sinister: Vampires" podcast will resume with brand-new content in 2023.

Rose lives in New Orleans. She isn't capable of surviving anywhere else.

RANDY WALKER

Randy Walker is a fiction and creative non-fiction writer based out of New Orleans. He gives ghost tours in the French Quarter and basks in the inspirational insanity of his city. His writing has appeared in the magazines Stuff and Maxim and the online literary publications Neutrons Protons and Scarlet Leaf Review.

Check out Randy's good reads at: **Randythestoryteller.com**

JONATHAN WEISS

"I was first introduced to New Orleans in the flesh when I was but 7 years old. Wandering through the old streets, looking at sights I'd never imagined outside of a storybook, while I didn't have the experience to understand that I was looking at my home for the first time, I do remember that my thoughts were these: 'This place is magic. I will live here when I grow up.' Now, decades later, I've been fortunate to have seen this city in her many moods over the years."

Jonathan Weiss is one of the city's leading historians and purveyors of the macabre stories that makes New Orleans the most haunted city in America. Licensed for two decades, he's one of the very, very few pre-Katrina guides still operating. Having lived in Boston, Philadelphia, Texas, Baltimore, D.C., Paris, and London among others, he still always returns home. Very few guides equal Jonathan in depth of experience, his knowledge of the old city and its neighborhoods, and in addition to his regular tours, he is able to accommodate private tours by request. Jonathan has appeared and consulted on The Vampire Diaries & The Originals, CMT, MTV, ATT Uverse, SyFy, Discovery, the Travel Channel, and for several films over the past decade, and most recently on William Shatner's "the UnXplained" on History.

For more info go to: **www.jonathanweisstours.com**

For the best selection of new and used books in the French Quarter, check out **Dauphine Street Books** and **Beckham's Bookshop**! Tell Steve, Katrina, Jason & Heather I said hello!

Available now at **Iron & Salt Press!** The book that launched the new vampire series you've been waiting for! *This Crimson Debt!*

The beautiful Rose Sinister courtesy of Rachel Clinesmith (Vampyre Cosmetics)

"This Crimson Debt by Rose Sinister is the type of book you can't put down. It's the type that makes you want to stay up all night reading, then go back to it during the day to finish it. It's a story that has real world connections, romance, adventure, horror and vampires - all in one book!"

Good Reads – January 27th, 2023

* Available at **RoseSinister.com** and by special order wherever books are sold—support your indie brick and mortar bookstore.

A heart-felt thank you to the many thousands of people who have allowed me the privilege of sharing this amazing city over the past 10 years! For you, I am eternally grateful! What a ride!

.

www.ingramcontent.com/pod-product-compliance
Lightning Source LLC
Chambersburg PA
CBHW032048020426
42335CB00011B/245